IT SERVICES BUSINESS MANAGEMENT

IT SERVICES BUSINESS MANAGEMENT
Concepts, Processes and Practices

Sanjiva Shankar Dubey
Asia Pacific Executive
IGA Service Delivery
IBM

PHI Learning Private Limited

New Delhi-110001
2012

₹ **250.00**

IT SERVICES BUSINESS MANAGEMENT: Concepts, Processes and Practices
Sanjiva Shankar Dubey

ISBN-978-81-203-4531-7

The export rights of this book are vested solely with the publisher.

Published by Asoke K. Ghosh, PHI Learning Private Limited, M-97, Connaught Circus, New Delhi-110001 and Printed by Mohan Makhijani at Rekha Printers Private Limited, New Delhi-110020.

To

My Grandparents

Late Gupteshwar Dubey

Lala Pyari Dubey

(Dada and Dadi)

Late Rajeev Nayan Mishra

Late Narayani Mishra

(Nana and Nani)

Contents

Preface

A book, like a landscape, is a state of consciousness varying with readers.
—Ernest Dimnet

IT Services Enterprises are leading India's growth story

IT Services (ITS) industry with almost a non-existent origin about 30 years ago, is now a thriving 70 B USD industry. Today, there is not a single home that does not boost at least one person related or working in IT Services industry. Most global ITSE[1] have leaders graduated from Indian Engineering colleges and B-Schools. ITS industry directly employs 2 million plus professional, 200,000 join its rank and file every year graduating from various universities. ITS industry contributes nearly 4% of India's GDP, and looked upon as premier industry where India has left a world leader's stamp. This burgeoning industry would need another 5 million trained youngsters in the next ten years doing variety of functions in diverse roles requiring wide range of skill sets.

IT Services Business Management is an upcoming subject

One of the challenge faced by the ITS enterprises is the readiness of the graduated and postgraduates joining them. Quality and preparedness of the fresher have been a subject of several studies and research in the recent times, which is impacting the ITS growth and threatening to loose India's advantage to other nations. It is estimated that about 2% of the IT Services industry turnover is spent in various induction programs for the fresher. IT curriculum of present times does not cover the business and management aspect of IT Services Enterprise.

This book comprehensively covers the management topics of IT Services business—from sales and marketing to delivery and quality management. Such a customized book can trigger an essential course in graduate/postgraduate level to bridge the gap between industry needs and academic output. The major topics covered under various chapters are as follows:

1. IT Services Enterprise (ITSE) landscape and current challenges
2. IT Services industry value delivery chain
3. ITSE business processes and function overview
4. Strategic foundation for IT Services business
5. Marketing of IT Services

---

1. Microsoft, IBM, Google, HP, etc.

6. IT Services business development
7. IT Services selling process
8. Delivery management of IT Services
9. Qualities assurance of IT Services
10. Measurement and monitoring of ITSE performance
11. Creating a high performing ITSE team
12. Managing innovation and enterprise learning of ITSE
13. Management of ITS Enterprises growth
14. Future trends of IT Services Enterprise
15. Summing it all

This book will equip students graduating from B.Tech, MBA, MCA and other programs with concepts, processes and best practices of IT Services business management. The book presents a well-researched compendium of deep knowledge of its various topics. The readers of this book are bound to be better prepared for good placement and subsequent successful career. It will also appeal to working professional in IT Services Enterprise to broaden their knowledge horizon, and the IT Services companies can adopt it as a part of their induction programs.

This book apart from prevalent theoretical concepts and processes, has cases, management stories and learning tasks (SALT) and review questions and assignments. Written in an easy-to-internalize manner, this book will be useful to the students and also IT Services industry professionals in their career growth. My humble attempt has been to present a comprehensive companion for younger IT professionals right from their placement time to induction program till they become specialized and develop a firm footing in the industry.

I hope that this compact book, with deep research about prevalent practices, will be welcomed by the faculty, students, practitioners and alike. Additional aids in the form of power point slides, answers to the questions, MCQs and case studies will be made available to the institutes and faculties on request.

Any suggestions for improvement are welcomed whole heartedly.

Sanjiva Shankar Dubey
itsm.ssdubey@gmail.com

Acknowledgements

This book is a culmination of several years of my learning and experience as a practising manager of IT Services Business. My learnings were enriched by seniors and colleagues of this wonderful industry. I acknowledge their contribution in shaping up my thoughts, honing my skills, and encouraging me to pen this book for the benefits of the young IT Services Business professionals. I am thankful to my employer IBM, for allowing me to pursue my academic interest in my spare time.

Being a visiting faculty at IIM Campuses at Indore, Lucknow, Noida and Rohtak, XLRI and other B-Schools, I have been able to share the concepts, processes and practices with the students whose interaction in the class and outside further provided a test of their suitability. These students are the silent contributors of this intellectual exercise and are worthy of my thanks.

In addition Directors, Dean and Faculty colleagues of these institutes are worthy of my gratitude for inviting me from time-to-time to interact with their students.

This book has drawn insight from the works of several researchers, authors, and practitioners. I consider my work as carrying forward their tradition and quote Bernard of Chartres[1], another dwarf standing on the shoulders of giants. Care has been taken to appropriately mention their work. However, if any such have been missed out, it would be incorporated into the future editions of the book, if pointed out.

Writing a book requires hours of solitude, and months of painstaking efforts which can only be undertaken with the support and encouragement from my family. They stood by me, while I burnt the midnight oil writing the book. I am fortunate to receive unstinted support and encouragement from my wife Vibha, son Priyamvad and daughter Devisha, who made this journey truly enjoyable. I am also indebted to continued encouragement from my elder brother Sri Ashutosh Dubey and sister-in-law Smt Riddhi Dubey, while pursuing this efforts.

Thanks are also due to the editorial and production teams of PHI Learning, whose dedicated and meticulous effort of editing and production process could make this book a reality.

Finally, as a true believer of destiny, my gratitude is to the supreme power that guides and shapes our thought and deeds. This book would not have been possible if it would not have been decided by the destiny.

Sanjiva Shankar Dubey

---

1. Bernard of Chartres was a twelfth-century French Neo-Platonist philosopher, scholar, and administrator.

Chapter 1

IT Services
Industry Landscape

So companies have to be very schizophrenic. On one hand, they have to maintain continuity of strategy. But they also have to be good at continuously improving.

—Michael Porter [Author and Harvard Professor]

1.1 Introduction

What is the business of IT Services? IT Services (ITS) business is a multi-dimensional business that functions in diverse spheres. It has many new things to learn, explore and unravel. The IT Services depends on other businesses, and now has become an integral part for most of them. For example, we cannot imagine a bank without the ATM facility and core banking solution or the airlines without internet-based booking. The most enticing feature of IT Services is, it comes up with newer prospects in new industries every now and then.

Though IT Services is an industry that is so central to most of our commercial and work life, something that is increasingly occupying most of our day time in one form or the other, be it checking our e-mails, buying books or movie tickets or changing our status on social networking site, but we know very less about how it functions. Let us take an example. We eat food and do cooking, but this does not guarantee our abilities to run a multi location fast food chain, as we do not know about serving quality burger and pizzas across the nations within same service levels. Similarly, knowing a computer language or two, writing program code or knowing how a module of ERP works and is implemented, is like knowing how to eat or cook a dish. This is not equivalent of knowing how business of chain of hotel, fast food, flight kitchen or restaurant works!

This book is about managing IT Services business for global clients. It builds the foundation concepts of how IT Services Enterprise (ITSE) work, and how each one of the professional joining them can lead a successful career. This presents a compendium of processes and best practices followed in various functions of a professionally managed IT Services firm, which most of us want to be part of. Such a body of knowledge is certainly required for anyone joining this coveted new age services industry.

1.2 IT Services Business's Conceptual Foundation

For building conceptual foundation of any business, one must be aware of its past briefly,

1

understand its present comprehensively and prepare for its future inquisitively. The history of computers, IT and its convergence with telecommunication is now a part of the general knowledge. Most of our readers would have learnt about it in their schools and undergraduate curriculum. History of IT and IT Services therefore, would not invite much discussion in this book. The main focus of this book is to enlightened our readers with the comprehensive knowledge of the present IT Services Enterprise and arouse their curiosity for its glorious future which they are going to be part of.

IT Services industry started with almost a non-existent origin about 30 years ago. It is now a thriving 70 billion USD industry in India and approximately 2.6 trillion US$ worldwide[1] in 2012 as per recently published Gartner report. All industries spend nearly 2–5%[2] of their annual turnover on IT. This is the most thriving industry that has emerged a major global source of improving efficiency and effectiveness of all other industries and has become a source of both growth and employment. Several research[3] have been conducted to unearth multiple advantages occurred to variety of industries due to IT systems and services. For example, airlines industry transport millions of passengers enabled through seamless interoperability of three or four airlines reservation systems. Now, banks do not open more physical branches to spread their operations linearly, but resort to online banking. Mobile call records are the newest reliable *Khabri*[4] to police investigators. Government ensures transparency and service level to its citizens through e-governance portals and systems. No one would ever precisely calculate how much extra remuneration millions of basic workmen like plumbers, electricians, mechanics, small traders and many others could generate with affordable mobile phone in their hands enabled through innovative information and communication technology. Every common citizen in India knows how the online railways reservation system has added several hours if not days in their life by eliminating the painful process of standing in the queue for booking the train tickets. Read the article by Suzanne Iacono and Rolf T. Wigand[5] to gather industry by industry impact of IT systems and services to enhance every industry competitiveness and efficiency.

As the IT industry grew, it adopted processes and practices from other industries and transformed it to suit its ever-changing requirements. Many of these concepts, processes and practices have become grounded in the last 20–25 years of IT Services Enterprise evolution. Remember, IT Services enterprises in addition to developing and maintaining IT systems and software also work like any other enterprise and have similar business functions. ITS firm also solicits business, manages customer relationships and operates large pool of workforce many of them with extremely good background and intelligence levels. Yet, the irony is that those concepts and functional management principles that have become standards for manufacturing, retail, healthcare or any other services in the last hundred years of management education are only relevant in parts for IT Services industry.

---

1. Source: http://www.gartmer.com/technology/research/it-spending-forecast/accessed 02012012
2. http://blogs.gartner.com/jeff_roster/2009/02/11/it-spend-by-industry-worldwide/
3. Johnston, R. and Gregor, S. (2000). A Theory of Industry-level Activity for Understanding the Adoption of Interorganizational Systems, *European Journal of Information Systems,* 9: 243–251.
4. A hindi word for informer, who provide leads to police about any crime or criminal.
5. Iacono, Suzanne and Wigand, Rolf T. (2005). Information technology and industry change: view from an industry level of analysis, *Journal of Information Technology,* 20: 211–212.

1.3   IT Services Business Management is Lot Different

Managing IT Services Enterprise is totally different than managing any other services firms such as healthcare or insurance firm. Services marketing are dramatically opposite to marketing retail products. While many IT Services Enterprise ultimately make or maintain IT products like any other manufacturing enterprise or provide services like other services firm, their process and methods are is quite different.

Take an example of IT Services selling. Unlike product services industry, selling skill of ITS is not only required amongst business development team but also within the delivery teams. In ITSE, everyone is expected to have sales orientation either to convince the customer or to colleague to sell their unique innovative idea or approach. The ever-changing nature of technology and consistent train of innovation makes IT Services a unique industry where half life of knowledge is less than 5 years. Such unique differences makes large number of fresh entrants to this industry fumbling to find relevance with what has been taught in their universities or have learnt while performing IT functions elsewhere.

They need to enrich themselves with various processes and functions of IT Services Enterprise, to bridge the last mile knowledge for their successful career in the IT Services industry. They must adopt process perspective to understand prevalent concepts of managing various functions of IT Services Enterprise. In addition they should read case studies and stories of successful IT Services projects lifecycle to build further foundation of thin knowledge.

1.4   Understand Concepts Process and Practices

IT industry is at a cross road in India. It has seen tremendous growth in last 30 years; employ 2 million plus professional directly and nearly 8 million indirectly in support functions such as administration, travel, employee care and real estate management. Currently, it contributes nearly 4 % of India GDP and looked upon as pride industry where India can safely and proudly say that they are the world leaders. What France is known for wine and Japan for electronics and cars, India is for IT.

Yet the brand India of IT needs to shed its low cost image and gain intellectual and innovation leader image. This cannot sustain India's leadership in IT Services for long. The simple reason is that Indian economy unlike the western counterparts is a growing economy where inflation and aspirations will continue to rise. This will call for higher wages, higher cost of logistics, infrastructure, power and many others, year after year. So the days are not far off when the cost advantage will no longer be attractive. So IT industry has to move from being a low cost commodity supplier of cheap labour to become a value added differentiators in front of the clients. They should be innovative problem solver to the businesses rather being a cost-effective supplier of technical services. It is no brainer to surmise that one of its reasons lies in the lack of formal preparation of professionals during their studies for this industry. All leading professions enhance its execution prowess and growth through continuous learning, research, innovation, adaptation of best practices and sharing experiences with fellow professionals. Medical professionals are known to combine their intellect to fight deadly diseases and complex patient situations. Unless the IT professionals both new as well as experienced are deeply endowed with concepts, skilled in processes and enriched with best practices, how will this profession get enriched?

To go up the value chain

Many companies, especially the major ones have tried (and still continue to do so) to develop business-oriented capabilities and make efforts to go up the value chain by setting up business consulting practices with varying degree of successes. They also need their sales team to be well-versed in consultative selling approach so that they do not come across box pushers or warm body suppliers. Yet large section of their sales team remains oriented or equipped to selling commodity services, partly because of historical reasons and largely because lack of efforts to reorient them. When you are successful in a particular way, it may be difficult to change your way to adopt a different way. That is where the younger generations who would be adaptable to learn new way of doing things should come up and gradually bring changes in the system.

To win and execute large services and solution contracts

Large contracts of IT Services are won when the IT Services company demonstrates deep understanding of client business needs and presents an appropriate, innovative and attractive solution to address them. Such capability would need the team to be equipped in adopting a process-centric approach for winning and execution. Managing IT Services business in the coming decades will be a far more challenging and difficult where India will compete with the low-cost peers like China, who can deliberately control the cost as in manufacturing arena. In addition there are small countries who are the followers like Philippines, Malaysia, Mexico, Brazil, Russia, etc. who can make the Indian IT industry dream turn sour. India needs large numbers of IT Services professional who are well-equipped in executing large value-added projects which can only done by adopting process-centric approach. Management of IT Services business as a subject must be taught mandatorily to any aspiring IT professional if this path of going up the value chain has to be pursued.

Finally, the word IT Services has been used in a larger context where it encompasses various types of services, including IT enabled services. Telecom and IT convergence has led to remote offerings, services on demand on many varieties, all of which requires consultative selling approach to make customer understand the value of the technology delivered to them. Here IT is seen as a covering to all types of technology sales to address a client business needs.

1.5 Transforming from Product to Services Enterprise

Let us start with the first and foremost process for sustaining any enterprise, sales to understand the differences. IT products especially hardware, software licenses are easy to sell. In such cases you have to explain the features to the right customer and if the customer has a need, the sales process culminates. It is not easy for a sales person to get welcomed with open arms by the customer waiting with a blank cheque. There will be chase and fight with competing products. But services sales process requires deep exploration of customer's need before being able to configure appropriate services to address them. We can call it solution selling or relationship selling where the sales process is designed to serve the need of the client and as soon as the sales deal is signed the process of further selling really starts through the services delivery process.

The challenge is the transformation of the sales workforce that comes from product selling mind set (velocity selling!), who are interested to push the product whether or not it meets the customer need. We have to change their mindset to services or solution selling. This is a complex transformation not easy to achieve unless the cultural change is brought about in the organization and the sales team is equipped with the necessary training and education. It requires sustained leadership, adaptations in supporting systems and process, political and cultural navigation, and most of all, communication. Not only it requires a clear cut definition of new Success criteria but also building credibility, and addressing road block during the transformation process. It might also mean practically rebuild the team, changing leaders and or the entire team. Lori Williams calls this an evolutionary process that requires painstaking building of processes and capabilities. While only 20% people are called to be born salesperson (eagle) the remaining 80% are successful as they follow process meticulously and smartly.

Remember in services business getting a customer order means nothing in terms of revenue. The revenue is realized only when the services are delivered. In fact in services business, selling is a continuous process. This approach is not limited for complex mega size contracts, but is also needed for small size short duration contracts as they lay the foundation of relationship for the bigger one.

Most companies want fewer suppliers and most suppliers want customers that give them repeat business. The same is true for ITS business as well. Unlike a product selling—the IT Services business—the value of the contract will be realized only when the ITS firm will deliver these services meeting all customers requirements and expectations. Only then the customer starts to pay based on the milestones or deliverables.

This is the precise reason many ITS firms with strong past history of product or just staffing services business fail to realize this paradigm change required in their approach. In staffing services, once the customer has vetted the resume and conducted interview of the resources the selling process stops. The candidate is placed to do the work with client, and his/her performance is totally the responsibility of the client to extract work out of the resource, the supplier company does not play any role afterwards other than billing based on the time sheet of the hours works by the resource person.

1.6 Keep Focus on Client Value

The job of IT Services Enterprise leaders is to make sure that every interaction of their team takes customer to newer heights of value delivery, new learning and something more useful. Client relationship, like any other, is never static or buried in the past achievements. The process in its first step recognizes the importance of creating value in maintaining a long-term customer relationships and taking action accordingly. In fact for every step of the ITS sales-delivery-account growth cycle the following activities need to be performed::

(i) Assess customer needs and expectations
(ii) Activities to meet these customer expectations

(iii) Identify techniques for improving the customer business process

(iv) Detail out strategic problem-solving approach

(v) Match customer characteristics with requisite profile of salespeople

(vi) Explain the outcome to customer

(vii) Convey the benefits and develop long-term relationship

1.7 A Brief Overview of Global IT Services Industry

Globally, the IT product and services market has crossed US$ 1.6 trillion in 2010, growing 4.0% over 2009. The IT Services share has increased from US$ 566 billion in 2009 to US$ 574 billion in 2010. Amongst all geographies, Americas still leads the IT Services market with 43.0% share followed by EMEA (Europe Middle-East and Africa) revenues 39.7% and AP (Asia-Pacific) revenues 17.3% in 2010. In BPO arena out of total US$ 158 billion 55.3% in 2010 was distributed amongst Americas. 25.9% has been distributed amongst EMEA and 18.8% distributed amongst AP.

IT Services is highly outsourcing based industry where the global customers take advantage of cost-effective skills from developing countries to provide IT Services. Due to increased robustness of telecom infrastructure and cost-effective rates in these countries, outsourcing of IT Services and BPO has become very attractive. It is no wonder that the outsourcing showed a growth rate of 10.4% in 2010 over 2009 and ended up being a US$ 102–106 billion size market in 2010. While IT Services sourcing grew at 10.3% to a market size of US$ 62–64 billion and BPO sourcing grew at 10.6% to a market size of US$ 40–42 billion. NASSCOM strategic review, 2008–2011 estimates a market potential of approximately US$ 550 B (US$ 280 billion for IT services and US$ 220 billion) which still remains to be tapped.

India amongst other countries is a leading service provider of Information Technology (IT) and Information Technology Enabled Services (ITES) for the global client. In addition domestic market of IT and ITES is also growing due growth in Indian economy expected to be around 8–9% in the years to follow.

Future of IT Services Industry is looking extremely bright. The expected growth of IT Services is likely to be to US$ 684 billion at a CAGR[6] of 3.9%. This will have US$ 239 billion as outsourcing portion by 2014. This includes US$ 42.8 billion of offshoring component in 2014 growing at a CAGR of 6.6%.

Overall BPO services will be US$ 201.5 billion in 2014 which is growing at CAGR of 5.8%. Analysts such as Gartner, Forrester, IDC and others predict healthy growth of IT and ITES industry.

1.8 Indian IT Services and Solution Industry at a Glance

Indian IT industry will grow to approximately US$ 70 billion in terms of revenue by end of 2011 and will account for about 5.8% of country's GDP[7]. Employing over 2.2 million professionals, this industry is grew at the rate of 19% last year (2011). This industry indirectly

---

6. Compounded Annual Growth Rate
7. http://www.ibef.org/industry/informationtechnology.aspx accessed 25072011

gives employment to about 8 million people more who support the professionals either in infrastructure management or logistics. Indian IT industry did export worth US$ 59 billion in FY2011 which is 26% of total Indian exports. In addition, IT industry in India is poised to grow to US$ 225 billion by 2020, and commensurately will need 30 million IT professionals.

The large part of IT industry revenue comes from IT and ITES sector. The estimates vary between 50 to 55% of the total IT industry revenue, this sector accounts for the majority of employment in IT industry.

The estimates[8] show that about 40% of IT Services are delivered to Banking, Financial Services and Insurance (BFSI) industry clients, another 24% to "emerging verticals" comprising of healthcare, retail, media and utilities, and 20% from the high technology and telecom sectors and remaining for manufacturing client. However, in the future as per Nasscom[9], the emerging verticals growing at 22% will outpace the rest by 1.5 times.

IT Services industry in India has always been in the forefront of quality led services. Majority of them have already established their processes based on international standards such as ISO 9000, CMM, Six Sigma, ITIL, TOGAF, etc. Over 500 Indian IT Services companies have obtained CMM certifications.

1.9 Future Trends of IT Services Industry

According to Dun and Bradstreet study[10] Indian IT-BPO industry from 2011 is likely to witness several important trends. Some of which are as follows:

(i) Trend towards acquisition and mergers leading to consolidation.

(ii) Cloud computing is likely to usher new opportunities for the IT Services and give rise to new offerings which can be used by small and medium corporations.

(iii) Remote Infrastructure Management Services (RIMS) is the next likely opportunity for marketing IT Services. While NASSCOM and McKinsey estimates global RIMS market to be USD 96–104 billion it is expected that nearly 70–75% of it can be offshored, and Indian IT Services companies can take advantage.

(iv) Indian government is likely to spend more on IT adoption leading to growth in the domestic market. Government of India has adopted a national e-Governance Plan (NeGP) through which USD 9 billion will be invested in NeGP projects till FY14.

(v) More opportunities will come from other verticals such as government, healthcare, retail and utilities and IT Services companies would de-risk their business from BFSI sector clients which was the worst hit segments due to the impact of 2009 global financial crisis growth in these emerging verticals is expected to be substantially faster than the core verticals.

(vi) IT Services companies will diversify from core markets (i.e. U.S. and U.K.) to other growing markets such as Mexico, Ireland, Netherlands, Philippines and Brazil.

(vii) Small IT Services players will be impacted as government is going to withdraw tax benefits for STPI (Software Technology Parks of India).

---

8. http://knowledge.wharton.upenn.edu/india/article.cfm?articleid=4573 accessed 25072011

9. National Association of Software and Service Companies; an industry body of software and services company.

10. http://www.stockmarketindian.com/highlights/IT_BPO_industry_outlook_for_2011.html

(viii) Rural BPOs will emerge as the new IT Services segment to be keenly watched. NASSCOM estimated that about 35 rural BPO centres employing over 5000 people are already in place.

(ix) Small and Medium Business's (SMB) will boost the new market opportunities for the IT Services sector.

1.10 IT Services: New Market Place Realities

IT Services market place is witnessing a phenomenal change in the last few years. Gone are the days when Indian companies were able to take the easy route to place manpower resources and bill them on a time and material basis. The customer is no longer interested in stand alone services, but wants an integrated solution that takes care of requirement definition, solution design, delivery and implementation. All this will now be under a fixed price contract and under stringent service level agreements and penalty clauses for delay or poor quality. Even when the outsourcing projects were awarded in the past most were of one-off variety. The service provider was expected to perform certain services under given parameters and the role of integration with other streams was left to the contracting firm. This has now given rise to an either mega outsourcing, covering all aspects of a firm or business or just focusing of selective outtasking covering a slice of work from amongst the entire portfolio.

Companies are now increasingly being asked to standardize their service offerings to maintain a level of quality of deliverables. More and more companies now understand the benefits and risks associated with the local labour vs global delivery models. Consequently, the benefits can no longer be camouflaged by the service providers and the contracting firms demand that these benefits in parts be passed on to them. Many firms have tried between keeping their own captive delivery centres, complete or partial outsourcing with varying degree of success. Only their experiences and results produced have been different.

Finally, most services and offerings are labour based where man hours/man days are billed without the regards of using intellectual assets that may help to shorten the delivery time and help the service provider gain more realization from his team.

1.11 IT Services Business: An Art or Science?

Decades ago the debate was on whether software development is an art or a science. This has since calmed down a bit after a concerted movement was undertaken in 80's and 90's to standardize the software development process, tools and come out with standards so that the customer can distinguish between one organization from another. However, IT Services is still struggling to break free from art form approach where every services contract is uniquely crafted leading to unpredictability of the end results.

According to Paul Horn[11], a senior IBM Research VP, the IT-services sector is in dire need of people who are talented in the application of technologies to help in the businesses of those people who understand the intersection of business and IT. A Science approach for IT Services can only address these complex issues surrounding the transformation of businesses

---

11. http://www.businessweek.com/technology/content/jan2005/tc20050121_8020.htm

by simultaneous development of both business methods and the technology that supports it. For this a new discipline is needed that is called services science. It is necessary therefore that IT Services adopt the services science philosophy so that the certainty of delivery is maintained.

1.12 Challenges Faced by IT Services Enterprises

It is very easy to start an IT Services company with or without any significant capital expenditure. But scaling it up to a critical mass and growing it to a significant level has been an eluding dream for many of them. As author has mentioned in some of his lectures most IT Companies remain *bonsai*[12] companies perpetually and never scale upto a self standing, weather proof and fruit producing full fledged tree, as they are not able to manage the growth challenges successfully.

Growth challenges can be categorized into the following major heads:

   (i) Customer acquisition and retention

   (ii) Capital and infrastructure woes

   (iii) People continuity

   (iv) Dilemma between strategic focus vs opportunistic billing

Let us discuss each one of them in detail.

Customer acquisition and retention

Small and emerging ITS companies will find it difficult to convince the customer to award bigger projects for want for any past track record of successful execution. Once having secured a contract they find it difficult to successfully execute due lack of experience, quality issue or manpower attrition. Larger ITS firms though able to win large deals run into rough whether of continuous push from competition who offer reduced prices and win over the customer.

Capital and infrastructure woes

Managing a healthy pipeline and order book is important, so that the utilization levels of the team remains high. As the ITS company's size grows it requires larger space and infrastructure to provide working space for the team. All this calls for capital investment to start with and maintenance cost thereafter.

People continuity

ITS companies face major issue of people retention. This dynamic industry with opportunities and growth induces experienced and skilled people to change jobs. All this impacts the quality and delivery ability of the ITS firm.

Dilemma between strategic focus vs opportunistic billing

ITS companies face a unique dilemma between preparing for deep skilled projects or run after easy to execute commodity services. The former requires strategy, planning and patience to be successful, whereas the later will give easy billing, but with no differentiation whatsoever.

---

12. Bonsai: The art of growing dwarfed, ornamentally shaped trees or shrubs in small shallow pots or trays

1.13   Future Risks and Mitigation Strategies for IT Services and Solution Industry

As the world economy is becoming increasingly globalized, the opportunities as well as risks are also increasingly been multiplied. IT Services industry is amongst the first one to get a hit in case of any disruption anywhere either due to economy, political or reasons of nature. Theses uncertainties, for example US debt crisis, falling European economy or natural calamities such as Tsunami or earthquake, impact the IT spent of the major clients. In the event of any budget cut, IT budget is amongst the first one to be cut and thus the impact is felt by the service provider firms. In the recent times, major markets have been slow to recover after the 2008 sub prime crisis. In addition, our economy has been showing an increasing sign of instability due to popular unrest in Middle East countries or sovereign defaults by Southern Europe countries. These are a few examples which has impacted cuts in IT budgets leading to IT Services demand compression, pricing pressure and enhanced credit risk from vulnerable clients. Major currency exchange rate fluctuation due to increasing export and foreign exchange remittances further impact the profitability of IT Services companies.

Most IT Services firms address these challenges by generating new customers through diversification across geographies especially developing markets such as India/South Asia, Africa and greater China. These firms also adopt further diversification of their product and services portfolio. They aim to build closer relationship by developing deeper understanding of client business so that they can get repeat and long term business and lower their sales and marketing cost.

Indian IT Services firms also face issue of protectionism by developed countries through work permit and Visa restrictions. This can only be dealt by bringing more business offshore, and making services into value-added products.

As competition is growing in the seller-buyer segment, it also gets heated up while hiring talent. The salary cost is continuously increasing due to inflation in India and shortage of good quality professionals in adequate numbers.

Major Indian IT Services firms want themselves to be seen as full service provider in line of the illustrious MNC peers like Accenture, IBM, etc. Only then they can put enhanced focus to win and execute larger, more complex, but highly profitable services contracts.

All this can happen if these firm make increasing investment in building deep expertise through continuous and relentless built up of domain expertise and intellectual capital. This can be in the form of newer business models or productivity enhancement tools and offering services that does not get impacted due to demand decrease. The role of these companies should be the early advisor of new technology adoption for profitable use. Example of emerging cloud based services business models which can deliver software on a pay-per-use basis is being touted by major IT Services firm[13], as the next growth opportunity.

1.14   Who are the Likely Beneficiaries of This Unique and Interesting Subject?

This book is intended gift to all those who want to join or have joined the IT Services industry.

---

13. Annual Report 2010–11, TCS : Key risks Impact and Mitigation

As we have discussed that IT Services is a fast growing industry which employs millions of professionals globally. Most of these young professionals join IT Services industry after finishing B.Tech/M.Tech, BCA/MCA or BBA/MBA courses. Many complete their graduations in wide variety of subjects such as civil, chemical or other branches of engineering, science or even social sciences. IT Services Enterprise gives an opportunity to all and embraces them with open hand. But they need to prepare themselves for it, sooner or later.

However, once they join the work force they realize that they are barely quipped and hardly prepared to understand how this industry works. Their past education must now be supplemented with understanding of industry, its processes and practices. Fortunately, many large IT Services Enterprise do provide a few weeks for orientation courses[14] to make them somewhat prepared. But they limit such induction to specific organization practices related to their immediate job which is neither exhaustive nor comprehensive. For other professionals, not joining these major ones or joining in small batches, lateral placements etc. are expected to pick up understanding on the job. Consequently, not only will you take time to be productive, but will find extremely difficult to understand the big IT Services picture of your enterprise. You will be grappling to relate how your current assignment fits in the overall success of the firms. It is no wonder that several young professionals find it difficult to navigate their career within these emerging IT Services firms according to their aspirations and abilities.

All IT professional must therefore acquire a comprehensive and exhaustive understanding of the business of IT Services. For them this book presents a clear, concise and comprehensive knowledge about it. With this knowledge of how IT Services firms work (or ideally it should), its various functions and processes and skills required, they will surely speed on to the accelerated expressway of their career.

This subject is an ideal course for the final year of any discipline (especially IT stream) and could be a great value addition for students' successful placement and greater productivity in this wonderful industry. For large number of IT Services firm who always look for creative and comprehensive content to groom their fresher, for them this book is a natural choice of induction curriculum or otherwise for skills building. Finally, those who have already started to work for few years; this is a ready reckoner for all time to act as reference and refresher. After all, where else would they get all the concepts, processes and practices of this mysterious IT Services industry at one place!

1.15 Summary

This introductory chapter lays foundation of the subject of managing IT Services business. It explores the need and the framework to understand the complexity of the IT Services business that has become the science of survival and competitiveness and art of innovation for other industries.

This chapter further defines the business of IT Services and then dwells into building the conceptual foundation of IT Services business. It also explains that IT Services business

---

14. A recent report quotes that IT Services industry spends 2% of their annual turnover on skilling the fresh recruits.

management is lot different than any other services or manufacturing enterprise, primarily due its close relationship with its wide ranging user industry and also due its continuous evolution arising out of technology, business models and innovative usages.

In also discusses that in order to enhance quality and agility of the IT Services industry its professional have to be deeply grounded in concepts, processes and practices. Only then these ITSEs will be able to go up the value chain and /or win and execute large services and solution contracts. Both these are proving to be an obstacle for the growth of Indian ITSEs. This means they have to abandon some of the existing processes that have come from product selling mind set and must transform to a true services enterprise. They need to keep focus on providing client value.

This chapter gave an overview of the global IT Services industry, and its Indian counter part. It also outlined some of the salient future trends of IT Services industry, covering new market place realities as well.

It was pertinent to discuss whether IT Services business is an art or a science form. Science makes implementation easy and standard whereas, art firm is associated with the creativity and uniqueness. Fortunately, as the IT Services industries are discovering new opportunities and creativity frontiers, it is also emphatically bringing in scientific principles in managing that has become proven and routine. This is great combination and needs large number of professionals who bring the knowledge of business as well IT to keep relevance of IT Services industry to its user industry.

This chapter also enumerated some of the challenges faced by IT Services Enterprises, most prominently being the issue of managing and achieving growth covering:

(i) Customer acquisition and retention

(ii) Capital and infrastructure woes

(iii) People continuity

(iv) Dilemma between strategic focus vs opportunistic billing

With this it was pertinent to outline future risks and mitigation strategies for IT Services and solution industry for the benefit to our readers. The chapter also clearly identified the worthy reader's profile of its likely beneficiaries of this unique and interesting subject.

Review Questions

1.1 Why do we study concepts processes and practices of IT Services industry. How will it help the industry as well as its readers?

1.2 Describe some of the challenges of growth faced by the IT Services industry.

1.3 Why IT Services industry is considered mysterious or complex? Explain by giving some examples.

1.4 What are the future trends of IT Services industry? What are the new market place realities which ITSE must be able to address?

Suggested Further Reading

'IT-BPO Sector in India: Strategic Review 2011', NASSCOM.

McKinsey Study for NASSCOM called 'Perspective 2020: Transform Business, Transform India'.

Tata Consultancy Services, Annual Report 2010–11.

Brynjolfsson, E. and L. Hitt (1995). "Information Technology as a Factor of Production: The Role of Differences Among Firms," *Economics of Innovation and New Technology*, 3(4): 183–200.

Websites

www.Nasscom.in

http://www.palgrave-journals.com/jit/journal/v20/n4/full/2000052a.html accessed 29112011

http://www.information-age.com

http://www.rolandberger.com/expertise/industries/it_industry/

www.mckinsey.com

www.ibm.com

www.accenture.com

www.gartner.com

Chapter 2

IT Services Portfolio

You have to be fast on your feet and adaptive or else a strategy is useless.
—Charles de Gaulle [French general, writer and statesman]

2.1 Introduction

We have seen in Chapter 1 how important and interesting it is to know about the IT Services concepts, processes and practices in a structured manner. While the earlier chapter answered the question why IT Services are important the present one will answer What it is? In this chapter we will spread our conceptual journey to understand the gamut of IT Services and how they are related with each other. No IT Services Enterprise (ITSE) can claim capabilities to deliver IT Services of all types with equal finesse and effectiveness. We are using the word portfolio[1] of service to discuss various IT Services their unique outputs, challenges and type of skills required to perform them.

IT Services spans across IT and telecommunication industry covering various services such as:

(i) Software development and maintenance

(ii) Management of IT operations and infrastructure

(iii) Network management

(iv) Business process outsourcing (BPO), Voice and Data Services (popularly called call centers)

(v) e-business services like portals, ecommerce and data based services

Most of these services are (and can be) performed remotely using telecom network. The rapid advancement with which its capabilities have grown has boosted IT Services delivery manifold. Yet the core services that enable management of network are not classified under the IT Services. These two, core telecom and IT Services have significant differences in terms of company sizes, market structure and the way in which they are managed[2]. The book is largely centered around the IT Services and solutions which further depend on telecom services to use it as a means of communication.

---

1. A term popularly used in financial area to denote the total holdings of the investments like shares, bonds, securities, etc., of a financial institution or private investor.
2. This is a subject in itself and requires broader discussion.

2.2 Categories of IT Services

Broadly, the IT Services can be categorized[3] into the following:

(i) **Advisory services** covering Consulting, Planning and envisioning and selecting appropriate IT solution

(ii) **Build services** spanning across Software Development and Installation and its maintenance which leads to software Product Development and/or implementation

(iii) **Perform services** where customer expects the IT Services firm to run the day-to-day operations. This includes

- Operations and maintenance of IT applications
- Operations, upkeep and maintenance of IT infrastructure such as hardware, network, switches and power infrastructure
- Business process services covering transaction processing of business processes, customer services where voice-based call centers occupy their prime place and also data services where customer query, complaints or new orders are resolved/acted upon when they come through e-mail or directly put on the client company's website

(iv) **IT Governance services** related to management of IT assets, functions and processes, outsourcing contract governance, implementation of Security polices, etc.

(v) **Management of quality** of software development services, Project Management services

(vi) **Software as service (SaaS)**, the latest development with its various *avatars* such as, PaaS, HaaS[4], where the IT product or infrastructure is allowed to be used to large number of small and mid size companies at a fee decided based on number of users, disk space used, hours used and so on.

We now elaborate on each one of them briefly and show their interdependence in Figure 2.1.

2.2.1 Consulting, Planning and Envisioning

Advising includes consulting, planning and envisioning which relates to high end consultancy services spanning across IT strategy, Business process reengineering, IT planning and budgeting and related areas. The scope of such services can only be defined broadly at the initial stages as neither client or the ITSE would be able to exactly specify the end deliverable in exact terms. This service requires a good amount of close relationships between customer and ITSE to successfully deliver them. While the client can exactly specify their problems in detail, and what their business needs and priorities are, an ITSE brings deep domain specific knowledge and how IT can help addressing these business issues. A good marriage of need and expertise can lead to a good solution when both work as one team.

In the recent past, most clients have been increasingly demanding from ITSE advice on business domain as well. Technology is said to be a great leveler and many business processes

---

3. Sector Report: No. 10-II (September 2005) ICT and Electronic Business in the IT Services Industry, European Commission Enterprise & Industry Directorate General.

4. HAAS, (hardware as service), PAAS(Platform as service) are new emerging IT Services.

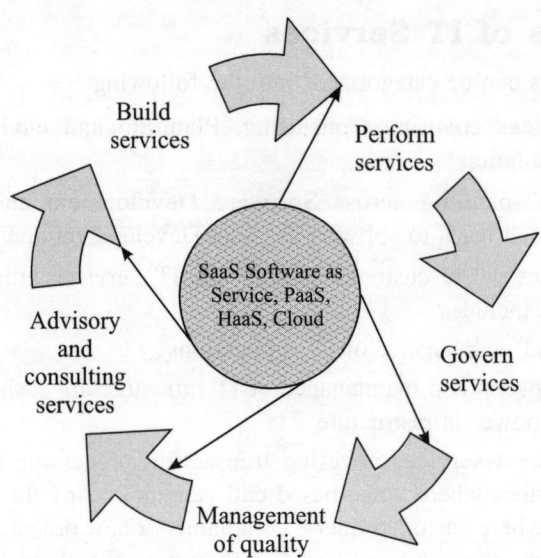

Build
services

Perform
services

Advisory
and
consulting
services

SaaS Software as
Service, PaaS,
HaaS, Cloud

Govern
services

Management
of quality

Figure 2.1   Interrelation of portfolio of IT Services.

are coming embedded in the technology solution. IT Services clients not only demand IT expertise, but also domain and operation expertise from IT companies. For example, as a user I expect my e-mail service provider (gmail or yahoo), to keep on informing me the best way of managing my e-mails, to manage the address book, view it on my cell phone and so on. In the same manner a retail chain of store would expect the ERP implementer to also educate and the best practices for operating a world class retail chain.

This demand shift from the *doer* of technology services as told, to trusted advisor of business best practices, are forcing ITSEs to embrace this type of services in their portfolio. Consequently, several larger ITS Enterprises have opened up consulting front end wing and several management consulting companies have integrated their consulting wings into their IT Services so that they can offer consulting-led, business solutions as the way forward for integrated IT Services.

2.3   Build Services

In this case the IT professionals create a software application for a client based on a given specification. In the initial days of IT Services, this was the most sought after IT Service to be offered to the client who may not have an adequate skilled resources and at times the necessary expected processes and techniques which are advanced and cutting edge. This service has several variants, some of which are discussed as follows:

Application development and installation

Application development and installation includes software development and maintenance services which IT Services company offer as contracted services. Majority of offshore IT

Services companies have focused on these types of services and have made their presence felt in global arena. Such companies can be further sub-divided into companies focused on offering:

1. **Standard software products:** These are sold as Commercially Off The Self (COTS) product to many customers offering standard features. Good marketing and sales ability through vast network of retailers and distributors help expanding this market segment. However, these companies also have to servitize[5] their products by creating services offerings so that the revenue from their product gets enhanced over and above their commodity-like products. Several other industries such as automobile know that the life time services revenue is far greater as compared to the initial sale value of a car. The cell phone industry is well on the way toward this path. Similarly, software products companies create new features, undertake annual upgrades and also customize their products to suit specific requirements to meet customer expectations and in the process gain more and more revenue.

2. **Custom built solution:** This is against the requirement specification to individual clients. Majority of IT Services companies working on outsourcing model fall under this category and offer professional services around several key technologies. This service can be offered by small to large size ITSE as starting new business is easy due to low entry barriers. However, for each one of them their success only depends on the quality of skilled professionals, and ability to develop good relationships with the customer by understanding their requirements well.

3. **Systems Integration (SI) services:** These services are provided across standard as well as custom built software. These companies focus on working with multiple standard COTS software to customize them appropriately for a given customer need. ITSEs also develop additional software modules and custom develop functionalities that helps complete the end-to-end need. These SI companies are authorized implementers of leading COTS packages (e.g. SAP, Siebel, People Soft, Oracle financials, etc). The closer co-operations between developers of COTS software and SI partners are well known and is a major source of revenue for the leading IT Services companies.

Product development and/or implementation

Instead of one-off application development, an IT Services firm may be engaged in developing software products for a client, which in this case may be another Software company who does marketing, brand building and selling. Small and mid-size product companies have followed this route to outsource this activity to contract product development companies. Like in the manufacturing say garments, leather, etc. hundreds of small and medium entrepreneur make products for leading brand who do quality control, strategy, brand building, selling and marketing.

The other variation of this service would be to do customization, training and implementation of some one else's developed product, especially when that someone else is a leading brand and the product has a wide market acceptance. Non-branded air-conditioners in India have been manufactured in unorganized sectors for several decades using branded compressors, fans (called kits) of established brands. In the same manner using standard modules of established

---

5. Cusumano Michael, The Changing Software Business: From Products to Services and Other New Business Models Paper 236, p. 9, MIT report http://digital.mit.edu accessed 25072011

software product companies are used to produce new software solution. COTS products, such as ERP initiated this trend.

2.3.1 Perform Services

This includes several services that operate and maintain the IT systems and infrastructure. The important ones are discussed as follows:

Application maintenance and operations

We have discussed about application development in the build services category, by extending the similar skills application maintenance and operations either onsite or remotely can be offered.

IT infrastructure operations and management services

These companies focus on operation of the ICT infrastructure which includes hardware and network infrastructure. These services are also known as IT infrastructure management or Remote IT infrastructure management (RIM) if done from a low cost location. The later type services (i.e. RIM) require more capital investment in setting up the computing centers and expertise to manage large infrastructure management facilities. Typically, this has been a forte of large corporations such as IBM or EDS who can demonstrate financial power and technical expertise to win and execute infrastructure management services. However, small and mid-size infrastructure management services companies have also started to make dent in the opportunity pie and are increasingly been considered for such services, initially by deploying teams at client premises and later at remote locations.

2.3.2 Governance Services (Security and Governance Management)

While the earlier segment of IT Services are related to IT application life cycle, there are other services that require across the life cycle and are specialist in nature. More and more IT functions are being outsourced, and this requires setting up a governance mechanism so that the service levels, contract deliverables and delivery standards are maintained. Such specialized services fall under this category.

IT Services pertaining to Security and compliance, leading to adoption and certifications standards such as BS 7799, ISO17799 and ISO27001 fall under these categories. In addition other specialist services which help IT systems to follow governance standards such as ITIL, TOGAF are offered by specialized IT companies or divisions of leading IT Services companies.

2.3.3 Management of Quality, Project Management

Software development industry is very large and while many are involved in software development few focus on advising the these development companies itself in managing quality, project management standards and setting up processes to implement best practices.

2.3.4 Software as Service

Software as a Service (SaaS) is an emerging as a newer offering of services where leading companies like Google, Yahoo, Salesforce.com, Amazon, Microsoft etc., provide software products to be used by paying a fee without having to buy them or worry about their installation and management. Such services are offered through Internet-based cloud infrastructure. These services as of now are built around use of standard software products and the users do not have to worry about the infrastructure availability or license fee or upgrades. So far simple and standard software have been deployed in SaaS model example, desktop applications, CRM,[6] etc.

This has several variations such as:

(i) *Hardware as a Service (HaaS)*: This has several sub classification, but primarily it means that hardware is available at free for use. Instead of buying a car you are renting it as taxi only in this case from the same service provider for longer duration that also takes care of the data security needs. While in HaaS means similar to licensing in managed services, in grid computing, HaaS is a pay-as-you-go model[7].

(ii) *Platform as a service (PaaS)*[8] gives facilities of a combined hardware and software environment (platform) so that a customer can deploy applications without investing in all the cost if done on standalone basis and also none of the complexity of managing it based on a yearly/monthly fee. PaaS service provider such as yahoo small business, Google, etc. give development as well as hosting capabilities for any application and support complete life cycle of and implementing web applications entirely available from the Internet. This include application design, development, testing, deployment and hosting and also services such as team collaboration, web service integration, database integration, security, scalability, storage, application versioning, application instrumentation and developer community facilitation.

2.3.5 IT Services Value Creating Chain

IT Services categorization can also be done on the basis of their industry domain focus such as banking, retail, and so on. Most IT Services companies offer wide variety of services and few remains specialized as that limits their ability to grow. While application development companies are getting into the consulting arena, the leading consulting firms are extending their services to software development, outsourcing and system integration as well.

If we probe deeper it will be crystal clear that all these IT Services are the part of larger IT Services industry value creating chain. Not all companies will have all the capabilities and maturity to provide services of all kind, and hence, have to limit to a few specialized areas. Take the case of medical services as an example to draw parallel from. At the most elementary level of medical services will be general physician practising independently offering medical advice to individual patients. As the complexity of the diseases increases, various types of hospitals are required to address the medical requirements. There could be small dispensary with a few doctors to multi-disciplinary nursing homes or hospitals. In addition, there are major referral hospitals

---

6. A very successful SaaS offering is from www.salesforce.com/ for mid size companies CRM needs
7. http://searchitchannel.techtarget.com/definition/Hardware-as-a-Service-HaaS accessed 02102011
8. http://en.wikipedia.org/wiki/Platform_as_a_service

or specialized medical centers at the upper end of the medical diagnostic and treatment. All are required to coexist to meet the varying need of the human population. Similarly, IT Services also have value creating chain meant to serve various types of customer needs. IT Services value creating chain helps us to understand how various types of IT Services are related to each other. By plotting them as two ordinates, business domain knowledge and IT Services process complexity, one can understand which IT Service will be valued more by its customer. IT Services value creating chain also enables us to understand how any IT Services company can expand its operations by either becoming more knowledgeable about customer business or taking up complex service task or both. When we mention about end-to-end IT Service providers as an example, we mean that these companies (IBM, HP, etc.) provide IT Services across the value chain. Figure 2.2[9] explains this in a very simple format.

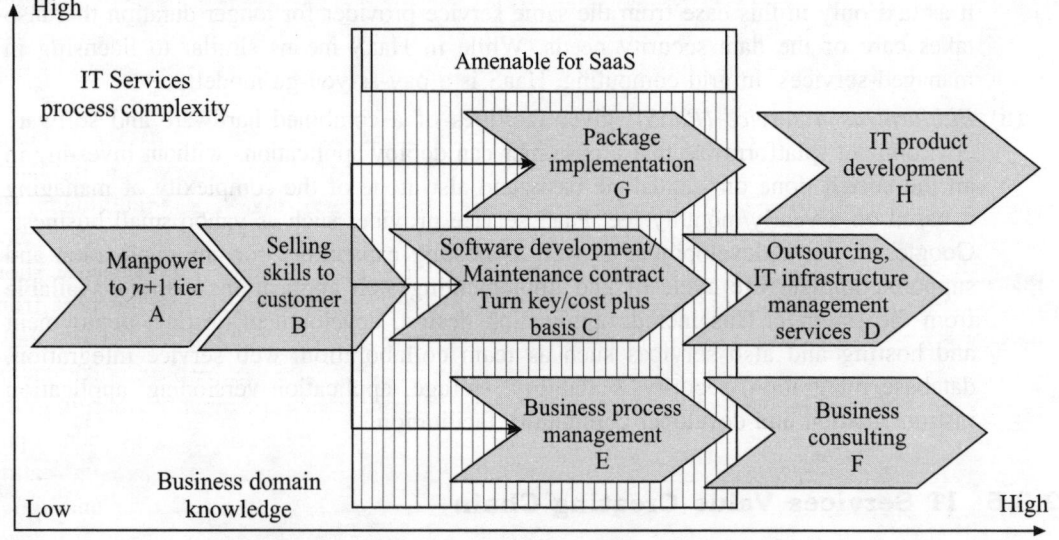

Figure 2.2   IT Services value creating chain.

Staffing services (A and B)

For most start up IT Services companies the first entry point of engagement with the customer is to provide skilled manpower. Call it resourcing, staffing or body-supply business where the client selects candidates after suitable test or interview and assigns work to them under their supervision. Since many small staffing provider may not have direct relationship with the end customer organization, they end up providing these skilled staff from their payroll to a bigger IT service provider (as shown in the diagram block A, manpower to Tier $n+1$). The bigger service provider then positions these skills (from either their payroll or partner's payroll) to the end customer as shown in block B of Figure 2.2. In both the cases, the responsibility of extracting work, quality of work output and end results would lie with the end customer. Skilled resources (i.e. staff) in such cases have to ensure that the customer is happy with their work and does not go back to their employer with any adverse feedback for their continued services. Most of the end customer organization would provide challenging and interesting work, congenial

---

9. Dubey, Sanjiva Shankar, *Innovation with IT*, Tata McGraw-Hill, New Delhi, 2008.

environment for work such a good office space, cafeteria services, hence the contracted staff would enjoy almost the same benefits and feel good despite carrying a contractor badge. Such resources while working on overseas assignments are extra careful to ensure their continued job, hence less worry to the organization that holds their payroll. At times these contract professional deliver extra work, spend long hours in lieu of a good feedback or added incentives such as overtime or free cafeteria facilities. The success of Indian IT industry through low cost contracting is legendary and many large players have thousands of skilled professional deployed under this type of service model.

Staffing services is great start up business model for any IT Services company to choose. This model is less risky to start, assured revenue without having to supervise work, low management overheads and easy to achieve the revenue numbers. On the negatives of this model is that it is highly un-differentiated (any one can do it), has low margins and does not lead to any residual value within the firm in terms of any intellectual asset or domain learning. This is a trading model that works of large volume turnover, with low return per unit of transaction. Issues like employees jumping one company to the other are more frequent as there is no significant feeling of identification with the employer.

Typically, this model of services works extremely well in demand driven situation. IT being an industry with ever evolving new technology will always have shortage of skills in the latest and rarest technology. Therefore, the end user firms would need such skilled individuals for project execution, trouble shooting, etc. at various intervals for varying duration. If the service provider firm has an aggressive and persistent staff that is able to locate such skills at short notice, gets their interview and short-listing done at a rapid pace they can win business from either tier -1 IT companies or the end user firms. In some cases as the business grows these service providers may have a small bench (staff doing nothing) who can be positioned against requirements due to the virtue of some of them being multi skilled. Remember the margin in the business is too thin and despite difference between the assignment-based pay or the bench pay (which would be substantially less) no company can maintain a large bench to prevent eating into its profits. Such larger IT Services firms, with multiple lines of business over and above staffing, redeploy these bench-staff on in-house software development projects if there is a need.

Software development/Maintenance services (C)

Next in line, across the central verge of services value chain is the services provided around software development or their maintenance. One would find under this category services firms ranging from multi-billion dollar IT leading firms to recently formed five friends entrepreneur unit just looking for a new business. Most businesses big or small, including large government and public sector units do have requirements for custom development of software applications. Specifications in all such cases are framed by the contracting company and the services firm has the responsibility to build software application as per these specifications. Previous track record of the team, adherence to quality standards and sometimes size of the firm do form a basis for selection by the contracting firm. In this type of services usually the specification becomes the basis on which the contractor firm would quote their efforts and consequently their price.

The service provider firm has to have the capabilities to deliver the project as per the specification, within the budgeted time and cost. However, given the usual challenges of incomplete specification, added functionality during the course of discussion (called scope creep) and frequent changes in the team composition (due to attrition), completing project on time and budget is a well-known problem.

A variation of this services model is contracting a service provider firm to do maintenance of the exiting software applications. Maintenance is the term used in software application for correcting errors (bugs), making changes to keep pace with the regulatory changes and of course adding new functionalities. Usually, the contractor firm undertakes such maintenance contract for a period assigning a team as per the contracting agreement. In some cases, the contract scope is specified in terms of size of maintenance work such as minor, major, etc.

Outsourcing of IT infrastructure management services (D)

The next type of IT Services along the same path is outsourcing of management of IT infrastructure. This included monitoring an upkeep of network, server and desktops including services for maintaining desktop equipments, installation of software, firewall maintenance, etc. Many end user corporations, who focus their IT team's efforts in managing business requirements and application development, tend to outsource these services much more easily. Falling under the pure technology task, it is easy to manage these services as an outsourced work through regular review of uptime, service levels and so on. A variation of this service is remote infrastructure maintenance where the contractor firm provides the same service remotely by taking access of the technology equipment through set of tools and processes.

Business process management (E)

IT Service providers are uniquely poised to undertake business processes work. Most of the business processes are performed using integrated IT tools (application software) which are developed or customized out of Enterprise Application (ERP). All such business processes that are standard in nature, routine and does not need the contracting firm's specialized skill sets can be outsourced. Business processes for employee and customer services, routine financial processes such as bills collection fall under these categories. One the contractor firm develops more capabilities and better relationship. More complex processes can be outsourced. The growth of Indian BPO industry[10] is a result of GE and American Express setting up their offshore business process management units in mid 90's. As a result of which many independent business process management service providers came up taking advantage of skills available in these areas. IT Services firms who were hitherto focusing on software development and management (maintenance) found a natural progression to undertake business process management work.

One must notice the fine distinction traversing this path of where the service providing firm of IT will have to also include skills that are needed to run the business processes. For example, for an accounting process, the service provider has to have trained accountants, cost accountants, financial analysts, Chartered accountants and other, over and above the IT skills to manage these services as a unit.

Business consulting (F)

Most IT Services firm talk about going up the value chain. This is the ultimate level of services that they want to provide to the customer as business consultant. Easier said than done, these

---

10. The readers should not get confused with call centers industry that focuses on customer care, telephone sales and other services through voice or e-mail.

services require the service provider team to build deep understanding of business domain of the order that these consultants can help the customer solve their business problem. This consultation may pertain to advising senior management of a firm about strategy, structure and initiatives for gaining more market share, reduction of cost, running focused and effective marketing campaign or many other advices.

Package implementation (G)

As the enterprise systems like ERP, CRM, SCM and others package software started to gain wide acceptance as a possible choice, large number of IT service providers developed skills around these packages. These services include business process mapping to these packages, identifying gaps and extent of fitness, undertake package customization to suit business rule of the user firms followed by other implementation activities like data conversion, pilot launches, user training, onsite support and trouble shooting.

Package implementation services of major ERP packages like SAP, Oracle, People soft and others are done by a large number of big and small IT service providers and is a big source of revenue. While implementing these packages the service provider firm has to have the skills to understand business processes and package module functionalities. Small teams of technical expert who can write additional code in package specific language are also needed.

Product development (H)

Most services company face difficulties to scale up. They keep struggling between the extremes of the two typical constraints, one being resources non-availability when there is a customer order in hand and the second being the resources sitting idle when there is no customer work to be performed. In the case of former, companies end up loosing opportunity, quicker revenue realization (as they are unable to mobilize adequate resources) leading to delay to project timelines and seriously affecting deliverable quality. In the case of later, where a company is able to maintain a resource bench and able to mobilize the resource, the bench eats up into profitability.

In order to address this problem few companies trade the path of developing a software product. This requires adequate upfront investment in building a software product based on likely customer requirements. Such products are then sold in multiple copies to many customers and charges such a user licenses, annual maintenance fee, future upgrades can be levied to the using organizations.

Building software product with universal appeal which can sell in multiple copies (hundreds or thousands) is always a dream nursed by most IT companies. But a few succeed. Besides the ability to come out with a product that will have universal appeal, selling and sustaining continuous development to add new features on a long-term basis is difficult task. Software, especially application software, face regular and repeated challenges from new players in the market who can easily come out with a look alike products at a lower cost to gain entry in the market. In addition, running and sustaining a company with product mind-set where one may have to keep doing product enhancement without a customer in sight, and thus, spending money to pay salaries, etc., requires a totally different approach.

There are several good examples of successful product companies like SAP, Oracle, Siebel (in ERP/CRM space) and several point solutions products. However, there are many more failure examples where product companies folded up due to either not getting enough critical installed base, or management lack of vision for making the product continuously enhanced on a sustained basis.

Some services companies do carve out a product after doing a successful custom development efforts based out of learning during the software development exercise. Such products (which are not strictly developed using a product development philosophy) are sold with heavy customization efforts wrapped in for every new customer. So barring the logo of the product most code may be different from one customer to other, thereby loosing the advantage of having common code across installed base.

Advantages of understanding IT Services value creating chain

By understanding how various types of IT Services are interrelated, an ITSE can chartout a suitable course for its future growth. IT professionals can also choose their career growth path by acquiring business domain knowledge or ability to perform complex IT Servicess process.

2.4 Summary

In this chapter we described the entire landscape of possible IT Services, yet we cannot claim that it is exhaustive.

While answering the question of what all IT Services constitute the entire landscape, we adopted the zooming in model to explain this for the benefit of the readers. As you see any map, more and more complexity, detail and relationship are shown as you zoom in, in the same manner we described the landscape in several increasingly detailed iterations.

The broadest classification of IT Services was covered as services spanning across IT and telecommunication industry covering various services such as:

   (i) Software development and maintenance
  (ii) Management of IT operations and infrastructure
 (iii) Network management
  (iv) Business Process Outsourcing (BPO), Voice and Data Services (popularly called call centers)
   (v) E-business services like portals, e-commerce and data-base services

They were further categorized into the following based on the nature of services such as:

   (i) Advisory services includes consulting, Planning and envisioning relates to high end consultancy services
  (ii) Build services covering
        (a) Application Development and Installation
        (b) Standard Software products
        (c) Custom built solution against requirement specification
        (d) Systems Integration (SI) Services
        (e) Product Development and/or implementation
 (iii) Perform services covering application maintenance and operations and IT infrastructure operations and management services
  (iv) IT Governance services covering all aspects of IT function governance
   (v) Management of Quality of software development and project management

(vi) Software as service covering newer variations such as Hardware as a Service (HaaS) and Platform as a Service (PaaS)

In the next level of detailing the relationship and positioning of these services were done by plotting them in an intellectual IT Services value creating chain. This section also detailed out the manner in which these services are sold or are popularly presented to the clients. These details will help readers to understand where an ITSE stands with respect to the value chain of services delivery and where it can go in course of time. This section covered services such as:

(i) Staffing Services

(ii) Software Development/Maintenance Services

(iii) Outsourcing of IT Infrastructure Management Services

(iv) Business Process Management

(v) Business Consulting

(vi) Package Implementation

(vii) Product Development

It may be easy now to note the increased level of sophistication and preparedness required for the companies to move along these levels. In addition, ITS professionals can choose their career path along the value creating chain for future growth.

Review Questions

2.1 What is the broadest classification of IT Services and how they are interrelated?

2.2 Which IT Services have the lowest entry barriers to get into? Do you think the model is long lasting for any ITSE for future survival? Explain with reason.

2.3 Draw the IT industry value creating chain and position the following ITSE companies; (i) Infosys, (ii) SAP, (iii) IBM, (iv) Amazon, (v) Salesforce.com

2.4 What is the difference between SaaS, HaaS and PaaS. Explain with examples.

2.5 What are the difficulties faced by any ITSE while providing all types of services?

Suggested Further Reading

Dubey, Sanjiva Shankar, *Innovation with IT*, Tata McGraw-Hill, New Delhi, 2008.

Dubey, Sanjiva Shankar, *IT Strategy and Management*, 2nd ed., PHI Learning, New Delhi, 2009.

Chapter 3

IT Services Business Processes, Models and Functions

The process of scientific discovery is, in effect, a continual flight from wonder.

— Albert Einstein

3.1 Introduction

This chapter will explain the various processes and functions of an IT Services Enterprise to give a summarized view of what is achieved by each one of them. There is a lot of confusion in the minds of students aspiring to join IT Services industry who think it is synonym to software development, in simple terms coding. While software development is one of the services, the IT Services industry is much more than that. This chapter will give the larger view of other important functions and processes. This chapter will also build the foundation to understand how an IT Services Enterprise functions. Accordingly, the students can very well start visualizing the opportunities for their career. This chapter will also clear a number of semantic confusion so that when the young engineer/MBA or MCA joins IT Services firm he/she can appreciate the roles played by the other departments. As we discussed earlier, this book is aimed at students, but is equally useful to those who are already in the job for a few years. They may have joined an IT Services firm and may have been slotted for a particular task, but those who want to grow within the organization will find it extremely useful to explore options, prepare themselves for internal job interviews and build capabilities for further growth.

3.2 IT Services Enterprise Processes

A typical IT Services firm will have several interconnected and interdependent processes. Depending on the maturity of the organizations, these processes will be performed by one or more departments either jointly or independently. We have taken the process view of the IT Services Enterprise to help our readers get customer-centric way to look at how an IT Services enterprise runs. In the subsequent section we will also describe some of the way IT Services firms are organized where we will discuss about the functions and organization structure.

The main Enterprise processes of an IT Services firms, irrespective of type of services it may be engaged in, can be categorized as the following:

(i) Strategy, planning and business model design
(ii) Managing finances, support infrastructure, administration
(iii) Business development which includes the following:
    (a) Marketing
    (b) Sales
    (c) Opportunity management and customer engagement
(iv) Delivery management
(v) Managing services business operations

Figure 3.1 shows all these processes and their relationship with each other.

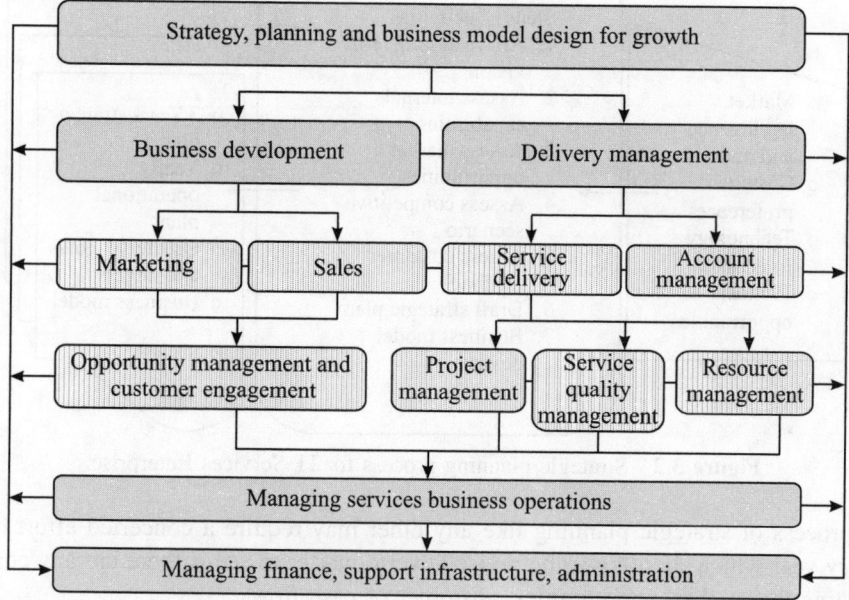

Figure 3.1 IT Services enterprise: key processes.

3.3 Strategy Planning and Business Model Design of IT Services Enterprise

Any enterprise must have a process to develop and maintain its long-term strategy. Based on this strategy the enterprise does planning for its execution. IT Services firms are no exception and also have to do the same for their long-term sustenance. Irrespective of the focus of IT Services a firm may have, the importance of strategy and planning process will have an important role to play in shaping up the enterprise future.

Smaller IT Services firm may run this as an informal process that the senior management perform over few days every year participated by CEO, COO, Head of delivery, and Head of business development. In large IT Services firm this task is assigned to full time responsible group headed by Chief strategy officer. In some cases, this process is also influenced and guided by the investment partners like venture capitalists who bring strategic inputs and give directions. We will examine this process through our input-activities-output framework.

As we can see in the Figure 3.2 strategic planning process takes inputs such as market potential and customer preferences apart from keeping a tab on the technology trends. These firms especially the smaller one also depends a lot on the tactical opportunities, such as customer relationship or key capabilities that may be in demand during a particular period.

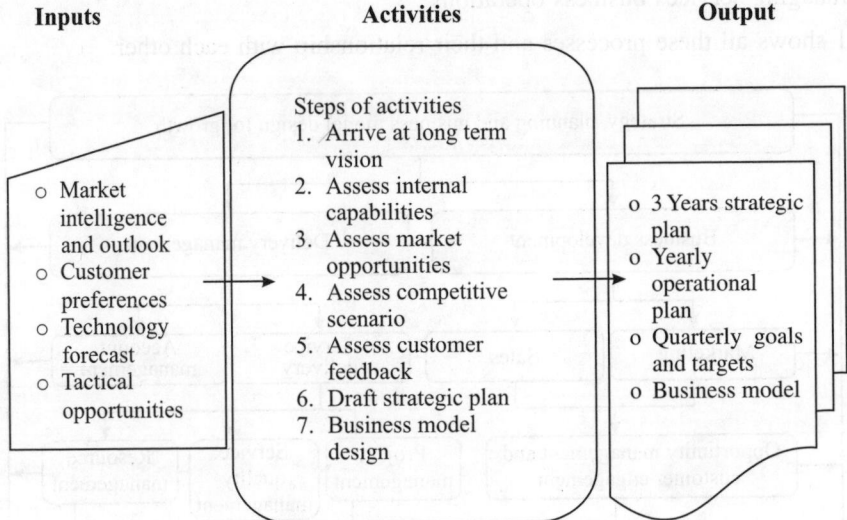

Figure 3.2   Strategic planning process for IT Services Enterprise.

The process of strategic planning like any other may require a concerted effort of about a week every year which should also be revised every quarter to see if there are any changes that are impacting the market, opportunities, customer or cash flows.

This process sometimes also merges with the business development process and several MBA find opportunities to work in these areas in a large IT Services firm.

3.3.1 Business Model Design for IT Services

This section will elaborate on business model redesign for IT Services firms. We have discussed that strategy formulation and planning being one of the important tasks for the senior management. Here we will discuss prevailing business models for IT Services firms to give our readers a perspective of this important aspect of IT Services.

Business model is a term referred to as[1] a method a firm employs to earn the revenue to survive and grow. A business model describes what a firm will do, and how, to build and capture wealth for the stakeholders. Effective business models operationalize good strategies converting great ideas into realistic revenue. This also includes deep understanding of aspects such as

---

1.   http://www.businessdictionary.com/definition/business-model.html

target markets, customers, and services offering types, cost incurred and profits.[2] However all IT Services business model can be simplified into the following:

(i) **Pure hourly based services:** This may form a wide variety ranging from hourly billing to monthly rates for attending a fixed numbers of work hours. While this model seems to be simplest of all (also known as staffing services) it is largely used for low end skills and has no scope for reaping the benefits of the software developed by the skilled resources.

(ii) **Fixed price against completion of a task**: Typically used for software development services where against a set of requirements, the IT Services firm is expected to be paid a fixed amount. This model has an element of risk associated with the scope creep (i.e. extension of work) due to poor requirements gathering and hold up of payments due to not completing the milestone work in time. However, this also has an advantage that the composition of project team can be controlled by the IT Services vendors, therefore it can use the entry level resources (trainee or fresher's) in the process to keep the cost down.

(iii) **Package implementation and customization:** Typically used for implementing and customizing standard Commercially Of The Shelf (COTS) available packages such as ERP. The services are based on estimated efforts based on locations, functions or user base expected to be impacted during the COTS implementation. This work will have functions of expected changes, reports to be customized or users to be trained. All these estimates are clearly specified as part of the proposal.

(iv) **Code plus services:** Many IT Services firm have software codes (called assets) which after some customization can be used by multiple clients. Such services are paid as combination of software licenses fee and implementation charges. Annual maintenance fee based on the original cost of license to give regular upgrade and trouble shooting services can also be levied to the clients.

(v) **Pay as you use services:** A new business model where the IT Services provider makes Software and infrastructure available and customers can use software based on number of user access facilities, data storage requirements or modules/functionalities to be used. A good example is salesforce.com that allows their CRM product to be used based on subscription and pay as you use basis. In this model these services are accessed by the client through internet. Since the application code runs from the IT Services providers end the environment is under their control, and therefore, the cost of running would be less. Google, 37signals, and many others fall under this category. The flip side of this model is the maintaining and running the application infrastructure and ensuring its availability. There could be other factors like network connectivity, speed etc. that can impact the users convenience. All this facility has to be maintained by the IT Services firm. In addition, the revenue levels are lower than those of other services type. One can add advertisement revenue in addition to subscription to supplement the IT Services revenue. Also this model is not very welcomed for data in sensitive industries such

---

2. Details discussion on Business Model can be seen in Chapter 5 of Author's book Innovation with IT, McGraw-Hill education.

as banking, tax authorities, and health care. Customers also have to limit their need as available in the existing versions and have to continuously change when the new versions are released by the IT Service provider.

(vi) **Risk and reward sharing:** In certain large and complex services contract there may be element of risk and reward sharing based on the outcome of the services provided. For example, in the case of business process services and outbound calling services, the payment is made based on the success rate of the call or culmination of end-customers requirements. Recently, IBM entered a revenue sharing services contract for outsourcing Bharti Airtel's entire IT operations. Such contracts require to be drafted very carefully and executed with great finesse, else it may end up with lot of risk for both IT Services provider as well as the client who gets into such contract.

(vii) **Services as product:** It is reverse of servitijing a product used in the pay as you use the services also called Software as Services (SaaS). In this model instead of developing customized development a standard software product can be developed by the IT Services product and sold in large quantity. Incremental costs of selling more copies of the product are negligible, leading to extremely high profit margin. Companies such as Microsoft, IBM, Adobe, ERP products, anti-virus software, point solutions etc. are great examples. Yet this is not an easy business model as it requires lot or initial investment to work on the product idea and then in its marketing. Lot of efforts for marketing and brand building will be required before the first copy is sold. It will also require regular upgrade and enhancement in the product feature to appeal large numbers of users. In addition to it, challenge of meeting competition remains greatest in successfully executing this business model.

In order to understand what are the cost elements and what how it is related with revenue and profit Table 3.1 has been created as a quick summary.

Table 3.1   A general appreciation of financial terms for an IT Services firm

Item	Description	Typical range (in %)	Remarks
Revenue	The amount charged from customer for providing services	100	It may include revenue for labour-based services, sale of intellectual asset (e.g. software licenses), pay as you use services, on line advertisement on websites. Also any risk and reward is also counted in revenue
Price	Charge of the services per unit based on the prevailing market conditions	Cost per unit	It may vary depending upon the customer, size of contract and type of service. One of the critical activity and decision point also dictated by market conditions as well

(Contd.)

Table 3.1 A general appreciation of financial terms for an IT Services firm (*Contd.*)

Item	Description	Typical range (in %)	Remarks
Cost of services	Cost of direct labour for performing the services, overheads, infrastructure cost, management cost	60–70 of price	Indirect component of labour services could be nearly 1.5 times the direct cost. It also includes cost of intellectual property at a estimated basis
Cost of sales	Efforts for sales, marketing, promotion, customer travel for business development	5–7	Salary of sales and marketing team, travel
Gross margin	Difference between revenue and cost	30–40	
EBITDA (Earning before interest tax depreciation and amortization)	Difference between revenue and cost excluding depreciation, loan interest, taxes and amortization	60–70	An approximate measure of a company's operating cash flow based on data from the company's income statement. Calculated by looking at earnings before the deduction of interest expenses, taxes, depreciation and amortization
General administration costs	Administrative expenses not covered in sales and marketing	6–8	Includes headquarter expenses, Directors fee
Marketing and promotion	Cost for brand building promotion, web presence	2–3	Online marketing cost is also included
Research and development, innovation projects	Cost of developing new services, technology development, innovation projects	2–3	

3.4 Managing Finances, Support Infrastructure, Administration

Based on output from the strategic planning process the ITS firm has to plan for capital investment, create infrastructure such as offices, administer several other activities such as company formation, billing, tax payments, etc. This process is a foundation process through which the rest of the organizational processes operate. This is the reason why in the Figure 3.1 this is shown at the bottom. Supported by CFO this process also covers other infrastructure processes like provisioning for IT infrastructure for employees, regulatory processes such as contract management, employees work permits, travel, visa, accommodation for onsite workers, etc. Figure 3.3 shows the input activities and output of this process.

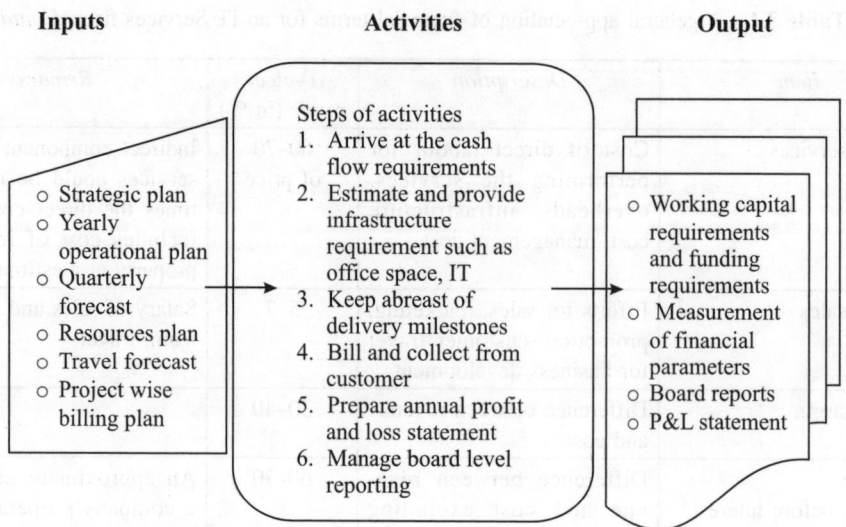

Figure 3.3   Managing finances, support infrastructure, administration process for IT Services Enterprise.

3.4.1 Managing Finances, Support Infrastructure, and Administration: Sub-Processes in Detail

IT Services companies need a very strong support team. Especially when they are working for the Global clients in using outsourcing model. This is also called Global Delivery model where the customer work is performed from IT Services firm's location in low cost countries (such as India). The teams working on client projects require office infrastructure space and network connectivity to be able to perform software development, management and maintenance task sitting remotely. All this requires a number of processes to be performed regularly and efficiently.

Let us use Figure 3.4 to explain them better. As we can see the IT Services enterprise support processes get triggered with inputs coming from strategic plan for the year. Support processes take time to build up and require meticulous forward planning, be it renting out new office space for the employees or implementing ERP for internal operation. Many of the outsourcing services firm operate out of Export Processing Zones (EPZ) created by the Government to boost export where they give certain concessions. However, such EPZ put in strict regulation of material movement, people access and many others that are required to be complied with. All this requires a well-oiled machinery to work round the clock. Most IT Services firms of reasonable size (say 1000 + professional staff) require a number of support processes. These include, access control, parking facilities, canteen services, fire prevention, power, lift and many others that cost money, management time and efforts. Compared to airlines business where two pilot fly an aircraft with 200 passengers require, host of other support processes like ticket booking, airport management, cabin management, maintenance of aircraft, air traffic control, baggage handling, and so on. All these are support functions but no less important for the successful running of the airlines business. Let us discuss some of these processes for IT Services enterprise in detail to explain to our readers, which are equally important for the success of any ITSE.

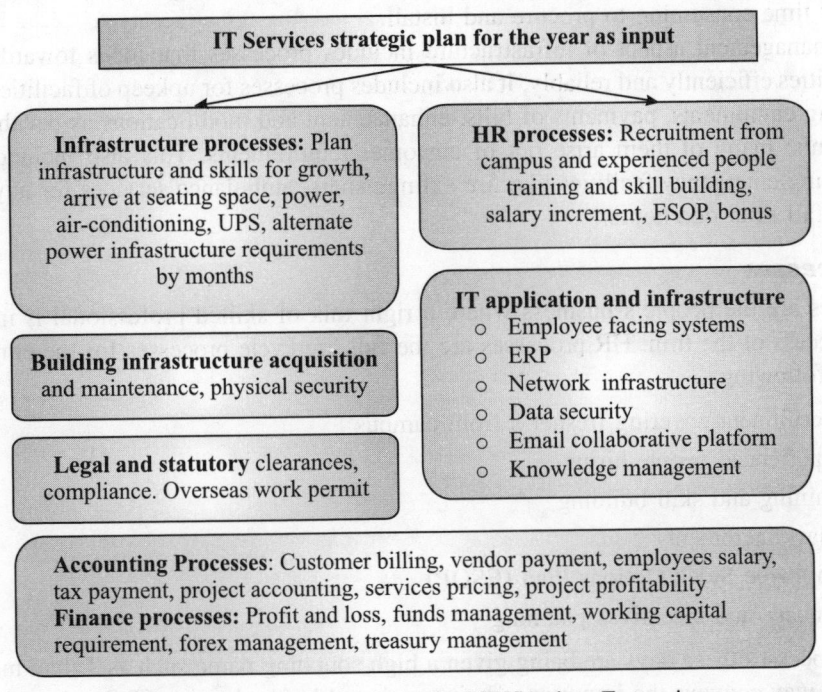

IT Services strategic plan for the year as input

Infrastructure processes: Plan infrastructure and skills for growth, arrive at seating space, power, air-conditioning, UPS, alternate power infrastructure requirements by months

HR processes: Recruitment from campus and experienced people training and skill building, salary increment, ESOP, bonus

IT application and infrastructure
o   Employee facing systems
o   ERP
o   Network infrastructure
o   Data security
o   Email collaborative platform
o   Knowledge management

Building infrastructure acquisition and maintenance, physical security

Legal and statutory clearances, compliance. Overseas work permit

Accounting Processes: Customer billing, vendor payment, employees salary, tax payment, project accounting, services pricing, project profitability
Finance processes: Profit and loss, funds management, working capital requirement, forex management, treasury management

Figure 3.4   Support processes of IT Services Enterprise.

Infrastructure processes

IT Services firms are like huge factory where people produce software and services for the global clients. Unlike offices which run only during the day time or shops or other establishments till evening, these services units run almost round the clock. Considering the increased percentage of women employees, these premises require good facilities amenable to them including security, rest rooms, etc. Most IT Services units operating in major cities provide facilities for employee welfare such as food, recreation, health care, concierge, transport. The reason of such facilities being the large number of young professional are part of IT Services industry who live away from their families, and many are working couples who depend on these facilities to take care of their day-to-day problems, and give more time to concentrate on the work, which at times requires coming in shifts and stay late to complete a complex task. All this leads to the high importance attached to the infrastructure facilities. Many a times, the clients especially overseas clients want to visit the infrastructure facilities to be assured that the team working on their assignments are working in well-provisioned facilities.

Infrastructure process has two parts, planning as well as management. In the case of former, lot of importance is given in ascertaining the requirements of the growing business pipeline of the firm. Real estate of suitable nature are always difficult to obtain at a reasonable rate and can be a huge drag on the companies cost. Building rent, power, air-conditioning, water, and so on cost a lot of money and need to be planned well in advance. Considering the uninterrupted operations requirements, most IT Services factories need UPS and generator sets, all these are costly and time consuming to procure and install.

The management aspect of infrastructure includes processes that focus towards operating these facilities efficiently and reliably. It also includes processes for upkeep of facilities, cleaning, maintaining equipments, payments of bills, enhancement and modifications as per the changing requirements; many of them arise out of customer requirements. This also includes planning and actuating emergency facilities like fire extinguishers, ambulance services for any employee who may fall ill at odd hours.

HR processes

IT Services are the people's business where a right mix of skilled professional is instrumental for the success of the firm. HR processes are the full life cycle processes for the employee that cover the following:

(i) Recruitment covering fresher's from campus

(ii) Experienced people hiring

(iii) Training and skill building

(iv) Salary increment

(v) Employee Stock Options Plan (ESOP)

(vi) Bonuses and incentives planning

HR processes these days are being given a high sounding name such as Talent management which in a way conveys the importance being assigned by the leading IT Services firms of this important function.

IT application and infrastructure processes

IT processes of IT Services firms are often misunderstood as it remains on the background, and enables the organization to run like a well-oiled machinery. Like a power plant utility that generates power for the city also requires power for running its pumps, turbines and other auxiliaries. Similarly, the IT Services enterprise that serves hundreds of customer, also requires IT application and infrastructure to deliver them precisely.

IT application and infrastructure processes cover all actives where IT support is needed. All business processes of the firm would require IT applications and hardware as well as network infrastructure. The later is most important as most IT Services outsourcing projects depend on remote connectivity. Network connectivity is a major cost incurred by most IT Services firms in global delivery model.

IT application and infrastructure process also ensure that IT applications which are meant for running the enterprise are developed (or implemented) and operated properly and efficiently.

This includes application systems such as

(i) Employee facing systems

(ii) ERP

(iii) E-mail and collaborative platform

(iv) Knowledge management

Security and compliance

IT Services firms have to observe and enforce several security measures as they deal with sensitive data for its clients. The most elementary one is the access control and physical security within the premises of the IT Services delivery centers in addition to the measures for data security, customer data privacy and compliance with the regulatory provisions. While working with the global clients these IT Services firms have to observe country specific regulations for obtaining work permits, VISA, Tax payments for services rendered and service conditions of employees from various countries.

Accounting processes

IT Services firms have to run error free and accurate accounting processes to manage the financial transactions for their stakeholders that include employees, vendors, business partners, customers, shareholders and others. For example, customers would expect accurate and timely billing for the services provided and the vendors would expect to be paid timely. All this would require robust accounting processes which can withstand the scrutiny of statutory audits from time to time as desired by the statutory laws such as company's act. In addition, the IT Services firm must closely account for the cost and margins for its services so that it can remain competitive and profitable at the same time.

Some of the sub processes of accounting process are as follows:

(i) Customer billing

(ii) Vendor payment

(iii) Employees salary

(iv) Tax payment

(v) Project accounting

(vi) Services pricing

(vii) Project profitability

Finance processes

These processes deal with sourcing and management of funds keeping the strategic objectives of the IT Services firm in mind. These processes include how and where the funds for conducting the business should be obtained from. The sources of fund could be loan, equity capital or investment from venture capital source. This process also makes the profit and loss statements, and briefs the board about the financial health of the firm. This process also is responsible for working capital, cash requirements and cash flow management. Since most IT Services firms also engaged in exporting their services and solutions, a proper management of foreign exchange (which keeps fluctuating due to international economy situations) called Forex Management, is needed. Finally, the retained income needs to be invested properly to yield additional income which is performed by the sub process called Treasury Management.

3.5 Business Development

Some one has rightly said that business is nothing but marketing. The business development process is one of the most important ones in the IT Services enterprise. This is process which has several combinations of activities and sub processes like marketing, sales and opportunities management. Each of these is further discussed in detail in Chapters 4, 5 and 6. However, a brief explanation about each one of them may be in order at this stage.

Whenever an enterprise starts functioning it has to announce and continuously communicate with the prospects in the market place. Product companies do it by putting full page ads in newspapers or running TV commercials using celebrity to endorse them. This generates curiosity and leads to customers coming forward to buy them. In case of the IT Services firms creating awareness and generating demand, process would be different as the company is not into mass marketed retail product segment. Creating awareness requires series of activities such as sending mailers, website development, personal contacts and meetings. In addition, it also requires preparation of services capabilities documents, collaterals, white papers, and so on to be used in customer interactions. We will discuss marketing process in more detail in Chapter 5.

Demand generated through marketing efforts needs to be channelized through a strategic business development process that is the bridging process between the overall Strategic vision and the actual opportunities available in the market place. Many a times in IT Services Selling situation a large services contract is generated by doing small pre-sales consulting work which is also engineered by the business development process. This has been detailed in Chapter 6.

Demand generated by the marketing process is also required to be further analyzed, evaluated and accordingly services and solution proposals are sent to the prospective customers. This process called opportunity management requires a fair degree of rigorous follow up and proactive approach to succeed. Finally, when the customers accept the technical proposal the sales team converts the opportunity into services contract. The process of sales is complex task which requires management of opportunities, proposals, customer relationship and giving the right price better than the competition. These process are further detailed in Chapter 7.

Accordingly, we have not included the I-A-O diagram for business development, marketing, sales and opportunity management processes here in this chapter.

3.6 Delivery Management

IT Services ultimately yield revenue when the services are performed. Any amount of sales effort only leads to a services contract (and may be some advance payment) but the real realization of revenue happens when services are performed (or delivered) to the client. Many IT Services firms falter by not ensuring that their delivery management process are well organized, and thus, loose out on customer satisfaction, fail to get follow on work and create intellectual capital for subsequent reuse. Managing a well oiled delivery management process includes service delivery, account management, project management, services quality and resource management processes. Delivery management process is like the engine room of the large ship that gives the power for the IT Services firm to sail further towards its destination. Figure 3.5 gives the I-A-O for the delivery management process. This process has been further explained in Chapter 8. In addition Chapter 9 covers IT Services quality assurance process.

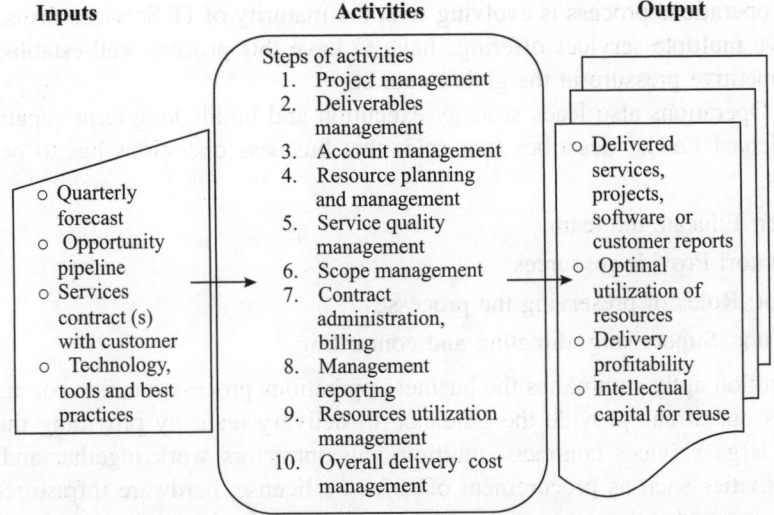

Figure 3.5   Delivery management process for IT Services Enterprise.

3.7 Managing Services Business Operations

Managing a large IT Services business requires a coordinated effort of its various functions and processes to achieve the strategic objectives. Managing services business operations is like the command and control of all operations of the IT Services.

The first step of business operations process is to make a detailed plan to operationalise strategy. This plan should be realistic and implementable and at times gives feedback to strategic planners. Business operations process owner not only has to understand the strategy, but has to contribute to decisions so that they are implementable.

Once the plan is made, the business operations has to make available the necessary resources, in case of IT Services it would mean hiring individuals with right quality of skills, providing for infrastructure and funds. This process drives the delivery management, business development and seeks support from finance and administration management processes. Business operations processes is the crucial link between these three processes as shown in Figure 3.6.

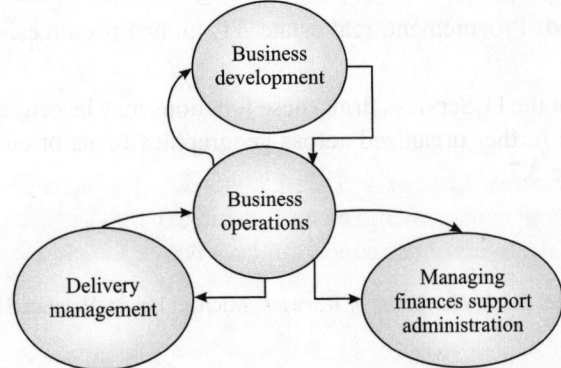

Figure 3.6   Relationship of business operations with other groups.

The business operations process is evolving with the maturity of IT Services firms. IT Services firms that have multiple services offerings have to have this process well-established so as to meet the competitive pressure in the global market.

Business Operations also leads strategy execution and builds long-term capabilities. Nigel Slack and Michael Lewis[3] describes four roles that business operations has to perform. They are as follows:

(i) Trainer: Educate the team

(ii) Facilitator: Provide resources

(iii) Curator: Roles of preserving the processes

(iv) Governor: Supervising, directing and controlling

This role definition aptly summaries the business operations process function for an IT Services firm. Business operations provide the guidance to delivery team by providing them the right resources. In large services contracts, multiple subcontractors work together and there are a number of activities such as procurement of software license, hardware infrastructure, all that processes are run under the aegis of business operations. It also maintains the right balance between the bench strength and pipeline of projects. Finally, it helps acting as custodian of performce metrics and helps the Chief Executive to drive the strategies for the firm's growth.

3.8 Functional Organization Structure in IT Services Firms

After having understood the processes and business model, the functional orientation should be easy to understand. Organizations structures are formed around function to facilitate specialization and accountability for performing a certain task. It also enables separation of duties so that different sets of people are responsible for different activities to ensure a check and balance. For example, a user department should only specify their needs to procurement department and refrain from selecting the supplier. In addition the payment of the bill is done by the finance department. Similarly, IT Services firm organize their operations in the following functions:

(i) **Customer related:** Marketing, business development, sales, engagement management

(ii) **Delivery related:** Project management, software development, infrastructure operations, process management, consulting, quality management, call centre, etc

(iii) **Support related:** Procurement, real estate, IT, human resources, training, accounts and finance.

Depending on the size of the IT Services firms these functions may be centralized or decentralized. Customer functions are further organized across geographies focus of customer industry focus. This is shown in Figure 3.7.

---

3. Operations Strategy Nigel Slack, *University of Warwick,* Michael Lewis, Prentice-Hall, 2003.

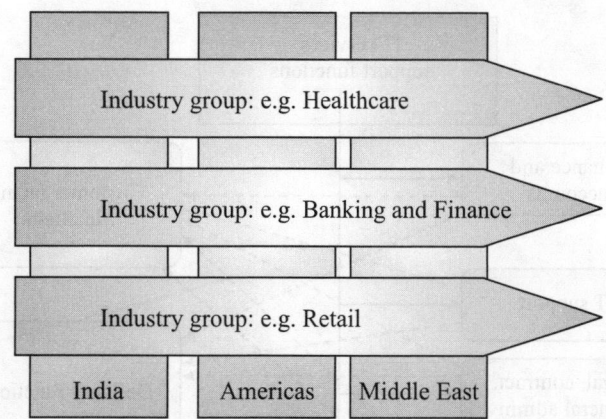

Figure 3.7   Customer facing functions organization in IT Services firms.

Delivery functions choose a mix of specialization where teams are organized across the specific skills and or certain industry. Sometimes, the delivery resources are pooled in one or more competency groups and released to work on customer projects for the duration of project. After completion of the project they return back to their parent competency group. Figure 3.8 gives a pictorial representation

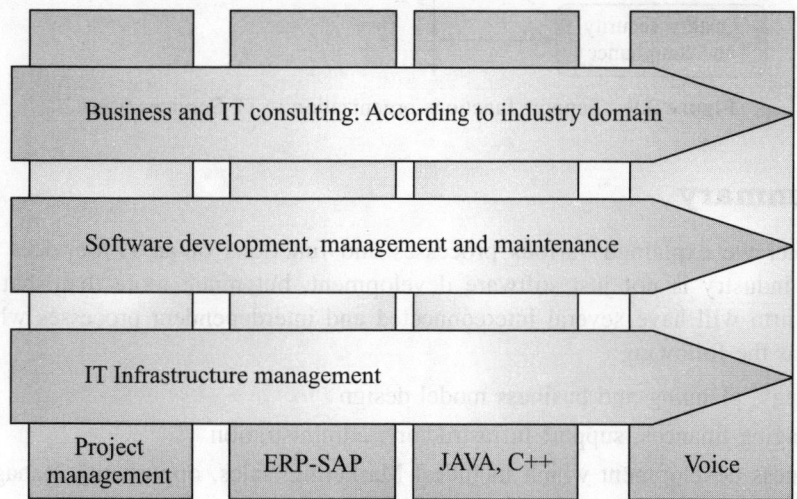

Figure 3.8   Delivery functions organization in IT Services firms.

Support functions are usually centralized even though the key individuals may be located in several cities to support that group. Figure 3.9 details this out further.

These diagrams does not contain all the sub functions, and these are shown for the representative purposes only.

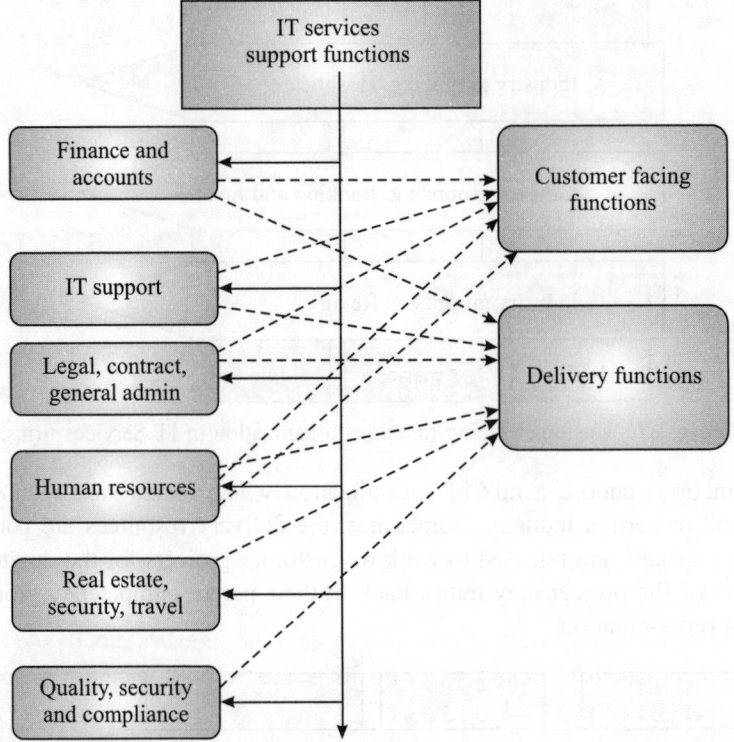

Figure 3.9   Support functions organization in IT Services firms.

3.9 Summary

In this chapter we explained various processes and functions of an IT Services Enterprise. IT Services industry is not just software development, but much more than that. A typical IT Services firm will have several interconnected and interdependent processes which can be categorized as the following:

- Strategy, planning and business model design
- Managing finances, support Infrastructure, administration
- Business development which includes: Marketing, sales, opportunity management and customer engagement
- Delivery management
- Managing services business operations

For each of these processes, a detailed input-activity and output diagram was provided to enable our readers get a clear view of the processes inputs, activities and outputs.

We further discussed several prevailing business model designs for IT Services. We surmised that Business Model is what a firm will do, its processes and approach to gain customer and in the process build and capture wealth for the stakeholders. IT Services business model were simplified into the following major areas as:

- Pure hourly-based services
- Fixed price against completion of a task
- Package implementation and customization
- Code plus services
- Pay as you use services
- Risk and reward sharing
- Services as product

We also summarized various cost and profit elements in IT Services for the benefit of our readers in a simple table.

Finally, functional organization structure in a typical IT Services firms are explained: After having understood the processes and business model the functional orientation were easy to understand. IT Services firm organize their operations in the following functions:

(i) Customer related: Marketing, business development, sales, engagement management. It was further explained that customer related functions are further organized across geographies focus of customer industry focus.

(ii) Delivery related: Project management, software development, infrastructure operations, process management, consulting, quality management, call centre, and so on. This was further detailed out to cover how delivery functions choose a mix of specialization where teams are organized across specific skills and or certain industry or pooled in one or more competency groups.

(iii) Support related: Procurement, real estate, IT, human resources, training, accounts and finance. Support functions are usually centralized even though the key individuals may be located in several cities to support that group.

Finally, the chapter ended with diagrams of sub functions of these major functions.

Review Questions

3.1 What are the major generic processes of any IT Services enterprise? Draw the enterprise wise process diagram and explain in brief each one of them.

3.2 What is input-activity and process diagram? What are its advantages to depict the process framework? Draw I-A-O diagram of the following sub processes as applicable to IT Services Enterprise:

(a) Project management

(b) Opportunity management

(c) Customer engagement management

(d) Account management

3.3 What are the prevailing business models for IT Services Enterprise? Discuss advantages and disadvantages of each one of them.

3.4 What is the relationship between business development, business operations, delivery management and support processes? How the business strategy does bind all of them together in an IT Services firm?

Suggested Further Reading

Boulton, R., Libert, B., Samek, S., "A Business Model for the New Economy," *The Journal of Business Strategy*, 21 (4), July–August 2000, pp 29–35.

Ghemawat, P., *Strategy and the Business Landscape,* Prentice Hall, 2001.

Hamel, G., and Prahalad, C.K., "Strategic Intent," *Harvard Business Review*, May–June 1989.

Hamermesh, M., and Piromohamed, "Note on Business Model Analysis for the Entrepreneur," Harvard Business School, 2002.

Website

http://www.quickarrow.com/news_events/serviceline_news/4020Myth.asp

Chapter 4

Strategic Foundation for IT Services Business

There is one thing stronger than all the armies in the world,
and that is an idea whose time has come.

— Victor Hugo

French poet, playwright, novelist, essayist, visual artist, statesman, human rights activist

4.1 Introduction

In this chapter we will examine some of the prevalent strategies adopted by IT Services Enterprise (ITSE) and also examine some of the innovation possibilities keeping in mind the emerging trends. IT Services Enterprise are driven by the spirit of individual brilliance like many other knowledge economy firms, and most successful one have shown that the individual brilliance has been gradually converted into enterprise abilities to carry the legacy forward. If we look around and notice some of the successful ITSE leaders we will notice the gradual transformation they had over the years.

For example, a most respected and IT industry leader, now in its 100th year of existence is IBM. IBM started as tabulating and recording company and at one time, and was synonymous to big main frames and hardware business. Today, this 97 B US$ enterprise[1] earns nearly 35% of its revenue through services sales. HP which is known for its market leadership on printing products is also a hardware and services company. Infosys which is one of the success story emerging from India is true reflection of Indian middle class aspiration, fighting spirit and entrepreneurial zeal that takes eight of its founders pooling their personal savings of less than 250 US$ (₹10,000) in 1982–83 to create a 6.5 B US$ enterprise[2] with over 170000 professional working across the nations on global projects.

Each of these giants have followed different approaches for their success, our effort in this chapter is to understand the strategies ITSE firms adopt for their growth, in a theoretical manner.

4.2 Strategy

Strategy is defined as the long term plan for any organization to achieve a desired goal. The

---

1. http://investing.businessweek.com/research/stocks/snapshot/snapshot.asp?ticker=IBM:US accessed 13102011
2. http://www.infosys.com/investors/financials/Pages/profit-loss-data.aspx accessed 13102011

world of business has several opportunities and ways to tap them. But the firm has to choose the most suitable one that they can execute with ease and can demonstrate better performance as compared to others (competition) for a long term sustenance.

A noted strategist and thinker Michael Porter, in his seminal book *Competitive Strategy* has described generic strategies as along two ordinates of scope and sources of competitive advantages. Further he described that the source of competitive advantage can come from either being cost focused or differentiation focus. Porter framework gives generic strategies applicable to any industry as:

   (i) Cost leadership (no frills)

  (ii) Differentiation (creating unique desirable products and services) and

 (iii) Focus (offering a specialized service in a niche market). Which is further subdivided into

       (a) Cost focus and

       (b) Differentiation focus.

Porter's framework is a widely used theoretical discourse to help understand the strategy concepts that can be applied in any industry. Figure 4.1[3] shows them in perspective.

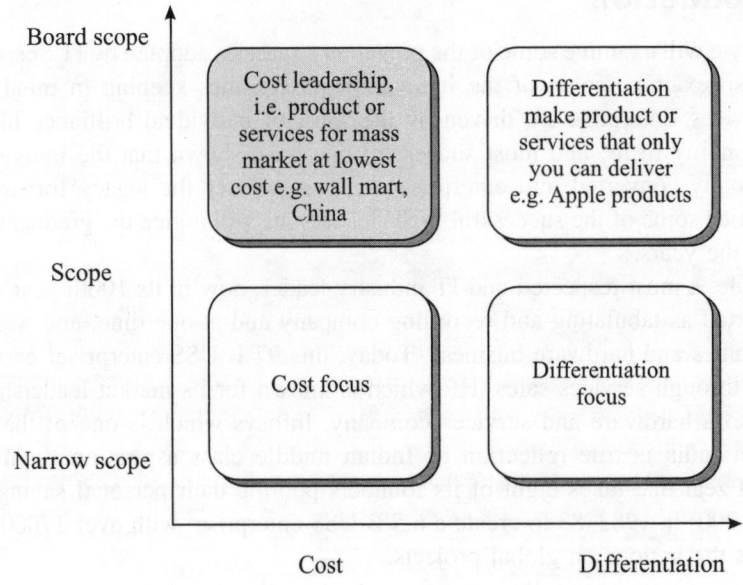

Figure 4.1 Porter's competitive strategy framework.

In most cases, companies choose a combination of these generic strategies. This choice will also depend on product and services capabilities of the firm.

3. Porter's Generic Strategies Choosing Your Route to Competitive Advantage. Adapted from http://www. mindtools.com/pages/article/newSTR_82.htm accessed 13102011

4.2.1 Generic Strategies for ITSEs

Let us discuss some of the common strategies that ITSEs have been adopting in the past to build foundation, of our understanding.

All generic strategies can broadly be divided into two main sub categories—organic strategy and inorganic strategy. We will discuss them in detail.

Organic strategy

This includes approaches that lead to expansion of the existing team and capabilities and building business around them.

The following discussion is largely pertaining to organic strategies adopted by most ITSEs companies.

(i) **Ride the demand curve:** Some times the market demand for certain type of work is so much that if a firm is able to possess capabilities to deliver; it will earn handsome revenue and profit. It has happened several times in the past with IT Services industry. It was like sailing a boat along with the flow and favourable wind. The passage of distance would seem to be much easier in such situation. In the late decades of 90s was a one such time when potential of Y2K[4] bug gave impetus of huge demand for IT Services professionals. So was the case of the onset of internet explosion when huge requirements were created for website and portal development and many companies came up offering these services. Once these waves subside, the companies that have only focused on this type of work face huge difficulties to stay afloat.

(ii) **Explore new technology for growth:** Information technology keeps adding new technology products which can become a source of potential services offerings around them like cloud computing, smart computing, collaboration tools, business analytics and so on. The problem is to visualize the ones which are not just going to be hype and will die down soon, but the one which will grow in the future.

(iii) **Explore new territories, markets and verticals:** This approach is slightly different than the earlier one where an ITSE expands its services into new countries or in new markets and new industry verticals. While the term territory represents countries, the other two terms are explained as
   (a) *Markets:* Represents customer segments, e.g., small and medium business (SMB) sector and large enterprise customer.
   (b) *Vertical:* Refers to the business industries, e.g., retail, healthcare, etc.
   The challenge in this model is building not only the new customer relationship, but also commensurate skills to deal with market conditions.

(iv) **Broaden the variety of services:** In Chapter 3, we have discussed the IT industry value chain. No ITSE can claim to have all the services offerings from day one. Typically the ITSE expands its services either towards more volume (e.g. BPO) or more complexity (end-to-end outsourcing) or deep capabilities for example Business Consulting.

---

4. Y2K bug arose due to abbreviating the our-digit year to two digits in computer digital files that would have turned 00 in year 2000 (that is why the name Y2K), leading to accounting errors. Massive changes to the existing mainframe programs were needed and data was also required to be converted into new format.

(v) **Diversifying the service portfolios to widen the client base:** Most client industries typically follow economic cycles with peaks of demand and slow down. Automobile, oil and gas are in such a category. In other sectors like banking and finance, there were some serious troubles recently leading to bankruptcy of some of the major ones. Given such vagaries of the industries performance most ITSE try to seek business from customers from different industries so that the slow down of one sector can be balanced with the growth cycle of the other.

(vi) **Anchor client strategy:** Instead of focusing on large number of small clients, many ITSE focus on a few large clients who are also popularly named as anchor clients. Any client can be called to be an anchor client if 30–40% of a particular ITSE, business comes from one such client.

The growth of Indian ITSE firms is also attributed to these large clients who gave significant portion of their IT Services business to these few ITSEs. Global firms like GE, American Express, and British telecom are well known for being anchor clients to several medium and small sizes ITSE during 90s and led these firms to grow. Many such anchor clients also made strategic investment in the ITSE firms though they remained passive partner in the day-to-day management.

The advantages of this strategy are less efforts and consequently less overhead on soliciting new business. The only drawback of following this strategy is that the ITSE will never come out of the shadow of the anchor client and at times may become complacent doing business with a few clients. This will also make the ITSE unfavourable with other competitor firms in similar industry as the anchor firm.

(vii) **Increase business from existing clients:** Soliciting more work from the same client is a natural strategy of any expanding ITSE. However, it should not lead to loss of focus and specialization of the ITSE firm. In order to solicit more business from the same client the ITSE firm has to *enhance its capabilities* which also become another strategic thread.

(viii) **Expand geographically:** IT Services industry is no longer location dependent. Expanding to solicit business in new geographies will lead to newer clients for more and more business. However, it will call for additional investment in hiring sales team who may have to be located in these new geographies.

(ix) **Growth through alliance with product vendors:** This strategy refers to becoming authorized business partners of Software or hardware product companies and offer services business around that product. A large number of big and small ITSE have followed this route and led to winning successful business. In order to adopt this strategy successfully, the ITSE has to invest its efforts and resources in getting them trained in the product features.

Inorganic strategy

This covers those initiatives that involves mergers and acquisition, creating join ventures and similar such initiatives.

Growth of IT Services firms can also be done through in-organic means where the existing ITSE firm acquires smaller firms or merges with another firm. There is several variation of this strategy comprising of:

(i) *Acquisition*

(ii) *Merger*

(iii) *Joint ventures (JV)*

In most cases, pursuing inorganic strategy will cost money to buy out the existing owners by the new management. Setting up joint ventures will also call for investment in the new business.

While in theory it may appear to be viable strategy for large ITSE with good cash reserve, in practice, the long term results are difficult to ascertain. IT Services being people business will have a complex cultural compatibility issues between the two firms. There may be loss of leadership as the seller firm management may have to relinquish control to the new management.

In the past mergers of like-sized firm also been tried out. Building synergy through two dissimilar capabilities have also been tried out and some of them very were successful and some not so.

Large ITSE sometimes buy very small boutique firms with unique specialization. These could be specialist firms in a narrow technology segment or business domain consulting firms. They have a better chance of getting along in the new culture.

Indian IT Services industry also witnessed some great successes of joint ventures in the decade of 1990-2000. Indian economy was opening up and many of the MNCs who have left Indian soil earlier in late 70s decided to come back following a Joint venture route. IBM and Tata formed TSIL (which is now IBM India/IBM Global Services) and Fujistu formed a JV with ICIM. On the other hand HCL formed several joint ventures during that time namely HCL-HP, HCL-Perot, HCL-Delux, all of them either parted ways or one of the partners bought over the other. In fact JV is one of the acceptable routes to enter new territories and new market using local partner's familiarity of the market and MNCs capabilities of technology. Over time as the growth opportunities become attractive it usually that MNC call the shot and decide to either buy the local partner or form wholly-owned subsidiaries. But these are the necessary steps of growth for any market place and industry. Examples of similar formations of JV and later a break up between the collaborating partners can be found in several industries such as automobile, pharmaceutical and financial services, both in India as well as at global scale.

4.2.2 Hybrid Strategies

Information technology is ever evolving and this gives enough opportunity for ITSEs to change gear and try out opportunities in different form and adopt strategies of growth that sometimes seems unrelated or going away from the core competencies. But if that strategy, howsoever opportunistic it may be, is successful than perhaps it is the right one to adopt. We have named them as hybrid strategies and will be using a metaphor like sunflower to explain them.

However, before we theorize the actual happenings (practices) some examples of the successful ones may be worth noting down. While there may not be any well publicized analysis of such success because neither these companies have widely circulated the detail that took them to these heights nor these have been researched in depth. We will take a note of some of the recent events and stories to capture the way ITSEs have been adopting a mix of strategies (call it hybrid strategy) to grow their businesses. The example list would be long, but we are limiting our discussion by picking some of them. This is neither exhaustive nor comprehensive list but is to give some more insights to how these companies have been using hybrid model of strategies.

IBM

IBM has completed its 100 years of existence in July 2011, a feat very few companies have achieved so far and perhaps no one has achieved it in the information technology areas. This journey can easily be traced through some unique characteristics such as anticipating the technology trends in advance and working towards it. At no time IBM can be called to be short term focus, through it may not have seen meteoric rise in certain technology verticals in some of its products or services. A company that boosts the maximum number of patents year after year for the last several years in a row is also the home of several noble laureates.

IBM gave the first personal computer and made its architecture available to all for use. Yet it decided to sell off the personal PC and desktop business to its manufacturing partner in 2004. IBM scientists gave principles of relational database, CMM model, e-business and now it is advocating smart planet and concepts of social business. Today, nearly two-third of its revenue comes from software and services, a company which was known as makers of mainframe computers about 20 years ago. It is one company that others listen to with respect as it brings ideas that become reality in times to come[5]. It is also considered by the leading analysts as a company, which has the ability to re-invent through several recessions and continued technological change facing intense competition[6].

The keywords to describe the big blue (as it is a popularly called) would be visionary, stable and always innovating itself. IBM also is known for high degree of corporate governance, employee care and ethical standards.

HP

HP[7] is the largest IT company of 2011 in terms of revenue and also the first one to cross the 100 billion dollar mark. It is a spirit of entrepreneurship which was established in 1939 by Bill Hewlett and Dave Packard in a garage in Palo Alto! Its net revenue in 2010 was $126.3 billion. While it remains a leader globally for inkjet, laser, large format and multi-function printers market and hardware industry, its history is chequered with large scale acquisition (or mergers) of related companies to fuel its growth trajectory. Some of the major ones have been Compaq in 2002, EDS in 2008, 3Com in 2010, Palm in 2010, Autonomy Corporation Plc in 2011 and Spinoff of Agilent Technologies in 1999.

The key words to describe HP would be—aggressive for growth, nimble footed and innovating its offering portfolio.

Iflex

Iflex[8], which is now called Oracle Financial Services Software Limited[9] has a history of being the captive unit of Citibank 20 years ago and then carving its independent identity. I-flex in

---

5. http://www-03.ibm.com/ibm/history/history/history_intro.html accessed 15102011
6. Krantz, Mark; Swartz, Jon. IBM Shows secret to corporate longevity. USA Today. June 16, 2011. p.1B-3B
7. www8.hp.com/us/en/hp.../about-hp/history/history.html accessed 15102011
8. http://www.expresscomputeronline.com/20011210/focus1.shtml
9. http://www.oracle.com/us/industries/financial-services/index.html

1991 started as Citicorp Overseas Software Ltd. (COSL) and later rechristened as Citicorp Information Technologies Industries Ltd. (CITIL). This is product-centric company which has successful products such as MicroBanker, Finware, Flexcube. CITIL changed its name to i-flex solutions to reflect its growing independence from Citicorp and to strengthen its Flexcube brand. It is one ITSE which is highly domain-focused, i.e. BFSI and product-centric. It was recently acquired by Oracle to create a dominant position in the BFSI space.

Keywords for Iflex are strong Domain focus in BFSI and product centric.

Micormax

A new entrant who moved from software services to mobile handset manufacturing became the third largest[10] after Nokia and Samsung is an example of a company spotting the opportunities of low cost, dual SIM handset market for masses. This is one of the examples where the rapid growth of mobile usage is giving rise to new types of converging services and products across telecom and IT. Keywords associated would be spotting the opportunities.

Google

Google[11] started in 1997 as a research project by Larry Page and Sergey Brin, Ph.D. students at Stanford which led to creation of search engine for World Wide Web pages. Today, it has created new business model of generating free searches paid by advertisement revenue. Google not only gives us all the information, but access to a number of online available applications, maps, translation features, emails and many others. They have launched the open source mobile OS called android that has ushered a totally new market for smart phones which was earlier limited by Apple's proprietary OS and Microsoft OS. Its earlier acquisition of YouTube[12] is a case in point as to how this company is enriching its portfolio through innovative acquisition with a larger game plan which is unfolding everyday.

Google is one ITSE which is totally focusing on new opportunities, retail customer needs and innovation. These incidentally are the keywords for this company. With recent $12.5 billion acquisition of Motorola Mobility takes this company to a new area, i.e. hardware (mobile handset)[13]. These developments also points out that ITSE firms cannot remain a pure play software or services firms after a certain stage. The keyword associated with it would be innovation.

Oracle

Nearly three decades ago, Oracle was founded by Larry Ellison as relational database company. After database technology, it was a natural progression to either acquire or create application that use database as part of its offerings, through Oracle database is also sold independently. Now Oracle's portfolio includes ERP, CRM, SCM applications, servers, storage, software, and networking products. It also was one of the first companies to make its business applications available through the internet through its Oracle Fusion Middleware products, and later have done a series of acquisition to make it not just Database Company but completing it as end-

---

10. http://articles.economictimes.indiatimes.com/2010-04-28/news/27625791_1_handset-market-mobile-handsets-music-phones

11. http://www.google.com/about/corporate/company/history.html

12. http://www.google.com/press/pressrel/google_youtube.html

13. http://www.google.com/hostednews/afp/article/ALeqM5h_s_y0pN3OcH4ahknfic0ZdNWpAg?docId=CNG. 3404e18b09e683dd9aaf2d6e60f080df.191

to-end hardware, software and services company. Oracle's strategy is claimed to be aimed to strengthen its product offerings, accelerate innovation, meet customer demand rapidly. Some of the acquisition in the recent past echo this thought;

- Sun Microsystems a high-end hardware manufacturer in 2010
- Hyperion Solutions Corporation 2007
- PeopleSoft (January, 2005)
- Primavera (October, 2008)
- Siebel (January, 2006)

Keywords associated would be enrich the portfolio around the core, database.

Apple

This is one firm is that has truly redefined the technology opportunities, and kept itself on the forefront by launching series of new products and services. Keywords associated would be innovations and convergence.

Igate

Another company being picked up for reference is iGate that has seen several transformations in the recent times. It was one company that was adopting innovative policies such as outcome-based pricing. iGate was originally incorporated as 'Mascot Systems Private Limited' in 1993 and was largely seen as mid tier generic IT services company. It was renamed iGate and in May 2011, iGate Corporation acquired an 82.4% stake in Patni Computers to become iGate Patni[14]. With new management in place and critical mass of employees due to merger of these two companies now it is aiming to be billion dollar turnover company by 2012. While its strategic success will be only seen in the future, it is good case to study inorganic growth strategy for a mid size ITSE[15]. iGate-Patni now positions itself as first integrated Technology and Operations (iTOPS) company and is focusing on giving a good competition to bigger Indian ITS players.

HCL

HCL is a shining example of Indian entrepreneurship which has changed its strategies and grown from strength to strength. HCL started as Hindustan Computers Limited has now grown into a multinational conglomerate, It has its DNA of deep hardware research abilities such as it was first to develop micro-computer in 1978. Please note that Apple developed its computer the same time and it was three years before IBM's PC. This effort is also considered as the birth of the Indian computer industry.

Apart from its R&D abilities in hardware it also led successful JVs to chart out the growth path, early joint ventures with, HP and many MNC players are well-known. In addition, HCL created its R&D unit as software services company as HCL Technologies in 1997.

HCL is perhaps the only Indian company that has between its various entities, a complete hardware, software and services portfolio akin to MNCs like IBM, HP, Oracle etc. According

---

14. http://www.cio.com/article/683817/First_Fire_the_Executives_iGate_Patni_CEO_on_His_Merger_of_
    Unequals?page=3&taxonomyId=3195
15. Another similar merger is Mahindra and Satyam computer services

to an IDC study, its value through verticalization strategy is recognized. A study[16] underlines its innovation-led strategy to tap uncontested market space—the blue oceans[17] where margins are high and competitors are non-existent. Another HBR case study[18] also underlines its employee first strategy led by its young CEO. HCL is known for being smart, innovative and homegrown ITSE firm that has ambitious plans for years to come.

Mobile VAS companies (One97/On mobile)

Mobile Value Added Services (MVAS) are touted to be the next wave of IT Services growth area where consumer-centric, mobile handset based applications and services arising out of the phenomenal growth of mobile users. These two companies we have picked up amongst many others are the leaders in Indian IT Services space in this vertical. These companies provide their services through a combination of cloud hosted, but client site operations or entirely deployed in customer networks.

The rules of the game is still evolving where the revenue sharing amongst, content providers, content generators, aggregators, telecom operators and infrastructure providers, all get a pie of the burgeoning revenue base.

The rapid growth of On mobile is a role model for many new age entrepreneurs. Its growth story also includes strategic acquisition such as Voxmobili (2007), Telisma (2008), and Dilithium Networks (2010)[19].

Innovation is the only vehicle that drives these companies. Such innovation is not only needed in technology area, but also around business models and understanding the evolving customer preferences. Keywords for mobile VAS companies are new business model and innovation.

4.3 Analysis Framework of Practiced Strategy

We will now propose a framework to analyze and evaluate strategies being practices and those which the companies may be proposing in the future.

(i) **Customer-centric or generic offering:** The first analytical parameter for any strategy for ITSE to be successful is to consider if it is customer-friendly. Customer demands better services at lower cost that addresses not only their immediate needs, but also the future needs. Customer wants flexibility and openness and wants to exercise choice, and does not want to be held captive to choose only the vendors products and services.

(ii) **Niche vs end to end offering:** The second parameter is the capabilities of the firms and its focus to serve the customers. On one end of this spectrum are the companies like IBM, HP, Oracle, etc. who have a very broad portfolio of offerings are stable and renowned for their brand. The second end is niche and focused players who do only a

16. http://www.managementlab.org/files/u2/pdf/case%20studies/HCLCaseStudy.pdf

17. Kim, W.C. and R. Mauborgne (2005). 'Blue Ocean Strategy'. Harvard Business School Press.

18. How the best Indian companies drive performance by investing in people. by Peter Cappelli, Harbir Singh, Jitendra V. Singh, and Michael Useem 1908 Harvard Business Review, March 2010

19. http://www.onmobile.com/docs/2011/annual_report11.pdf

few things to selected industry, and they do it rather well. Any ITSE has to choose its place accordingly.

(iii) **Disruptive innovation vs continuous innovation:** The third parameter is the innovation. One such approach is the incremental innovations or innovation along their own vision pursued by most established players. The second type belongs to game changer innovation done by the new players that come up every now and then. Examples of Dell's direct selling, Google, Facebook and many others fall in the disruptive category. Whereas the companies like IBM and some others established players pursue the path of continuous innovation.

(iv) **Organic, inorganic or hybrid growth:** This refers to the parameter where the ITSE approaches growth in organic means or by mergers and acquisition.

A simple analytical chart using three major dimensions of innovation, range of offerings and customer centricity is presented in three-dimensional charts in Figure 4.2.

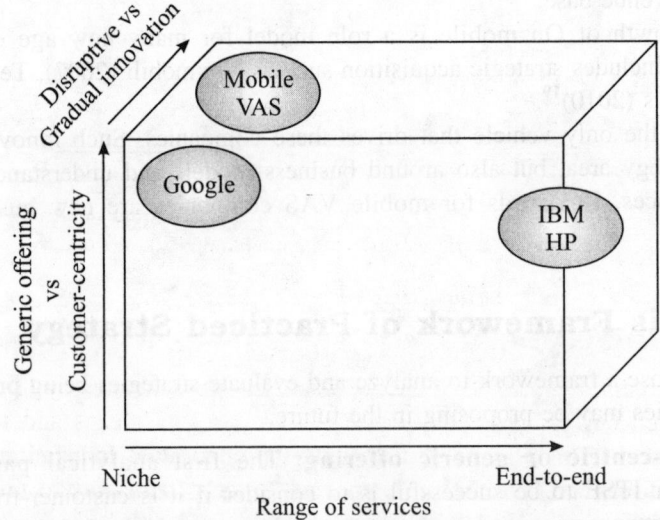

Figure 4.2   Strategic analysis diamond frameworks.

If we take all the eight dimensions then we can use a multi-dimensional strategy assessment diamond framework.

The strategic analysis diamond is presented in Figure 4.3.

For example, ITSE 1 provides specialized services to niche customer verticals and it follows a largely organic growth model. This is shown by the shaded polygon in the background. (Can you spot this company amongst the list of companies described?)

ITSE 2 follows inorganic growth model, disruptive innovation and gives services to the masses as shown by the cross shaded diagram.

Please note that no strategy is bad as long as it is yielding results and is risk free. We can use this framework to analyze each of the practiced strategies by the current firms and also the future ones.

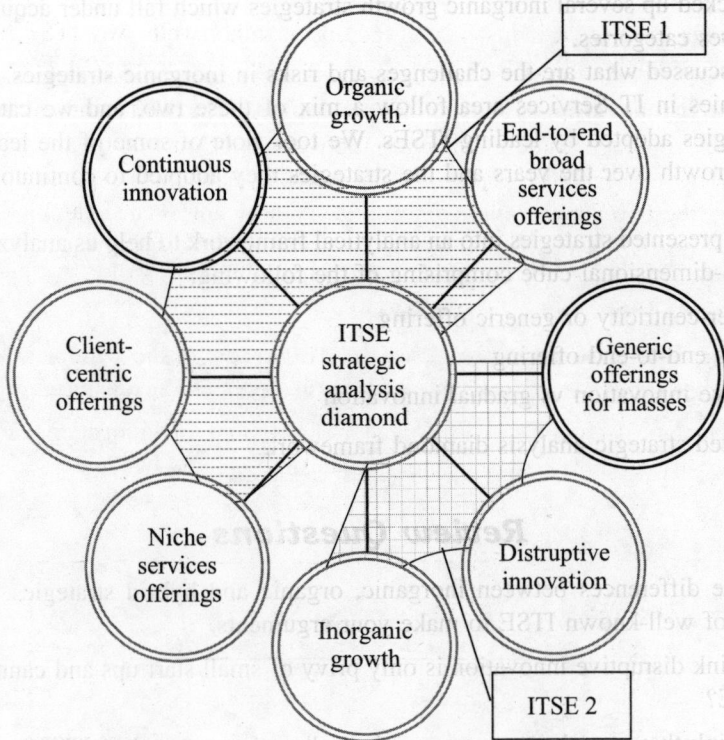

Figure 4.3 Strategic analysis diamond framework.

4.4 Summary

In this chapter, we discussed some of the prevalent strategies adopted by IT Services Enterprise (ITSE). We started our discussion by defining what strategy means and what is the generic analytical framework. This was needed to build the conceptual foundation and not purposed to be a detailed discussion. We took reference of Porter's framework to underline the generic strategies as the following

(i) Cost leadership (no frills)

(ii) Differentiation (creating unique desirable products and services) and

(iii) Focus (offering a specialized service in a niche market) which is further subdivided into
   (a) Cost focus
   (b) Differentiation focus.

We then focused our discussion on generic strategies for ITSE firms which were divided into organic, inorganic, and hydride strategy.

We discussed with example several organic growth strategies for ITSE firms such as ride the demand curve, explore new technology for growth, explore new territories, markets and verticals, broaden the variety of services, diversifying the service portfolios to widen the client base, anchor client strategy, increase business from existing clients, expand geographically, and growth through alliance with product vendors.

We then picked up several inorganic growth strategies which fall under acquisition, merger and joint ventures categories.

We also discussed what are the challenges and risks in inorganic strategies.

All companies in IT Services area follow a mix of these two, and we categorized them as hybrid strategies adopted by leading ITSEs. We took note of some of the leading ITSEs to examine their growth over the years and the strategies they adopted to continuously transform themselves.

Finally, we presented strategies into an analytical framework to help us analyze and evaluate them. The three-dimensional cube comprising of the following:

(i) Customer-centricity or generic offering

(ii) Niche vs end-to-end offering

(iii) Disruptive innovation vs gradual innovation

We also presented strategic analysis diamond framework.

Review Questions

4.1 Outline the differences between inorganic, organic and hybrid strategies. Take suitable examples of well-known ITSE to make your arguments.

4.2 Do you think disruptive innovation is only privy of small start ups and cannot be done by large ITSE?

4.3 Do you think that growth is a necessary ingredient for survival of ITSE?

4.4 Analyze why and how IBM has reinvented itself to remain a leading ITSE for the last 100 years.

Sugested Further Reading

Michael Porter 1985 *Competitive Advantage: Creating and Sustaining Superior Performance.*

Websites

http://www.nytimes.com/2010/09/22/technology/22oracle.html accessed 02012012

http://www.bostonanalytics.com/leading_thoughts_research/ba_mvas_in_india_research_report_10_07.pdf accessed 02012012

Chapter 5

Marketing of IT Services

I was an IBM customer...leaders want a solution to their
problem and they need someone who can help

—L.V. Gerstner 1994
Chairman and CEO, IBM Corporation

5.1 Introduction

In this chapter, we will discuss the concepts of IT Services marketing from theoretical as well as process perspective. Most of the marketing literature and research currently available are biased towards retail consumers and product. Service marketing researches especially of the IT Services marketing is of recent origin. We will take reference of the prevailing concept of services marketing and attempt draw parallel and espouse new conceptual foundation to enrich our readers.

5.2 Theoretical Foundation for IT Services Marketing

Marketing theory that too for IT Services marketing perspective is a complex framework to understand. Quoting Gummesson,[1] marketing is combination of scattered claims, derived from fragmented research of various microeconomic theory, social sciences, experiences, observations, and hype and success stories, but there is a little effort to generate comprehensive, grand theory for the service. The same is true for IT Services as well. In this chapter, we will attempt to distill various research approaches into a holistic framework, for the benefit of the students in the context of IT Services marketing.

Marketing

According to AMA,[2] *marketing is an organizational function and a set of processes for creating, communicating, and delivering value to customers and for managing customer relationships in ways that benefit the organization and its stakeholders.* Further Gummeson (2005)[3] extends

---

1. From One-to-One to Many-to-Many Marketing in the Network Society, Professor Evert Gummesson Stockholm University School of Business ACADEMY OF MARKETING and AMA CONFERENCE Dublin Institute of Technology July, 2005 SE-10691.
2. www.marketingpower.com
3. Gummesson , as above

marketing being a culture, an organizational function and a set of processes for creating, communicating and delivering value with customers and for establishing relationships in ways that benefit the organization, its customers and other stakeholders. This is a comprehensive definition and forms the basis of our further foundation of this subject.

IT services marketing is different

Unlike many other forms of marketing used for products marketing, it is the relationship marketing approach that is largely relevant for the IT Services. The word value creation is the sole objective of marketing for the benefit of the organization. This brings us to realize that in the case of IT Services, the process of marketing is not over unless customer is able to realize the value expected out of the services. This makes the role of IT Services provider much larger to help their customer realize the value they are looking for. An organization attempts to implement ERP, but this will need efforts of education, handholding, managing the change and inducing appropriate technology by the IT Service provider. For millions of smartphone users but for the enrichment and innovation brought by Apple, who would have demanded that such a gadget be made available! Before Steve Jobs gave i-phone and i-pad none of its users would have ever visualized its experience, remember these are product but what they offer is the service and associated experience, ultimately.

ITS is intangible, subjective and co-created

Like any other services, IT Services are intangible in nature and are difficult to execute as the underlying technology will always pose one challenge or the other. IT Services also suffer from subjectivity in customer evaluations. It is this very factor of intangibility that requires IT Services to create a proper image, a critical prerequisite for the ITS firm's success. When Grajek[4], et al. (2002) defined marketing as means of effectively transmitting information to potential users to communicate the quality and availability of a firm's services to impact the potential client attitude towards the firm, they also meant that this cannot be one way process of high decibel advertising by celebrity endorsement but also listening actively to the customer needs. Good IT Services marketing entails good listening to the prospective users, establishing a process of dialogue to unearth their needs rather than just promotion and awareness campaign. Unless the ITS marketer listens to the need and understands it well it will be impossible to create and deliver good IT Services. A popular name used for this approach is called co-creating of IT Services.

IT services is heterogeneous and complex

IT Services are heterogeneous in nature and are complex to manage, and therefore, need different models for marketing and communication. With business processes, and technology being the two ingredients the people factor makes this ITS much more complex to deal with.

Processes are prime

All these factors discussed above make IT Services success highly process-centric. Berry,

---

4. Why to Market IT Services and how to do it, : SusanGrajek, Patrick, Laurie Cagnetta, susan.grajek@yale.edu, Patrick.lynch@yale.edu,laurie.cagnetta@yale.edu, SIGUCCs'02, November 20–23, Providence, Rhode Island, ACM 1-28113-564-5/02/0011.

Bennett, and Brown (1989)[5], argue that customers judge a IT Service as much or even more on the service process than on the service outcome. Processes in IT Services form the '*how*' part of service delivery and make it the key differentiator for the services delivered. This is precisely why leading ITS Enterprise are extremely focused on the process and skills be it marketing, selling or delivery.

Finally avoid overhype

Yet, IT Services Enterprise should not fall in the trap of making overhype promises for routine services. This will raise the customer's expectation and lead to their dissatisfaction.

5.2.1 Marketing as an Integrative Vision of the ITS Enterprise

Having a services vision is important and lessons must be learnt by the IT Services enterprises. This will drive their marketing efforts in the right direction. Taco Bell a company frequently cited in the literature broadened its service vision by changing itself—from preparing food to feeding hungry people. By outsourcing large part of its operations and reducing its kitchen, it freed up space and employees to serve customers better[6]. This precisely means that IT Services firms must change their marketing vision from being technology service provider to being specialist of problem solving of particular variety.

Noted author Phillip Kotler defines that marketing concept takes an outside-in perspective where the focus is on customer needs and their achievements through coordinated marketing efforts. This leads to the conclusion that marketing process must be focused on customer's needs. IT Services firm achieve this by driving integrated marketing efforts that combines services design and development to convert customer's needs into suitable services offerings. Once the customer needs are met, the firm will easily be profitable through customer satisfaction.

Heskett (1987) argues that a strategic service vision requires marketing and operations to be operated as one function, something that is true for the IT Services firms leading to formation of their strategic service vision. Services vision comprises of identification of a target market segment, development of a service concept to address targeted customers' needs, codification of an operating strategy to support the service concept, and design of a service delivery system to support the operating strategy.[7]

5.2.2 Services-Dominant Marketing

In light of these critical factors for IT Services, the concept of services-dominant Logic of Marketing[8] comes in handy to explain what approach should be adopted for IT Services

5. Berry, L.L., Bennett, D.R. and Brown, C.W. (1989). Service quality: A profit strategy for financial institutions. Homewood, IL: Dow Jones-Irwin.
6. Henkoff, R. (1994). Service is everybody's business, Fortune, 229(13), 48–50, 52, 56, 60.
7. Heskett, J.L. (1987). Lessons in the service sector, *Harvard Business Review*, 65(2), 118–126.
8. Vargo, S.L. (2007), "On a Theory of Markets and Marketing: From Positively Normative to Normatively Positive," *Australasian Marketing Journal*, 15 (1), 53–60.
—— (2008b), "Why "service"?," *Journal of the Academy of Marketing Science*, 36(1), 25–38.

marketing. Vargo and Lusch[9] define services as the application of specialized competencies (knowledge and skills) through deeds, processes, and performances for the benefit of another entity or the entity itself. This definition is most appropriate in case of IT Services where the emphasis is on application of specialized skills and co-creation of value through the process of service delivery.

Vargo and Lusch proposed ten foundational premises (FPs) of service-dominant marketing as follows:

   (i) Service is the fundamental basis of exchange

  (ii) Indirect exchange masks the fundamental basis of exchange

 (iii) Goods are distribution mechanisms for service provision

 (iv) Operant resources are the fundamental source of competitive advantage

  (v) All economies are service economies

 (vi) The customer is always a co-creator of value

 (vii) The enterprise cannot deliver value, but only offer value propositions

(viii) A service-centered view is inherently customer oriented and relational

 (ix) All social and economic actors are resource integrators

  (x) Value is always uniquely and phenomenological determined by the beneficiary

How true theses fundamental promises are in the context of IT Services can be gauged by examining each of these points in the following example.

5.1 SALT IT Services
Need of a bank

A large bank wants to transform its operations that is largely manual and run across the country through large numbers of branches. They hire an IT Services provider to undertake the task of transformation. The IT Services provider installed hardware, network, and software programs for the banking operations. They designed their websites and enables the ATM machines, develop mechanism for the issue of debit and credit cards and also add features of mobile banking.

What is the need of the bank?

Bank primary job is to serve the customer for their financial needs. Bank does not want any hardware or software. All it wants is an IT system that helps them to serve their customer better. Their transformation is aimed for overall process efficiency improvement not just automating the old processes at higher cost in sophisticated way!

Can the bank claim that by installing the new IT system their customer service will improve?

Can the bank achieve transformation by just changing the IT system?

Most banks have now reached similar levels of automation and computerization. Why one bank is more liked by the customers than others?

The answer will depend on how the bank employees are able to realize their objectives using all these facilities. If the employee's attitude and service orientation has not changed a new IT system would not make the customer fond of the bank.

---

9. Stephen L. Vargo and Robert F. Lusch, Evolving to a New Dominant Logic for Marketing, *Journal of Marketing*, Vol. 68 (January 2004), 1–17.

5.2.3 IT Services is Customer Co-created

Prahlad[10] (2004) opines that marketing is experience-centric co-creation of value, a fact that is very apt for IT Services marketing. For the reasons well known, most IT Services and solution are futuristic in nature and even if they may be using proven tools and methods its end results will always be unpredictable as the organization seeking the service is different than others. Service-centered view propagated by Vargo & Lusch[11] states that marketing is a continuous processes in which the firm is constantly striving to make better value propositions than its competitors. Service-centered view of marketing perceives marketing as a continuous learning process helping the firm to improve its financial performance by:

   (i) Identifying and developing core competencies which are better than the competition.

   (ii) Identify potential customers that could benefit from these competencies.

   (iii) Cultivate relationships with customers in developing customized, competitively compelling value propositions to meet specific needs.

   (iv) Continuously seek market feedback by analyzing financial performance.

   (v) To learn how to improve the firm's offering to customers and improve firm's performance.

In the case of ITS marketing, the customer is user as well as co producer of the services. ITS marketing process heavily depends on the customer interaction. The value of services a customer receives is the perceived value in use. Vargo and Lusch emphasizes that interactivity, integration, customization, and co-production are the hallmarks of a service-centered view, and its inherent focus on the customer and the relationship. It also shows that:

   (i) Service delivery and customer satisfaction depend on employee actions

   (ii) Service quality depends on many uncontrollable factors

   (iii) There is no sure knowledge that the service delivered matches what was planned and promoted

   (iv) Customers participate in and affect the transaction

   (v) Customers affect each other

   (vi) Employees affect the service outcome

   (vii) Decentralization may be essential

(viii) Mass production is difficult

5.3 IT Services Marketing is Different

Many researchers[12] have distinguished services marketing from product marketing, sighting

---

10. Prahlad, C.K. (2004) "The Cocreation of Value," Journal of Marketing, 68 (January), 23.

11. Stephen L. Vargo and Robert F. Lusch, Evolving to a New Dominant Logic for Marketing, *Journal of Marketing*, Vol. 68 (January 2004), 1–17.

12. (Regan, 1963; Rathmell, 1966; Shostack, 1977; and Zeithaml et al. 1985). Quoted in An Investigation Into Four Characteristics of Services, Russell Wolak, Stavros Kalafatis and Patricia Harris* Kingston Business School, Kingston Hill, Kingston upon Thames, Surrey, KT2 7LB, Phone 0181 547 2000 Fax 0181 547 7026, E-mail p.harris@kingston.ac.uk: *Journal of Empirical Generalisations in Marketing Science*, Vol. 3, 1998, pp. 22–43.

several other characteristics such as intangibility, inseparability, heterogeneity and perishability. Let us discuss them in the context of IT Services and establish new meaning for our understanding.

Intangibility in services

While Regan (1963) introduced the idea of services being activities, benefits or satisfactions which are offered for sale these are nothing, but promises that a service provider gives to the client. This is highly perception dependent. In case of the IT Services, most often, the client may not have any prior experience to set and check a benchmark against.

Inseparability of services

Refers to simultaneous delivery and consumption of services, which to some extent may not be totally applicable in IT Services. Unlike physical services, in IT Services there may have time-delay between production and consumption of the output. For example, if the contract is for application development and maintenance, the production may be separate than the consumption which may happen over a period of time.

Heterogeneity of services

It refers to high variability in service delivery as outlined by Zeithaml (et al. 1985) due to high labour content. Consequently, the service performance is dependent on people, process and performance measure ability of the service provider firm. This characteristic is more pronounced in the case of IT Services as the Information technology is ever evolving, and therefore, the importance of heterogeneity factor. Seeking the cue from Onkvisit and Shaw (1991) who opines that heterogeneity offers the opportunity to bring flexibility and customization and even a considered as a benefit and point of differentiation as postulated by Wyckham et al. (1975).

Perishability of services

In case of physical services, this characteristic of services highlights the fact that in general, services cannot be stored and carried forward to a future time period (Rathmell, 1966; Donnelly, 1976; and Zeithaml et al., 1985). Not only these services are time dependent and time important as opined by Onkvisit and Shaw (1991) which make them very perishable. Hartman and Lindgren also mention about the issue of perishability being the prime concern of the service producer. The impact to client is felt only when the insufficient supply leads to wait and delay.

In case of IT Services as well the time lost cannot be recovered. Wait time or not productive time utilization does impact bottom line of the IT Services firms. Yet IT is all about automation of other services, and hence, IT Services also can be automated to make less and less dependence of human workforce. For example, tools are increasingly replacing human intervention for providing services, IVR (Interactive Voice Response) tool can help customer get to know about his account balance, status of reservation as well as train information. All these were earlier being performed by human agents. Monitoring of complex network infrastructure is no longer human dependent but is hugely automation assisted where rows of computer hardware equipments are monitored by specially written agents that flag of any issues. IT Services has potential to breed intellectual capital and software that can be put to reuse. So while agreeing that IT Services too has perishability as characteristic but has also got potential to produce intellectual capital for reuse.

5.4 New P's for IT Services Marketing

Most services marketing concepts are driven from the product marketing history. Product marketing concepts talk about traditional 5P's of marketing—Product Price Place Promotion Position.

Services, especially IT Services, differ from product marketing as well as other services in many ways. Given these analysis of IT Services Characteristic it may be useful to summarize the new 6P's of IT Services as

(i) Promise

(ii) Process

(iii) People

(iv) Performance measure

(v) Past experience

(vi) Price

We will discuss each one of them in detail.

5.4.1 Promise

Most IT Services are promise to address a customer problem. More articulated and detailed the promise will be, better will be the clarity of what the customer is ultimately going to get. Statement of work, proposal document, services catalogue are but a few means through which a service provider can promise what it is going to deliver.

Having a well-written services proposal document (promise) also helps in setting up the customer expectations. Predictably, such expectations would not be believed as the client knows what it is going to get and when. Services delivery lead passes from several hands, right from marketing folks, to business development, sales and finally to the services delivery team. Keeping the promise in same letter and spirit as the discussion progresses towards agreement and execution is an important means that can be achieved by documenting every step and discussion in a meaningful manner.

5.4.2 Process

The next question after the award of contract arises as to how the promised services will be delivered by the IT Services firm. Even before the contract is awarded the client gets supreme confidence if it gets glimpses of the processes and its adoption maturity to be adopted by the IT Services firm. This is the reason why IT Services firms of repute undertake process certifications of CMM, ITIL and many others to distinguish themselves from others who have not, especially the most recent start ups who would not have chance to go up the process maturity curve. We have devoted the remaining chapters of the book to create a process framework of all the functions of an IT Services Enterprise. Running an IT Services Enterprise with a process-centric approach makes its operations far more predictable and results sustainable.

5.4.3 People

Success of services enterprise is through people and IT Services is no exception, despite the fact that it may have higher degree of automation built in the services delivery process. Skilled people take less time to understand customer's requirements and are able to guide the customer far better in the usage of new technology. There are several factors that need to be considered such as skills, retention, training, and motivation etc. to create a good people team. Most IT Services contract are awarded based on examining the key personnel profile and in most situation submitting the resume of these key people along with the contract document is almost mandatorily followed. We have devoted Chapter 11 Building IT Services Management team to discus this aspect in detail. Please see (Story and learning Task) 5.2 emphasizing the differentiation through of people in getting a large service contract.

5.2 SALT (Story And Learning Task)
People are the key in services

Summer afternoons are usually not the appropriate time to go out for customer meeting, in Delhi. By the time Principal consultant parked his car in the busy Bahadur Shah Jafar Marg and walked upto the express tower, he was drenched in sweat. He needed to cool down and wanted to head straight to the cafeteria to pick up a bottle of chilled soft drink.

From the corridor across the hall he saw his room had a small crowd, but he ignored and continued to walk towards the pantry.

"Hello sir... we need you quickly...." A young associate came running to him.

"But I need chilled soft drink... I am thirsty... you know" he chuckled... "but what happened?" he replied.

"I will fetch that for you... the MD office has called five times since you were away and the her Secretary is holding line for you.." and she ran to fetch his cola drink. (Those were the days when mobile phones have not become so ubiquitous.)

"Professor, the ABC Power CIO would like to talk to you urgently. Apparently, the IT consulting and implementation they awarded to MNC Consulting has run in rough weather. I met the ABC Power MD on a social gathering last night and he was sharing his plight of how the MNC consulting team is not working along with theirs". MD spoke slowly. She had nicknamed him Professor due to his habit of explaining things in detail and grey hairs or both.

"Not an issue. I am back in the office with no desire to leave till the city cools down in the evening. Do ask him to call after an hour or so..." he said "But what do we do... the contract is with other company what way we can help" he added.

"Professor don't worry about the future. You just explain his questions the best you can and leave the rest to me and tomorrow!" She laughed at the other end.

By the time he was half way though his chilled cola and 30 mails his secretary announced that the CIO of ABC Power was on the other end waiting for him. He asked her to transfer the call and signaled to close the door.

The CIO surprisingly had no technical question to ask. He was concerned about the way the incumbent IT Service company has staffed the team. He was curious as to how he would have staffed his team in terms of skills, attitude and experience if a similar project would have been assigned to his firm. Talking ideal situation it was no brainer to visualize why the ABC Power was unhappy. It was clear case of bait and switch which means the services firm puts different sets of people than the one who were paraded during the engagement cycle of selling the services contract. In addition, the CIO wanted to know how the client team should staff themselves as any IT Services project is nothing, but co-creation of value by client and IT Service provider. The discussion went on about managing change that IT project would bring and what initiatives are needed, thereof.

The three-hour long conversation got over by 6.00 p.m. Luckily it was not on mobile phone else the call would have dropped ten times and battery would have gone in between. The sweet old land line phone with powerful speaker and microphone worked beautifully. At home late night he received a call from his boss that ABC Power has decided to cancel the contract of IT consulting and services with MNC Consulting. They now want to seek their services and insist that the Principal whom CIO spoke must lead the project. "And I have no reasons to disagree, you plan for execution I will work the contract details with them and keep you in the loop" she said.

His wife and two children were animatedly trying to listen what was going on. As he finished the call, the younger amongst the two asked "which city now you will going to?" "Nashik. You know why it is famous for?" He asked the elder one.

The ten year old quiz master spoke "it is the Wine Capital of India, situated at the bank of Godavari where Kumbhmela is held every twelve year and is also famous Jyotirling Trimbakeshwar and Shirdi Shrine are close by that is why it is also called Holy City" came a prompt answer. The principal consultant was soon engrossed to think as to who he would select as the Engagement manager, who else should be in the team and so on.

The ideal team composition he suggested to the CIO of ABC power in the afternoon will now have to come in real... in next few days at the most!

Questions

1. Why would a CIO take decision to cancel the contract with an exiting supplier?
2. Did a three-hour conversation helped CIO to firm up his ideas of an ideal team that will steer his company out of the problems being faced?
3. Will this change be easy or risky, what way the Principal consultant should mitigate the risk?

5.4.4 Performance Measure

The major challenge in any service delivery is to ensure whether its services are performed consistently and efficiently. There is a need to ensure service quality (detailed discussion in follows in Chapter 8) is maintained and the performance is measured against the standards set in the promise document. Measuring IT Services performance is an emerging discipline which requires continuous filed inputs. If these performance measures are articulated well and also shared with the customer, the satisfaction quotient will go up manifold.

5.4.5 Past Experience

There is nothing more effective and useful than to share the firm's past experience of successes to a new prospect while IT Services marketing. Not only it gives confidence to the customer that they are not in the hands of novices who are being paid to learn on client expense, but also gives a fall back on experience for better execution of services delivery. Past experience gives useful insight, working templates, report outline and many other useful intellectual capitals which can improve efficiency and reduce learning curve. SALT 5.2 shows what way the past experience helped in winning new consulting services.

5.4.6 Price

This is only P that transcends both product and IT Services marketing. Pricing in services vary from firm to firm, but is also a reflection of what skills and quality of processes and people the IT firms does possess. IT Services have to be configured according to the customer needs and meticulous details required to produce the services. There is no point giving high priced services to medium-sized customer whose needs are simple. Accordingly, taking the right call for pricing is critical while selling IT Services.

5.5 IT Services Marketing Processes

IT Services marketing processes are a close knit group of processes to achieve two objectives:

  (i) Creating mindshare about the firm with customer

 (ii) Generate opportunities which can be further converted into sales

In order to meet these objectives the marketing processes will be closely working with the delivery management processes to understand and create capabilities, and with sales processes to convert them into firm service contracts. Figure 5.1 gives the schematic view of the IT Services marketing processes.

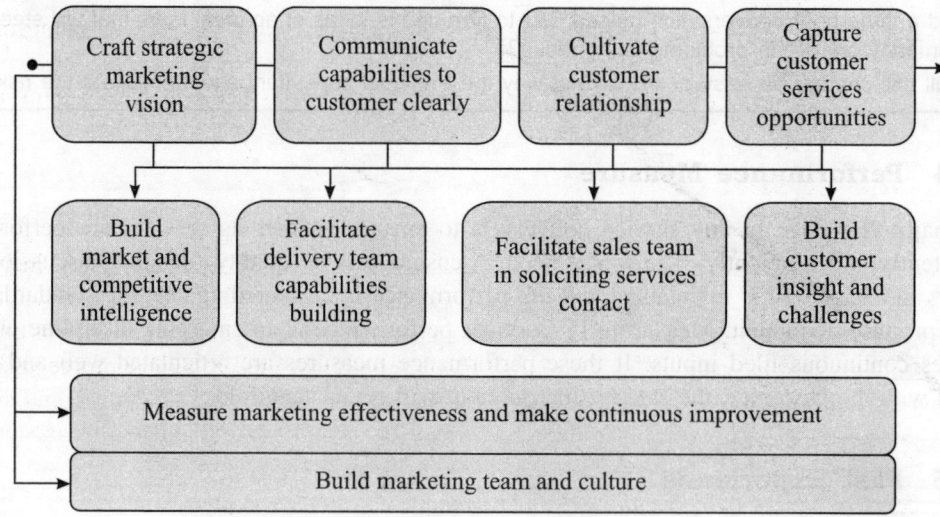

Figure 5.1 IT Services marketing processes.

The IT Services marketing processes are as follows:

5.5.1 Craft Strategic Marketing Vision

Also called marketing strategy this process answers the questions around what services the firm is going to offer to which customer segment and at what price. This needs a careful understanding of the IT Services market as well as the capabilities the services firm has built up or is in the process of building up.

Develop services offerings

The process interacts very closely with the delivery team experts and develops services offering[13] documents. These documents or contents of the services firm's website usually under the section our services, also help the marketing sales and business development team to understand and propose them in customer interactions. These documents are often the starting piece of information sent to prospective customers with details such as past experiences.

Define target segments

The second important activity of this process is to define the target segment of customers where the firm would like to solicit opportunities. Once the target segment is defined then the marketing communication process takes over. Segmenting the market gives the IT Services firm a focus so that their efforts can be better utilized.

Positioning and branding

The third activity of this sub process is to decide the positioning the form wants itself to attain in the mind of the customer. Jack Tout in his seminal book *Positioning—The Battle for Your Mind*[14] refers to identifying a market niche for a brand, product or service utilizing traditional marketing placement strategies (i.e. price, promotion, distribution, packaging, and competition). In case of IT Services the positioning is a key factor which attracts the customer. Many IT Services firms find it difficult to get away from a low cost, low quality tag because they positioned themselves as such to gain quick contracts. Use of services positioning matrix as advocated by Collier[15] is useful to create a linkage between what a customer expects and accordingly design services capabilities to meet them. The matrix helps managers think about marketing and operations linkages, roles of the customer and service-provider in creating and delivering services, facility design and process choice, and the different types of management challenges at each position in the matrix.

Positioning processes also leads to creating a brand image that conveys the value the firm brings in clearly. Building brand in IT Services enterprise is the most necessary. Brand increases familiarity and comfort level with the customer especially when selling is being done of intangible IT Services. Thorough Brand the IT Services firm can convey its service attributes such as quality, cost-effectiveness, innovativeness, simplicity, etc. Brands help deliver and reinforce essential message what the company wants to convey and helps in increasing awareness and recall. Infosys is one prime example of IT Services firm that created a brand image that is standard for delivery predictability, financial transparency and corporate governance[16]. Something every stakeholder from customer to employees, partners to investors and shareholders would like to be associated with. Sustaining an image and positioning requires not just glossy presentations or advertisement but living upto its elements by ensuring delivery. In many situations as the story goes, Infosys did not compromise on ethical or pricing issue and some of these decisions were

---

13. Offering document are short non confidential documents to convey what the IT Services will cover and what benefits the customer is expected to get.
14. Al Ries and Jack Trout I "Positioning—The Battle for Your Mind." McGraw-Hill, 1981.
15. David A. Collier, Susan M. Meyer, (1998) "A service positioning matrix", International Journal of Operations & Production Management, Vol. 18 Iss: 12, pp.1223–1244.
16. http://www.business-standard.com/india/news/building-brand-infosys/400295/ accessed 1092011

vetted by the Chairman himself. Building brand also means conveying a simple message, not making it cheap by overuse. Finally, it is the delivery team that makes sure the brand promises are lived upto. Finally, this process must help in preserving, propagating and establishing the brand.

5.5.2 Communicate Capabilities to Customer Clearly

Once the strategic vision of the IT Services firm is in place it needs to be conveyed and clearly communicated to the customers and other stakeholders. Many-a-times, firm's marketing strategy and its brand philosophy needs to be communicated internally as much as it is required externally.

This sub-process covers the following activities:

  (i) Defining and articulating value proposition

 (ii) Choosing right communication tool

(iii) Collecting and receiving feedback, potential prospects

Initial communication tools will include non-confidential marketing summary, key service offering profile, white papers covering experiences, insights from similar industry or similar services. Use of Information Technology tools such as intelligent and smart website, subtle advertising in media, and participation in tech fairs, networking, etc., also helps in marketing communication.

The age old e-mail does work in conveying what the IT Service provider is doing. In addition, the use of electronic IP exchanges helps in reaching out to unknown territories and locations.

Then there is the usual direct contact or Cold Call to reach out to prospect with information. One can start with reaching out to the network of contacts which needs to be constantly followed-up.

Campaign management is the theme based communication program where the IT Services provider reaches out to prospective customers. Unlike product marketing, these campaigns are around new services offerings and new technology. Theses campaigns may need sending mailers, conducting workshops, participating in blog and other events.

Best practices for Customer communication[17]: Brad Cleveland a noted expert in the area of Customer Relationship Management describes 12 principles many of which are applicable in the context of IT Services management as well. These principles are transposed into following best practices for customer communication:

  (i) Use plain and simple language, avoid jargons and do not explain technology in minutest detail.

 (ii) Focus on what benefit the customer will get not what the services will do. The effort should be relate the customer need with the solution not explaining how great the IT Services firm is.

(iii) Be precise and to the point to address customer needs.

---

17. Adapted from http://www.icmi.com/Resources/Articles/2007/October/12-Principles-that-Drive-Profitable-Customer-Relationships.aspx bcleveland@icmi.com accessded 01092011

(iv) Must explain and present your services or solution in as simple form as possible. Use of jazzy power points gives an impression that you are hiding truth behind packaging.

(v) Must quote supporting data, especially if it related to customer benefits, you need by precise to last decimal but state a range. But avoid too much of data in chart which is very crowded.

5.5.3 Cultivate Customer Relationship

This sub-process starts reaching out with customers and develop relationships. While seminars, mailers, executive briefings, personal visits, etc. will lead to new contacts some of them will seek services and become exciting customers. We have used the word cultivate rather than manage to convey a sense of growth of relationship from strength to strength for IT Services firms. Not only we need new customers to be identified, but we must also need to cultivate existing customers, who are sometimes ignored. Very early on in my career one of my senior gave me a simple formula to priorities my marketing and sales attention. She said we will first serve the customer who pays (existing) then we work for the customer who is about to pay (those who have signed contract) and finally those who are likely to pay (i.e. prospects).

Once a customer or prospect comes in touch with the IT Services firm this process keeps track of their needs and interaction history so that at an opportune time the customer may like to seek the services. After attracting new customers is important for business growth, but should not be overemphasized as the acquisition process is always costly as compared to doing business with the new customer. Sometimes, in order to win the new customer against stiff competition, IT Services firms give hefty price discounts or free services leading to lower margins of profits and cost of acquisition.

By focusing more on existing customers and building meaningful and lasting relationships the IT Services firm will be able to restore its profitability and can significantly improve the customer lifetime value. Howard[18] suggests that cultivation of customer relationship can be done by

(i) Keeping regular and meaningful contact, observations, and ongoing interactions

(ii) Ensuring that through atmosphere of exclusivity, competition is not able to come closer

(iii) Expanding relationship with offering new services some of them could be complimentary on regular basis

(iv) Surprise the customer with innovation in services

(v) Analyze customer behaviour to anticipate new needs, any change and taking corrective actions.

Cultivating customer requires a useful blend of strong leadership, clarity of marketing vision, and an effective measurement system. It has significant potential of reward in the long term.

---

18. Cultivate relationships to increase margins by: Robert Howard, http://customer-relationship-mgt. bestmanagementarticles.com/a-30155-cultivate-relationships-to-increase-margins.aspx accessed 01092011

Best practices for cultivating customer relationship

Some of the best practices which can be adopted are as follows:

(i) Know your customer well and update your knowledge regularly, this also means to find opportunities to interact with the customer more often, not only when there is an opportunity to address. Ideally using a single face of an account management team helps the customer.

(ii) Customize your response based on customer profile; never paint all of them with the same brush. Value those customers that are close to your strategic vision, politely disengage with those who are not, without antagonizing them.

(iii) A good marketing manager is able to anticipate customer needs, through analysis of customer profiles.

(iv) Communicate marketing insight about the customer back to the delivery team as well as the management team. Involve them in the process of account planning.

(v) Increase the base of revenue by retaining the customer, doing more with the existing one. This is why most IT Services firm want to become full-service provider.

(vi) Add value to customers as well as to the IT Services firm by continuous innovation.

(vii) Create simple yet effective processes to deal with the customer requirements, inquiries, complaints and ad-hoc requests.

(viii) Build a competent and enthusiastic team and marketing culture within the enterprise. Make them responsible as well as accountable by giving them guidelines for decision making. Create a culture of cultivating customer relationship which may be more than having a good technology and tool.

(ix) Build an atmosphere of trust, cooperation and collaboration with the customer.

5.5.4 Capture Customer Services Opportunities

Marketing activities would lead to response from the customer either explicitly or implicitly. In the case of later, the customer may indicate their plans for the future which could act an opportunities for the IT Services firm. All such opportunities which may come through, e-mail, RFP, verbal feedback or letters are required to be captured in an opportunity management database. Further these opportunities are assigned to business development team to act on.

5.5.5 Build Market and Competitive Intelligence

One of the prime functions of marketing is to keep the company abreast with what changes are taking place in the market and how competition is positioning themselves. For example, what impact the slow down in Americas will have on the IT Services market especially the offerings that the company is putting forward will be one of the exercise that the marketing team has to do.

There are several research agencies like Gartner, Meta, Kennedy Research, etc., who regularly publish market research data. The marketing team should read and absorb them and interpret them for the benefit of the rest of IT Services firm's staff. All such reports which can be purchased or gathered from secondary sources (website, Google search etc.) need to be interpreted in the context of the firm's strategic vision. Marketing is like a race where the firm has to speed ahead of the competition by positioning themselves better informed about the customer.

Gathering market insights is a comprehensive process that gives information about competition, customer and consumer preferences. Apart from the traditional sources the use of social media and networking sites has become more useful for gathering market insights.

Use of social media in IT services marketing

According to Wikipedia, social media is information content created by people using highly accessible and scalable publishing technologies that is intended to facilitate communications, influence and interaction with peers and with public audiences, typically via the Internet and mobile communications networks. Monitoring of the social media is important to keep a track of what is being said and discussed. Use of social media helps find the competitive landscape, community building, leveraging the network and outreach. It is an important source for brand monitoring covering what are the key feedback and emerging trends. Social media mining is another source to get competitor weakness and strength. There are some references given in the reference section for these tools.

5.5.6 Facilitate Delivery Team Capabilities Building

One of the important marketing processes is to facilitate the delivery team. Marketing team is like the captain sitting on the top deck of an ocean liner, who is in control of the destination and direction of the ship. Delivery team are the people in the engine room who run the engine so that the ship can move forward. It is the task of the marketing team to tell what all type of opportunities are coming up in the market, how customer demand is changing and for which what preparation are required by delivery team. Conversely, by learning from delivery team from their recent project successes the marketing team can reach out to the new customers.

This exercise is done through a regularly installed process where the delivery team managers and the marketing team sit together and create join action plan.

5.5.7 Facilitate Sales Team in Soliciting Services Contract

The marketing leads generated need to be converted in actual projects. This task is usually done by the sales team. They would depend on the insights and research of the marketing team to do successful selling.

5.5.8 Build Customer Insight and Challenges

Using this focused process the marketing team builds enough understanding about the customer business and challenges so that the customer starts accepting the service provider as a trusted advisor.

5.5.9 Measure Marketing Effectiveness

Marketing processes must not be implemented without proper measurement otherwise it may end up being a white elephant and marketing team that socializes without any apparent results.

The task of marketing is to convey the firm's value proposition so that the customer is attracted to solicit services. Ultimately all this must lead to opportunities or leads which must get converted into projects or service contract. Some of the marketing effectiveness measures could be the following:

(i) Number of leads generated monthly and its growth by each marketing person

(ii) Incremental revenue per marketing expense

(iii) Lead conversion ratio to qualified opportunity

(iv) Average cost of leads generated

(v) Number of new leads from new customers vs repeat customers

(vi) Return on investment of marketing spends

5.5.10 Build Marketing Team and Culture

Invest in people as marketing requires human capital investment. Berry and Parasuraman[19] say that in service businesses the least effective marketing department executives strive to be clever marketers themselves whereas the most effective executives strive to turn everyone else in the organization into clever marketers. Several studies have established a link between the satisfied customers and a culture of motivated market-driven employees. IT Services industry is no exception, where companies with lower attrition amongst its employees and sense of pride and association lead to enhance customer satisfaction, long-term relationship and larger revenue. If the employee feel they have the skills to satisfy the customer requirements their approach would be totally different than the one that has low confidence levels. Leading IT Services companies also figure in the best place to work surveys from time-to-time. Several studies[20] have directly linked satisfied customers with a culture of motivated market-driven employees. A good ITS firm cannot achieve its strategic vision unless its employees are highly motivated as employee/customer interaction is much higher than any type of marketing. Attainment of a strategic vision for IT Services organizations needs greater degree of employee and customer interaction, not necessarily the marketing or sales team alone.

5.6 IT Services Marketing Research Themes and Their Applicability for IT Services

A research by Furrer and Sollberger[21] has identified 27 conceptual themes for services marketing research. These are given in Table 5.1 and their applicability and criticism for IT Services are

---

19. Berry, L.L. and Parasuraman, A. (1991).Marketing services: Competing through quality, New York: The Free Press, p. 78.

20. Linda M. Gorchels, Executive Marketing Management Programs, University of Wisconsin, Madison Management Institute, 975 University Avenue, Grainger Hall, Madison, WI 53706 LIBRARY TRENDS, Vol. 43, No. 3, Winter 1995, pp. 494–509 @ 1995 The Board of Trustees, University of Illinois.

21. Trends in Service Marketing Research: 1993–2003 Olivier Furrer, Radboud University Nijmegen (The Netherlands), Pierre Sollberger, University of Neuchâtel (Switzerland), October 2004. Source www.escp-eap. net/conferences/marketing/2005.../Furrer_Sollberger.pdf accessed 30082011

presented to excite our readers to probe further this new age services that has led India to the world map!

Table 5.1 Services themes applicable to IT Services

1.	After-sale/customer service	Applicable to IT products such as hardware where after sales service includes installation and maintenance
2.	Business-to-business services	Most IT Services are b-2-b services and therefore all learnings are useful
3.	Consumer behaviour	IT consumers are becoming more sophisticated and technology savvy. They also want increasing speed of response and various options. For example, e-mail services are desired on desktop, mobile phone and now on television
4.	Innovation, new service development	Innovation is the main stay of competitive differentiator. It also helps reducing cost and increasing customer satisfaction
5.	Internationalization and export	Undoubtedly IT Services are leader in internationalization and export
6.	Methodology and measurement	Established framework of delivery methodology and measurement is an evolving discipline
7.	Operations and service design	With growing usage of IT Services this aspect is becoming very important
8.	Performance	By articulating and measuring services performance IT Services companies can demonstrate their unique differentiation
9.	Pricing and yield management	Applicable in totality, all services are price sensitive. Conveying the benefit is as much important in IT Services is to provide the benefit
10.	Service quality	Measurement of IT Services quality is gaining importance, more discussion is in Chapter 9
11.	Service failure and recovery	The parameters like MTTR, MTBF are too applicable especially for operational services for IT infrastructure
12.	Relationship marketing and customer retention	Most applicable in IT Services area for achieving success in ITS marketing
13.	Customer satisfaction	Would lead to repeat and newer requirements from customer
14.	Communication/promotion/advertising	More subtle it is better
15.	Service offering	Well-defined offering is good tool for communication and managing expectations
16.	Ethics	Of high order is needed as IT Services provider at times get access to sensitive personal or business competitive data
17.	Internal marketing and service employee management	Key for IT Services success
18.	Competition	Will always be after services that are well-defined and in use. Hence, continued innovation is needed
19.	Environmental context	Cloud computing, virtualization and green computing are the source of new service offerings that are making IT Services to transform itself

5.7 Summary

In this chapter, we discussed the concepts of IT Services marketing from theoretical as well as process perspective. We started by defining Marketing is an organizational function and a set of processes for creating, communicating, and delivering value to customers and for managing customer relationships in ways that benefit the organization and its stakeholders. However, we noted that that IT Services marketing is different for several reasons. IT Services is intangible, subjective and co-created and is heterogeneous and complex. Given these characteristics Processes are prime and make it the key differentiator for the services delivered. Yet, IT Services Enterprise should make routine services simple and not overhype it.

A good marketing must start with an integrative vision of the ITS enterprise. We took note of prevalent research in this context and drew relevance from them in the context of IT Services marketing. Typically, customer plays a very important part in co-creation of IT Services. Here, the customer is a user as well as co-producer of services. We coined the new P's for IT Services marketing as—Promise, Process, People, Performance measure, Past experience and last but not the least Price and discussed each one of them in detail.

The process of IT Services marketing achieves two objectives:

(i) Creating mindshare about the firm with customer

(ii) Generate opportunities which can be further converted into sales and covers the following steps:

    (a) Craft strategic marketing vision covering
- Develop services offerings
- Positioning and branding

    (b) Communicate capabilities to customer clearly covering
- Defining and articulating value proposition
- Choosing right communication tool
- Collecting and receiving feedback, potential prospects
- Campaign management

We also discussed best practices for customer communication.

IT Services marketing depends a lot on cultivating customer relationship by

(i) Keeping regular and meaningful contact

(ii) Ensuring exclusivity to keep competition away

(iii) Expanding relationship with offering new services

(iv) Surprise the customer with innovation in services

(v) Analyze customer behaviour to anticipate new needs

Cultivating customer requires a useful blend of strong leadership, clarity of marketing vision, and an effective measurement system. It has significant potential of reward in the long term.

We ended this discussion by outlining some of the best practices for cultivating customer relationship.

The other processes discussed in the sequence were capture customer services opportunities and building market and competitive intelligence. Use of new age tool such as social media was also espoused for the benefits of the readers.

A successful marketing also means facilitating the delivery team capabilities building and facilitating sales team in soliciting services contract. We ended the discussion with the necessity of building customer insight and challenges so that the customer starts accepting the service provider as a trusted advisor.

The chapter also outlines measures for marketing effectiveness and how continuous improvement can be made in this process. One of the important success criteria discussed was to build marketing team and culture. We ended the chapter with services marketing research themes and their applicability for IT Services.

Review Questions

5.1 Explain in brief how IT Services marketing is different as compared with other services.

5.2 Quoting prevalent research explain how IT Services marketing can act as an integrative vision of the ITS enterprise?

5.3 Explain the relevance of the concept foundational premises (FPs) of service-dominant for IT Services marketing.

5.4 Do you agree with noted Guru Late C.K. Prahlad opinion that marketing is experience-centric co-creation of value in the context of IT Services marketing? Give a suitable example to support your argument.

5.5 What are the new 6 Ps of IT Services? Explain each one of them in brief giving examples.

5.6 What are the IT Services marketing processes two prime objectives? Explain with example.

5.7 What are the various IT Services marketing processes? Explain them in brief with a suitable diagram.

5.8 Summarize in the form of a table at least 7 IT Services marketing research themes and their applicability for IT Services.

Suggested Further Reading

An Investigation into Four Characteristics of Services by Russell Wolak, Stavros Kalafatis and Patricia Harris, Kingston Business School, Kingston Hill, Kingston p.harris@kingston. ac.uk, *Journal of Empirical Generalisations in Marketing Science*, Vol. 3, 1998, pp. 22–43.

Rathmell, J.M. (1966). "What is Meant by Services?", *Journal of Marketing*, 30, 32–36.

Regan, W.J. (1963). "The Service Revolution", *Journal of Marketing*, 47, 57–62.

Shostack, G. (1977). "Breaking Free from Product Marketing", *Journal of Marketing*, 41, 73–80.

Zeithaml, V.A., Parasuraman A. and Berry L.L. (1985). "Problems and Strategies in Services Marketing", *Journal of Marketing*, 49, 33–46.

Wyckham, R.G., Fitzroy P.T. and Mandry G.D. (1975). "Marketing of Services—An Evaluation of the Theory", *European Journal of Marketing*, 9, 1, 59–67.

Website

http://blog.hubspot.com/blog/tabid/6307/bid/4553/5-Ways-to-Use-Social-Media-to-Find-B2B-Influencers.aspx accessed 01092011

Chapter 6

Business Development of IT Services

Stay Hungry....Stay Foolish
—Steve Jobs[1]

6.1 Introduction

This chapter is about how business development, i.e. soliciting new untapped business potential can be carried out by ITSE firms. It is different than marketing or sales as it combines several aspects and competencies to be able to reach out to new customers, new opportunities and even new product or services that may give further impetus to the exiting business. Sometimes it is also called whitespace marketing which refers to creating new opportunities from totally new market space.

For ITSE, given their nature of business being continuous innovation this function takes supreme importance to pave wave for next growth opportunities through strategic thinking, customer understating as well as positioning the existing and future capabilities for new business opportunities.

6.2 Business Development

A few months ago the newspapers and TV headlines were full of reports about the death of Steve Jobs. Most of us are aware of the iconic status of this visionary innovator and entrepreneur, but his spirit is an embodiment of a finest business development professional, this world has ever produced. He was able to visualize the anticipated needs of the consumer, was full of conviction that he would be able to deliver it and he delivered it just right many times! As you read this chapter remember the stories of how Steve came out with successful new businesses that his peers could neither think nor capture. This will help you to understand the spirit of successful business development person that he was.

Business development of IT is a holistic function that combines strategic thinking and planning, continuous marketing and sales, leading to opening up of new revenue stream for the

---

1. Steve Jobs 1955–2011, Co-founder of apple Inc., a visionary innovator during his Commencement address on June 12, 2005 Stanford University http://news.stanford.edu/news/2005/june15/jobs-061505.html accessed 07102011

firm. This may include new customer accounts or new opportunities with the same customer. It may also lead to branching out in different market or product segment through acquisition or merger with like size companies. In simple terms business development encompasses all activities that help IT firm generate new business opportunities as well as growing the existing ones. In most cases business development entails expanding the canvas of opportunities and working on white space for those solution and services opportunities that are either related with new technology or new business possibilities using power of IT.

Business development also enables strategic planning and corporate development functions. While strategic planning is used in large, established companies to expand and diversify their business, corporate development is used in startup and mid-size firms. In the case of later it may be carried out by the corporate finance department covering mergers and acquisitions.

6.2.1 Business Development Need for ITSE

Business development approach is most suited for ITSE firms in professional services areas by developing relationships with the client. Suitably carved out business development strategies help grow market share, increase revenue and drive profits. Business development has the inherent dependence on client relationship that leads to building trust. Business development also needs creating a culture within a firm that reward behaviour that drives new-revenue-building activity. It requires a rigorous approach of a tracking and measuring effort and success produced by the team.

Accordingly, an ITSE Business Development Manager (BDM) role involves taking a wide variety of initiatives such as marketing strategies, sales leads generation and exploring clients' requirements and positioning services and solution of the firm. The end objective an ITSE BDM achieves when he/she leads proposal of services and solution to client followed by negotiating and closing of deals.

ITSE business development is mix of marketing and sales though it may be a separate group within the organization chart focusing on non-routine marketing and sales. This function is over and above the establish channel of marketing and sales that the company may have. Andrew[2] defines that BDM approach with a client (or a partners) is a win-win value proposition approach and is not the same as pitching what you are already selling. It is a collaborative approach to help clients and partners achieve their goals in conjunction with your own. It is about partnership between two companies more than a vendor-customer relationship.

6.2.2 Tasks Performed as Business Development

Some of the tasks performed by an ITSE business development function include the following:

(i) Identifying new business opportunities.

(ii) Keeping a tab on developments in the industry in the focused market segment, and movement of competitors. This may mean gathering intelligence on competitive offerings, pricing, marketing strategies.

---

2. Andrew Jenkins Strategist, Design Thinker, Specialist: Social Media/Web 2.0, Wireless/Mobile, E-business/ E-commerce, Software, Internet http://www.linkedin.com/answers/marketing-sales/business-development/ MAR_BDV/289019-25901 accessed 5082011

(iii) Deep understating of ITSE company's strategy, its offerings and how it compares with competitors and its perceived standing in the marketplace. While as a sales person, one may pitch everything to everyone, a good BDM would take only selected clients where he feels that chances of winning the deal is most.

(iv) Innovate all possibilities to improve the firm's sales through new market segments, new sales channels or through driving synergies through partners. ERP companies partner with system integrators and hardware companies with application development companies routinely, as a part of their business development strategies.

(v) Prioritizing new business opportunities by comparing potential returns.

(vi) Pushing all new opportunities into deals. This needs their participation in proposal preparation, pricing and negotiation to closing deals.

(vii) Identifying and signing synergistic partnership to enhance value of solutions.

(viii) Establish partner channels to expand the reach of market.

(ix) A mix of sales and strategy to focus on getting new accounts or new services/solution in the market.

(x) Targeting smaller companies as acquisition target to enhance capabilities and revenue stream.

BDM role gives a good opportunity to acquaint with business strategy of the firm and getting hands-on experience in negotiating deals and managing partner relationships. It is a highly cross-functional role which needs close collaboration with various internal and partner-company teams such as sales, delivery, application development, solution development and marketing to close a successful deal. ITSE BDM team steers the strategic direction of a company as theses opportunities will become the future directions of the firm.

Business development includes a wide gamut of activities which are shades of

(i) marketing, leading to generation of interest and cultivating relationship

(ii) sales leading to proposing a solution, pricing and closing the sales

(iii) client engagement management and servicing leading to continuous relationship for more and more opportunities.

The difference is in the approach with which an ITSE BDM addresses his/her task. ITSE business development cultivates relationships with potential as well as existing clients using one-to-one marketing with decision makers either through personal contacts or tools such as social media. Business development activity is to open up the new doors, work with the new clients or new opportunities with existing clients. ITSE BDM increases the opportunity pipeline and fuels the growth of sales activity.

Business development is the finest capability which requires deep attention to detail for client requirement and understanding of ITSE firms capabilities that can be positioned and superb personal and communication skills. ITSE BDM not only has the ability to sell but bring the rest of the organization to come as a team while working on new opportunities. All new opportunities for IT Services requires collaboration with not only own team, but with partners as well a client team. ITSE BDM is responsible of the entire process right from spotting to converting into sales. In case of any slippage, it is the BDM who debriefs what has gone wrong for taking lessons for the next opportunity.

Business development is a continuous process and the engagement with client and partners is continuously evolved. Till a time client becomes so familiar with the ITSE firms capabilities that they start asking them services without prodding and probing from the ITSE BDM.

ITSE BDM also keeps a watch on the client industry as well as the IT industry, and accordingly positions new ideas, new solution for the client's benefits. In a way, BDM is compared with an explorer whereas, sales people are compared as hunter and the delivery folks as farmer. Business development process is multifaceted one that requires cultivating relationships with the clients, partners and at time competitors as well.

6.3   Business Development Process

Business development process follows several steps which are coordinated in a well-orchestrated fashion to meet the end results of the ITSE firm. We will use Figure 6.1 to define these process steps in pictorial fashion.

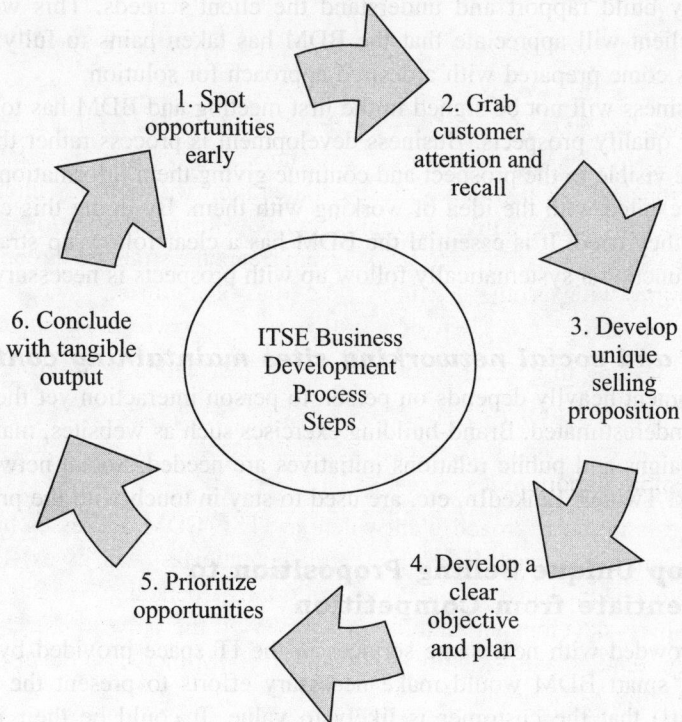

Figure 6.1   ITSE business development process steps.

6.3.1   Spot Opportunities Early

The first step of any business development exercise would be to spot opportunities earlier than the competition. A BDM must articulate what would be the ideal prospect and the services that prospective clients would need. Such identification will help in focusing on qualified prospects, early enough in the business development cycle.

There are several examples where the early movers maintained the market share and customer mind set which the second and subsequent firms could never break the barriers. I-phone, Blackberry, SAP, etc., are a few examples of such leadership created as soon as the opportunities were spotted and acted upon.

6.3.2 Grab Customer Attention and Recall

In the course of business development opportunities spotting exercise for ITSE, BDM would meet the prospective customers. They must focus to grab client attention and interest through a clear marketing message. This may include discussing typical problems that ITSE solves or the solutions they provide. BDM must engage the client in an interactive dialogue rather than giving a non-stop sales talk. They must make an impression about their firm's approach and services so that when the customer needs them, he is able to recall them. This is called building customer recall in the minds of the customer.

An important part of grabbing customer attention is through proper structuring of conversation to simultaneously build rapport and understand the client's needs. This will help building the trust as the client will appreciate that the BDM has taken pains to fully understand their problems and has come prepared with a desired approach for solution.

Note that business will not be signed in the first meeting and BDM has to keep in constant touch and further qualify prospects. Business development is process rather than an event, and the BDM must be visible to the prospect and continue giving them information to help them get comfortable and excited with the idea of working with them. By doing this customer will call ITSE firm when they need. It is essential the BDM has a clear follow-up strategy for the next meeting. In this function a systematically follow up with prospects is necessary for the business growth.

Role of tools and social networking sites maintaining contact

Business development heavily depends on person to person interaction yet the role of new age tools cannot be underestimated. Brand-building exercises such as websites, marketing materials, advertising campaigns and public relations initiatives are needed. Social networking initiatives such as Facebook, Twitter, LinkedIn, etc. are used to stay in touch with the prospective clients.

6.3.3 Develop Unique Selling Proposition to Differentiate from Competition

The market is crowded with near same services in the IT space provided by the similar type of companies. A smart BDM would make necessary efforts to present the unique attributes (not just the cost!) that the customer is likely to value. It could be their unique approach, process or model that they utilize. It could be the expertise in the niche area. This is to help answer the question "Why not I hire someone else?" Remember the BDM is trying to make an entry here, hence he and his firm has to look different so that the existing service provider is either displaced or a new opportunity is granted to a new service provider. David Miller[3] opines that BDMs must give a compelling offer that a client find difficult to refuse and motivates them to close the action for the sales. This may includes free pilot project, onsite demo, guarantee for results, attractive prices, etc.

---

3. David C. Miller FSA, MAAA Business Coach dave@translifecoach.com, www.BusinessGrowthNow.com.

6.3.4 Develop a Clear Objective and Plan

A good BDM clearly defines a vision and goal covering how much revenue from which types of clients and assignments are ideal for his firm.

Several year's ago, a well known ITSE BDM met the managing director of a large corporation in India while the pleasantries were going on the ITSE BDM quipped, "sir we have decided to sell our solution to you!". The ITSE BDM was meeting for the first time and it might have appeared arrogant on his part but he added, "the only part remaining is to explain and convince you of its benefits". It was natural that this conversation generated lot of curiosity and the client was tempted to examine it, and finally, bought multimillion dollars IT solution. Every customer is unique and for winning new business a BDM must develop a clear objective and plan suited to that very customer.

6.3.5 Prioritize Opportunities and Time

ITSE BDM will have to work on several possibilities (opportunities) at any given point in time. It is important that he prioritizes them and allocates his time and efforts accordingly. Unless he is able to manage his time well and prioritize pushing each one of them to the next step of decision making, he can end up just being a PR person. ITSE BDM ultimately is measured on the new revenue generated, hence all such development activities must end up with the real dollars.

6.3.6 Conclude with Tangible Output

All opportunities must be concluded with either a contract, pilot work or an understanding that when the client would be ready they would give a fair chance to the new vendor. That is where the importance of customer recall comes in. Once the contract is obtained, the BDM passes the baton to the sales and execution team and recedes in the background.

6.4 Approaches Followed for Business Development

Business development is a holistic activity that is focused towards generating more and more revenue opportunities for the firm. One of the simplest ways to kickstart this function is to use 7 W and one H as follows:

  (i) Who could be the target customers?
 (ii) What services and solutions can be sold to them?
(iii) Where are they located?
 (iv) When is the opportune time to reach out to them?
  (v) Who in the client organization should be approached?
 (vi) Why would the client be interested for the solution and services?
(vii) What business issues does it address?
(viii) How should the business development effort be directed?

6.4.1   Identifying Target Opportunities

ITSE BDM can identify new business opportunities in any or combination of account mining, replicating the success, and white space development. These are described as follows:

Account mining

As discussed it is positioning new solution and services (i.e. Opportunities) to existing clients. We all know that the approaching existing clients are far easier than looking for someone new. All existing customers must be fully developed and all possible opportunities be explored with them. This is also popularly called account mining. However, success in such existing account will also be governed by the quality of work performed in the past. That is why in ITSE sales it is important that the delivery work is performed flawlessly. This approach is also used for multi-divisional, multi-location corporations. In the case of public sector units, success of one can be easily repeated with others without having to go through the tender process. Exploring opportunities with the sister companies or group companies are done using this approach. One must politely ask this question frequently with the client senior management whom the ITSE BDM meets" do you think any other department/division could be interested and whom do I go and approach?" However, the existing services must be delivered flawlessly so that client is willing to engage repeatedly with the ITSE firm.

Replicating the success

Once an ITSE is successful doing a services to a customer, it desires that similar services to be proposed to new customers. Typically customers within the same industry or location are tried out. Sometimes, the non-compete clause may prevent the ITSE to approach a competitor of the existing client in the same location but proposing similar services to a new region (or country) is fairly acceptable. This is easiest amongst the three as there is past success record and the new customer may be convinced by examining the references.

Exploring new opportunities or white space development

Exploring entirely new opportunities is a toughest part for any ITSE BDM. First of all, the BDM team must do the target selection for type of customers/clients who fall under the selection criteria. Business development team typically visualizes an ideal customer profile suitable for the solution and services of the firm. It could be based on the specialization, market presence or established relationship with the client segment. Based on this profiling the exact clients are targeted and approached.

6.4.2   Establishing Contact

This is the next step of reaching out to the new clients through direct mail, telephone calls to seek appointment or meeting them in industry seminars or events. E-mail campaigns or use of social networking sites are also used. One can also seek referrals from the existing clients which could be better qualified leads. In addition, subtle and soft advertising by publishing white papers, newspaper articles and publishing success, stories can also be resorted to.

6.4.3 Using Partner and Channels

Many large ITSE firms leverage their partner network to reach out to new opportunities and clients. Typically, these partners could bring relationship, client insight and intelligence and also can participate as sub-contractor while delivering the IT Services. In some cases, these partners could be independent business development consultants who participate in the business development process and charge a retainer fee or % of the order value upon success.

6.5 Capabilities and Skills Required for Business Development Function

Business development process entails understanding client's industry requirements and matching them with the ITSE firm's capabilities. It will need fair bit of strategic thinking and close involvement of the solution design and development team from the ITSE firm. In practical terms it includes leading marketing strategies, building opportunity funnel and converting them into revenue generating projects.

Sometimes, this role is played by people in sales and marketing or business consultants. BDM is holistic job profile which has flavour of creativity, strategy formulation, execution, relationship building, marketing and communication and most importantly selling. The BDM profile will vary with the portfolio of services and solution the ITSE firm has and how capable it is to add new capabilities to meet new opportunities coming up in the market that ITSE BDM is spotting.

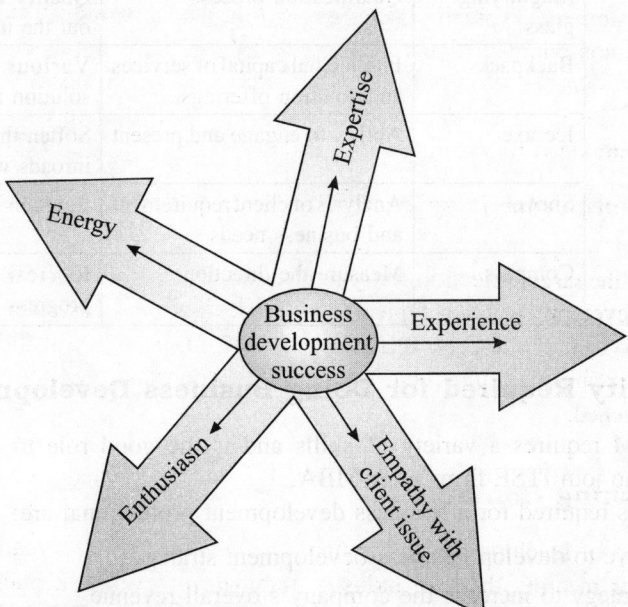

Figure 6.2 Business development successes—5 E framework.

Figure 6.2 shows the necessary ingredient that makes a business development process successful. While expertise is the starting point for any business development professional, he has to combine it with his ability to empathies with client issues and ultimately solving them. He has to possess necessary energy and enthusiasm to go after new opportunities, many of them would initially look infeasible and may look different from the current market trends. But that is where the job of BDM differs from that of sales person does who focuses on short term and immediate requirement. Finally, he has to gain experience after every interaction with customer, whether it leads to success or failure and builds his capability. Remember everything else can be acquired but one has to undergo experience. Finally, a true BDM must develop a winning mindset by pursing the opportunities with utmost tenacity. All this will take efforts, time, energy and money. Always keep improving the approach, collaterals, BDM checklist, and presentation, etc. relentlessly.

An ITSE BDM always has to deal with the new situations like a mountaineer who always climbs a new peak, after conquering one. Like mountaineer, the ITSE BDM has to face new situation in every expedition and that is why this metaphor has been chosen to depict the challenges he is supposed to face. Table 6.1 draws the parallel of a role BDM has to play and the tools that he has to have in his kitty to be successful BDM as compared with a mountaineer.

Table 6.1 Drawing a parallel of ITSE BDM with a mountaineer

BDM as a mountaineer	Tool used by a mountaineer	Parallel for a BDM	Used to
	Binoculars	Industry research reports and trends	Spot opportunities earlier before the competition
	Magnifying glass	Qualification process	Qualify opportunities, weeds out the unproductive ones
	Backpacks	Intellectual capital of services and solution offerings	Various presentation and solution approaches
	Ice axe	Ability to engage and present	Soften the target, make quick inroads with the client
	Shovel	Analysis of client requirement and business needs	Solution design techniques
	Compass	Measure the direction	Review of opportunity progress

6.5.1 Capability Required for Doing Business Development

A good ITSE BDM requires a variety of skills and is the good role to play by generalists especially those who join ITSE firms after MBA.

Key capabilities required for a business development professional are:

(i) Be innovative to develop business development strategy

(ii) Develop strategy to increase the company's overall revenue

(iii) Have entrepreneurial spirit and expertise to build brand and reputation.

(iv) Ability to identify and target potential corporate clients

(v) Develop and complete proposals and scopes of work

(vi) Address incoming leads

(vii) Manage client sales meetings, calls, and reach out frequently

(viii) Collaborate with delivery team for timelines and expectations

(ix) Serve as client liaison

(x) Ability to spot new opportunity in the market for a new services or solution or an adaptation of an existing one

(xi) Ability to formulate and implement plans to pursue these opportunities

(xii) Ability to develop relationships with key opinion leaders of the client organization

(xiii) Client acquisition consisting of prospecting methods, methods of engagement, qualification and discovery, proposal, presentation and closing

(xiv) Client retention consisting of strategic account management, customer service and cross-selling

(xv) Ability to conduct successful negotiation

(xvi) Sales planning

(xvii) Sales activity tracking and reporting

(xviii) Time management

(xix) Management and leadership

6.5.2 Skills Required for Business Development

Business development professionals will require a wide variety of skills to be successful. Some of these skills are as follows:

(i) Strong business acumen and strategic thinking

(ii) Strong research skills to understand the competitive landscape

(iii) Excellent quantitative and analytical skills

(iv) Problem solving abilities

(v) Technology skills

(vi) Killer deal-closing instincts and negotiation skills

(vii) Communication skills

(viii) Customer service and sales ability

(ix) Emotional intelligence and people skills

(x) Strong people and communication skills

Specialized ITSE companies may require strong technical background, or sales experience in a related field for their business development team.

6.6 Career Tracks for Business Development

Business development opportunities are growing in Information technology firms who want to go up the growth path through new opportunities, new alliances and partnerships. There is a growing need for ITSE BDMs who can develop the market and also close business deals in the new markets. Most companies want to keep business development as core and can outsource non-core functions, even the delivery.

Business development role has blend of at least three themes (or types) of work. The first of these themes is the strategic thinking and planning activity to find opportunities where the ITSE firm's capabilities can be positioned or developed to meet them.

The second theme is the ability to strike a long and mutually beneficial relationship with the leading and large number of clients progressively to build a large portfolio of business. Finally, these efforts should lead to getting services and solution contract for which meticulous selling activity is needed. In most of the cases, depending on the organization maturity and the position of the growth curve, all the three activities will be prominent in the ITSE BD career track.

This is why the nomenclature of the BD team may be different in different organization. In some, it may be a part of sales and in some it may be called business-to-business sales. In many cases, the business development team and the sales team are one and the same. Fresh hires are often asked to do cold-calling or prospecting for potential clients. In addition business development also has a flavour of account management which requires coordinating a variety of partner relationships as well as internal team. Since larger ITSE firms are building their businesses around partnerships, the responsibility to manage this is led by and it is business development team.

In case you are considering this role and applying for a job, make sure you understand the role requirement clearly and answer questions demonstrating your potential as a successful BDM. It will be of help if you also network with friends or alumni to understand about the prospective organization offerings and its potential.

In the process of interview you must do the following:

(i) Demonstrate your knowledge and familiarity of the employer's business and its competitive landscape

(ii) Show any experience in closing deals or managing relationships

(iii) Solid communication skills and analytical ability

Your success is assured if you have done all these recommended preparation and presented yourself well.

6.7 Tips, Traps and Pitfalls to be Avoided during Business Development

The following tips traps and pitfalls must be considered during ITS business development task:

(i) All IT Services must address a deep customer pain, stated or hidden. Hence, deep research is needed for unearthing them. Bring compelling insights about the client industry while explaining the value of your IT Services. Also make sure the customer pain is significant enough to warrant investment in IT and patience to address through its implementation.

(ii) Do not stuck to your technology. The real benefit comes in how the technology is applied to solve a business problem.

(iii) Be conscious of when you are entering the market, early stages, growth or late stages. The strategies for business development would be different which will also depend on what are you bringing to the table, your brand, technology, expertise or a combination of these.

(iv) Pricing in IT Services is toughest, under pricing not necessarily means winning as it will lead to quality compromise. The smartness is in demonstrating the value and being efficient. Don't hesitate to pass the benefit of efficiency to the customer and tell that fact clearly.

(v) Keep the customer's customer 'end users' in mind for IT Services, the chances are that the IT Services will be sold to a company that in turn provides services to the end consumer, say a bank or Telecom company. If the services are going to make the end customer's life better, it will be well-received.

(vi) Business development requires rigor and relentless follow up of new leads and new opportunities. Consider partnering with proven and profitable businesses first.

(vii) Instead of holding expensive CEOs workshop, glossy brochures or too jazzy website, try to meet, interact and listen to the customers as often as you can.

(viii) Even if you have to partner, which you have to in your technology space, ensure that the roles and value delivered by each partner is clear. No one should be considered more than equal for any good partnership to succeed.

(ix) Remember the ultimate decision while awarding a new business to a new company, new technology to an old company (or its various combinations) is made by a human being. There would be some personal glory, need and motivation hidden behind it. If you are able to touch that chord, the business is yours!

(x) Stay focused, and stay hungry for the new business. The last of this trilogy stay foolish represents that never adopt a "know all" attitude. Consider that you may be wrong, and therefore, check with customer, partners and your own team, but make your own decisions based on your own hunch.

(xi) Focus on a narrow niche of opportunities; leave the pots of silver while chasing the pot of gold. This is key to effective business development.

(xii) Always be ready to receive the feedback and use it to improve the next steps. All clients will not always be happy, but would be willing to share why they are not. Their feedback is simple and cost-effective improvement charter for your business development efforts.

(xiii) Try penetrating to the inner trust circle of the client. Only then the client will call you for more and more services. Try to become an advisor by helping in technical, professional and sometimes personal needs as well.

(xiv) Network regularly and effectively. Always invest in people to reap rewards later.

(xv) Some of the traps and pitfalls to be avoided are:
   - Lack of teaming amongst the business development team
   - Not enough role clarity and goal clarity
   - Procrastination in taking decision or action for the next steps

- Avoid commoditization of your services
- Not keeping track of market development and what competition is doing with your customer and elsewhere

6.8   Summary

In this chapter, we started our discussion by defining what business development of IT Services is. We summarized that business development of IT is a holistic function that combine strategic thinking and planning, continuous marketing and sales, leading to opening up of new revenue stream for the firm.

The most suited approach for business development for ITS firms is by developing good relationships with the client. Business development task includes identifying new business opportunities to establishing partnerships. Business development is the finest capability which requires deep attention to detail for client requirement and understanding of ITSE firm's capabilities that can be positioned and superb personal and communication skills. It is a continuous process and the engagement with client and partners is continuously evolved.

We then discussed the various stages of business development and activities performed at every stage. We also described various approaches followed for IT Services business development such as:

(i)   Account mining which are the new services and solutions for the existing clients

(ii)   Replicating the success that are the existing solution and services for new clients

(iii)   White space development are the new solutions and services for the new clients

In addition we also discussed the use of partner and channels in generating new opportunities. The next concept brought out in the chapter was about the success criteria for business development. We outline a 5E framework for business development successes, covering Expertise, Experience, Empathy with client issue, Energy and Enthusiasm. In order to explain this concept better we took a metaphor of a mountaineer and drew parallel to various tools used by them in business development context.

Our next conceptual thread was underlining capabilities and skills required for doing business development. We also mentioned what traits should be demonstrated by people who are vying for business development role and listed key skills required for business development professionals.

Finally, the chapter ended with a short summary of tips, traps and pitfalls to be avoided for a successful business development.

Review Questions

6.1   What is business development of IT Services? What are the tasks performed by an ITS business development professional?

6.2   What are the key capabilities and skills needed to be a good ITS BDM?

6.3   What are some of the tips for successful business development? What are the traps and pitfalls to be avoided?

Suggested Further Reading

Penrose, E.T., 1959. *The Theory of the Growth of the Firm*. London, UK: Basil Blackwell.

Websites

http://hbswk.hbs.edu/item/6596.html accessed 09102011

http://www.varjan.com/white-papers/ten-warning-signs-of-dysfunctional-business-development-departments.pdf accessed 09102011

David C. Miller FSA, MAAA Business Coach dave@translifecoach.com, www.BusinessGrowthNow.com. On Business Development tips.

Chapter 7

IT Services Selling

There is one rule for industrialists and that is: make the best quality goods possible at the lowest cost possible, paying the highest wages possible
—Henry Ford

7.1 Introduction

We have discussed in earlier chapters the importance of marketing and business development for the success of any IT Services Enterprise. The process of IT Services sales is the culmination of the earlier efforts when customer finally decides to award the services contract to the service provider. By far, this is the most crucial process which must go right to conclude the efforts in the form of a written contract. In this chapter we will examine the process of IT Services sales in detail and will answer the following questions:

   (i) Who are the likely buyers of the IT Services in any organization?

  (ii) What preparations are required to convince theses potential buyers?

 (iii) What are the specific traits that are useful in any sales person while going through the sales process?

 (iv) What are the various steps of the sales process?

  (v) How to conduct the sales process?

 (vi) Some useful tips, traps and best practices for the successful sales.

7.2 The IT Services Buyers

Understanding the buying process of the customer organization and the IT Services decision making process is the first step for IT Services sales. Typically the IT Services buying decision is led by the head of IT function in any organization. These individuals may carry a title of Chief Information Officer (CIO), VP, Director or GM (IT). The head of IT in the organization usually reports to Chief Finance Officer (CFO). This reporting relationship continues due to historical reasons as IT used be heavily oriented towards servicing finance and accounts function in the past. In new age organization, where IT is considered strategic, this reporting is usually to the Chief Executive Officer or Chief Operating Officer. Reporting relationship also explains how much the IT function is considered important for the overall business, higher reporting level of CIO shows increased importance of the IT function and independence of its decision making.

The reporting relationship of IT department in the hierarchy of the client organization is an important input for the IT Services sales person. This will help him to steer buy-in of all decision makers during the sales process. Typically the IT functional head (CIO) is the prime mover of the IT Services requirement yet the ultimate approval will come from the supervising authority above him.

However, the requirements (needs) of IT Services invariably get generated from business functions, such as operations, marketing, finance, etc. All head of these functions become one of the influencer of the services sales process, though the ultimate responsibility of gathering and conveying these requirements to the ITSE will lie with the IT head.

Interestingly, certain IT Services such as outsourcing of entire IT functions or part of it, is steered by the CFO or CEO. The reason for this lies in their ability to see the business justification of such moves far more dispassionately than the IT functional head. CIO or head of IT may not be convinced to slice away fully or a part of his/her responsibility to an ITS vendor and in the process loose authority and control. However, this mind set amongst the CIO community has also changed over time. New generation of CIO now see such outsourcing of long term advantages for their firm. IT outsourcing has now reached an acceptable level and consequently CIOs also have started to champion the need of IT outsourcing.

In many organization, especially the mid size one, there is another set of individuals who act as influencers during IT Services/solution selection process. These are consultants or advisors whose play an active role in the decision making cycle. Many mid size firms or public sector enterprise may not have enough experience or expertise in IT area. Consequently, the buying process is delegated to a consultant. Large public sector enterprise or government department routinely appoint another consulting firm to steer through the sales process. This is to ensure objectivity in the process of vendor selection. Similar model is adopted in large corporations which constitute IT procurement committee, comprising of the members from IT, Finance, Business and procurement departments.

A smart IT sales person does the necessary homework to understand the buying process of the client organization and tries to find out the concerns or objectives of each of the decision makers, influencers, their likes and dislikes.

Please note that it will also depend on the scope and size of the contract that will ultimately decide who all need to participate in the decision making. For example, if the need is to hire 10 Java programmer for a short term of 6 months to meet the programming backlog requirement, the decision can be made by the IT head and procurement manager jointly. However, if the decision is to award a multi-location multimillion ERP implementation services, the decision will need participation from all stakeholders.

Figure 7.1 gives pictorial representation of the IT Services buying stakeholders and the likely role they play.

It is clear from the figure that CIO plays the most important role in any IT Services decision making process, and therefore, must be influenced by the IT Services sales person. The shaded area shows the participants of a typical IT procurement committee.

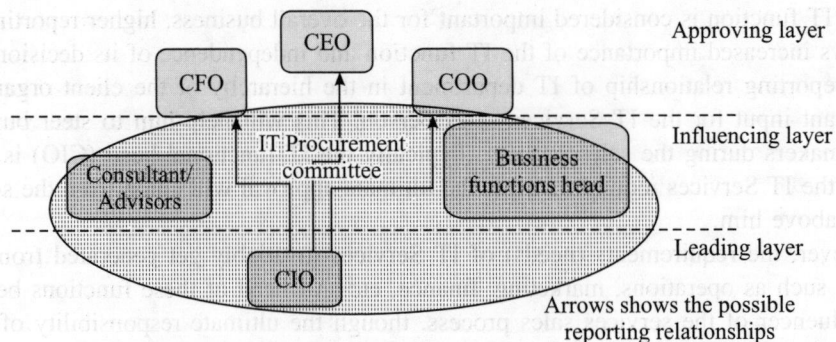

Figure 7.1 IT Services buying decision making layers.

7.2.1 Understanding CIO Buying Orientation

The role of CIO (or head of IT) vastly differs from organization to organization. These positions are occupied by the people with wide spectrums of background and past influences. Some of them would have worked in IT Services and Consulting organization, therefore carry some likes and dislikes against a particular ITSE. The task of an ITS sales person is to understand these background information about the client and accordingly present the ITS firm's capabilities to address the client needs and develop relationship for successful sales. ITS sales person also has to alleviate the apprehensions of the CIO.

A sales person typically knows a lot about their own firm's capabilities and does a good research on the negative points of their competitors. However, that is not enough. One has to penetrate the minds of the CIO and find what he/she wants to achieve through these services. Just beating one's own trumpet (which most of the ITS sales people do!) is neither enough nor helpful beyond a point.

Ancient historical strategist and writer, SunTzu said that, "if you don't know the opponent then for every battle won, there will be a certain failure[1]." The opponents in the context of IT Services sale process are not just the competing firms but also the decision makers in the client organization; the chief amongst them is CIO or head of IT. Let us dissect what goes on in the minds if the CIO while going through the IT Services sales process.

CIOs also have to sell IT concepts internally

A seasoned IT Services sales person understands that ultimately CIO is the custodian of the IT requirements for the functional people of his organization. Consequently, any new IT method, technology or approach (say business reengineering, cloud computing, mobile applications, etc.) has to be internally and convincingly sold to the functional people (and their unit heads) by the CIO. In this process the CIO needs the IT Services provider to enable him with the necessary pointers as to how these new services will benefit the business, not just its technical niceties. Consequently, ITS sales person must focus on how the new services will impact the business performance rather than quoting capabilities of its firm or technology features alone.

CIOs go beyond the internal users of IT

Most progressive CIOs have a larger business perspective that includes not only the IT users within the enterprise working in various function but the impact the IT Services will create on

---

1. The Art of War, by Sun Tzu, a sixth century B.C. ancient Chinese military treatise.

the end consumer of their firm. For example, a CIO of any telecom service provider, especially the leading ones, do not stop their requirement gathering for call centre agents, but visualize the need of actual users from the proposed CRM system. With this end-consumer requirement approach will lead this visionary CIO to seek more and more provisions for consumer self service in the CRM. The requirements will therefore change to providing for end users generated query on balance talk time, making fresh recharge, etc. ITS sales person's value will surely go many notches up if she explains how her program or services will help the consumer of the client's firm rather than just the business users of the client firm.

CIOs are also unique individuals

Like any functional manager a CIO will also have unique personality trait and style that needs to be taken into account while engaging in the ITS sales discussion. They may be, as David Miller[2] a psychologist describes, a

(i) commander's type who should be addressed with precise and to the point information as asked, quoting data and results with documentation and proof;

(ii) expressive type who engage in discussion and seek big inputs and must be dealt that way;

(iii) amiable ones who want to make everyone happy, and therefore, need an IT Services provider who ensures that all interests will be protected including theirs; and

(iv) analytical ones who would have too many if and why questions therefore must be confronted with good amount of preparation. Just engaging in weather discussion as expressive ones or relationship talk like amiable will not help.

The challenge is that no CIO will fit exactly in any one of these types and will always be a mix of them. Worst still they change their colours like a chameleons at different stages of the sales cycle, so doesn't go with standard product presentation with a risk to return empty handed.

CIOs juggle multiple priorities

A well-groomed CIO is not a technical person who gets mesmerized by the newest gadget or technology announced in famous Comdex[3] fair. CIO has to balance between contradictory needs from business users who want the latest's and fastest, CFO who focus is on cost and his own priority that may range from standardization, maintainability, security issues etc. The role of ITS sales person is to find out what these contradictions are and how the proposed services will be able to address. Gives these answers to the CIO and be in his good books the very next day.

CIOs are evolving in their perspective

Newer breed of effective CIOs are not just happy with the ROI of the services they seek, but want to evaluate the ultimate business results. They are now more and more innovative in their choice, focused on improving productivity across the organization not just the business functions but also of their own IT department. This way they look forward to new pricing models some of them are discussed elsewhere, such as pay for use, revenue sharing, etc. So if your sales proposal

---

2. *Personal Styles and Effective Performance: Make Your Style Work for You*, Merrill, David W., Reid, Roger H., Chilton Book Co, 1983.

3. Between 1979–2003 COMDEX was the "must visit" trade show of IT industry held in Las vegas every year in November. Now being held in addition in its virtual *avtar*. More details see, http://www.comdex.com/ accessed 24092011

is age old inflated cost with fat margins with huge upfront payment without any performance guarantee then your sales efforts will simply not work.

7.2.2 Understand Approver's Needs

Approvers are the CEO/CFO and COO of the organization, who finally authorize IT department to seek services from a vendor. The first question any approver typically asks to the IT head/ CIO is why these services are being sought from outside IT Services firm and why it is not being performed by the in-house team. ITSE sales person has to help CIO in addressing this question at the early stages of the sales cycle.

For most CEOs, IT function remains a mystery that always seems to be complex and difficult to manage. CEOs want IT to be simple, easy to use and of course flexible to accommodate new changes, which something IT is not always able to live up to. In addition, most CEO/COO come from functional discipline (sales, marketing, operations) where they have criticized the IT for not being fast enough to meet their changing needs in the past. Their new responsibilities to lead IT function as superior authority, proves to be daunting to most of these executives. While in many cases they are not averse of authorizing IT budget, but they are unable to understand frequent investment required in IT for technology upgrade, annual maintenance charges etc. CEOs are less equipped to manage unpredictability of IT cost, want lesser management intervention for issues like employee attrition, or know little about IT skills shortage. These reasons help outsourcing services being more welcomed by the CXOs (i.e. CEO/COO/CFO etc.).

An IT Services sales person must take into account of these factors while presenting their case to the C-level executives. Not only they should talk on how the technology will make the difference to the business outcome but also how the proposed services or solution are easy to administer, predictable in cost and reliable in use.

7.2.3 Understand Other Stakeholder's Needs

IT Services buying decision also has other stakeholders as well. These individuals, if not managed properly, can create problems during execution and delivery of the services. These set of people will have different requirements and aspirations, all of which must be ascertained to make a winning IT Services proposal. Now, let us discuss the needs of business functions heads, end users of IT and consultants/advisors role in the sections to follow.

Business functional heads

Business functional heads are keener to get their functional requirement met and more options of reporting and meeting their information needs. They often like that the new IT does not impact their authority of decision making and helps them with the growing information needs for running their business function. They should be interviewed during the requirement gathering and proposal making stages of the sales process and their apprehensions or objections should be handled and responded adequately.

End users of IT

The end users of IT always distaste complex systems that increase their data feeding or information retrieval time or in simple words their work load. You can visualize that these expectations are easily solvable by proper requirement gathering and good IT solution. However, some of these end users may be more accustomed of using a particular technology and would resist switching to the new one. They may turn hostile in feedback sessions or in procurement evaluation discussion. While it may be impossible to get views of all such people, the views of key opinion maker's amongst them must be solicited, addressed and explained either during open presentation or in one-to-one meeting. Remember that during the service implementation stages their role will be too crucial and their inputs extremely valuable. IT Services selling just not ends by signing the service contract, but goes on till the delivery is complete and customer pays. So if any or many of these end users are unhappy with the services of the firm then it is certain that the final payment will hit a road block.

The role of consultants/advisors

Expectations of these individuals are the trickiest of all to understand and address. If managed properly, they can become the advocate of the ITS sales efforts and if not managed well they can turn into adversary. In such situation, they may side with the competition! The other extreme situation created by the consultants is no action, deferring the decision or maintaining the status quo without IT implementation so that their continued importance is maintained. A successful ITS sales person makes all efforts to neutralize such consultants/advisors who become a hidden mine fields (possible problems areas) in order to make his sales. This is achieved through series of efforts such as building relationship with them, answering their technical questions with finer details, paying respect to their opinion and taking into account the hidden authority that they wield.

7.3   IT Services Offerings

Let us now understand various types of IT Services demanded by the customers. A detail discussion about various variation of the services portfolio has already been done in Chapter 2. This short recap will help us to decide the suitable sales approach.

(i) Bottom of the IT Services offering is the **manpower augmentation or resources staffing** services, where the services firms offer skilled resources on hourly/daily or weekly rate basis. Here the resume of the candidate is of utmost importance in selling these skills. By far this is the simplest way of selling services, where the candidate once selected is at the disposal of customer organization, who instruct them for work to be performed and also do the supervision of the work content and quality. If the selling services is being done by the small IT Services firm, then this is the most appropriate offering to the customer. Also if the need of IT Services is very specific and the customer organization has the necessary project management and supervision skills then, this is the suitable option to consider. Other advantages of this services offering is that it would be cheapest of all.

(ii) The second services offerings is the **fixed price project** based on the RFP specification as stipulated by the customer. Based on the requirement specification the vendor organization submits their proposal which includes their technical as well as commercial offer. The customer organization takes a decision based on quality of the proposal, vendor reputation and experience apart from looking at the price. The payment terms of such services offering is based on completion of project milestones.

(iii) Third and less common service offering is **complete outsourcing of implementation and running** of the ERP application based on either monthly/yearly fee or based on usage parameters such a number of users, duration of usage (8 hrs/24 hrs), number of customer locations, etc. Customers usually accept this type of offering only from reputed and established vendors who would have developed long-term relationship with them.

7.4   IT Services Selling Process

IT Services and solution selling requires a process to be adhered. Unlike selling a commodity services (for example man power resources) where the customer is clear about the requirement and exactly specifies the need, in most others the ITSE sales team has to closely work with the customer either to develop the requirements or understand exactly what their needs are. All this will need a consultative selling approach. Selling any services needs the understanding of the customer requirements as expertise/experience to serve to these requirement lies with the ITSE firm. The customer may specify the outcome but how to achieve that outcome needs to be defined by the ITSE team. Unlike product selling, in ITSE the firm not only sells capabilities, but the perceived value (expected end result) as well.

Process stages of IT Services selling as shown in Figure 7.2 are as follows:

   (i)   Identifying and qualifying the prospective customer
   (ii) Ascertaining their requirements
   (iiii) Preparing a response and proposal presentation
   (iv) Closing the deal
   (v)   Kick off the services

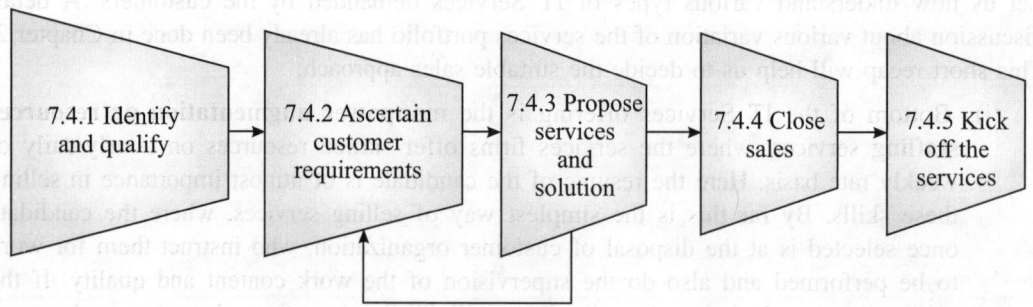

Revise, address objections and handle customer concerns

Figure 7.2   IT Services sales process.

Let us examine each one of these stages in detail.

7.4.1   Identifying and Qualifying Prospective Customer

The age old selling principle expressed in the form of AIDA dated around 1910, stands for Attention, Interest, Desire, and Action. This is still useful and can be applied to the IT Services selling situation as well. For any meaningful prospecting, IT Services firm has to get attention of the prospecting organization, arouse their interest and desire to deal with them and follow through with their action to submit proposals. Participating in industry group meetings, CEO forums, IT seminars/exhibitions (e.g. NASSCOM, Bangalore IT.com), and seminars run by IT product vendors, are the good occasion to grab attention of the customer. Process remains very much similar to other sales situation and starts with prospecting stage where a salesperson identifies qualified potential customers after participating in these meets. The other way to identify the prospect is to skim through the tender or EOI (Expression Of Interests) notices published in the newspaper and websites (like tender.com) on a regular basis. The third way of getting to know the prospects is by working closely with IT vendors who get direct requests from the customer and also advertise their product in IT journals and websites, etc.

The second step is **qualifying** the prospect, to ascertain whether it meets the criteria of the vendor organization. This is the process of identifying good prospects and screening out poor ones. A good prospect for one company may be poor for another. This decision would be based on the type of services and specialization the ITS firm has and its ability to mould the customer in their direction. Prospects that are considered poor are those customer organizations which take long time to decide, have poor payment records.

The third step is **pre-approach**, where a salesperson learns as much as possible about a prospective customer before making a sales call so that the sales call is made effective.

The fourth step would be **making the approach** where a salesperson meets the buyer and gets the relationship off to a good start. Without meeting a customer one can never be sure of the exact needs and therefore, for a start up ITS firm as many approach meeting should be carried out to gain the customer requirements that can be used while proposal making, not only to this client but elsewhere. The author always used to recommend its sales team to do "net practice" meeting with suspects to gain understanding of the customer issues. The good news was that many of such unlikely suspects got converted to IT Services deals finally. If these approach meetings turn out to be good, customer develops liking to the sales team and the discussion moves to the next levels.

7.4.2 Ascertaining Customer Requirements

The common factors in all sales process is to ascertain customer perceived need which can be met through proposed services. In this respect IT Services selling are no different. It's all about customer, their needs, their problems, their pain and making customer the focal point of all selling efforts. Most sales persons walk up to a customer and begin telling only about what he has to sell without enquiring what the business issues are faced by them. Compare this situation when a patient meets a doctor who without asking or examining the patient only talks about how good a surgeon is he and how he conducts the operations efficiently! While the patient may need to be operated upon, he would certainly loose respect to such doctor who has not bothered to enquire about the patient's problems. All sales process must start with ascertaining customers needs and must end with how these needs will be met. The sales person must add value at every interaction. We will define the steps for ascertaining customer requirements as follows:

(i) The first step is always to know your customer, what is their business, their key business drivers and their competitors. In addition knowing their competitive advantage, current business areas of concern is as much necessary.

(ii) Secondly, it is necessary to find your champion or advocate, within the customer organization (or make one). Such a person will help in understanding the customers' requirements in a much better manner and also will give tips in managing relationship with the decision makers.

(iii) Thirdly, ascertain how purchase decisions are made. One can't presume to prescribe a solution for a customer until you know something about them.

(iv) Fourthly, gather data from secondary research and find facts after meeting customer, their dealers and suppliers.

(v) Also meet as many people as possible in the customer organization. If possible meet end customers of the client firm as well as their competitors. If you are selling IT Services to a retail store meet the buyers who come to the store or visit other stores to see how they use these (or comparable) services. Selling IT Services starts with understanding the customer's business as well as knowledge about customer's customer. The customers actually want an advisor in the garb of IT Services provider who can help solve their problems.

In public sector or large enterprises, all requirements are included as a part of the tender document, yet it is recommended that IT Services firm sales people must meet significant set of people from customer organization to gather information that can be used as part of the proposal.

7.4.3 Propose Services and Solution

This step includes preparing response to customer requirement and presenting it in front of the customer evaluation team. This step is conducted after the requirement gathering phase is over. The key features of the response includes the following:

(i) Task to be performed as understood by the service provider

(ii) Time it will take to perform them

(iii) Team that it will deploy

(iv) Commercial terms and condition, includes price, payment terms, etc.

Normally, the commercial terms are submitted under a separate sealed cover and only in one copy to finance department or as advised by the customer. Some of the salient points for a good IT Services proposal are as follows:

(i) Client likes when the ITS firm complies with letter of RFP requirements and provide tailored approaches to their needs (not just standard approach).

(ii) Client always appreciates the strength of project team with experience pertinent to client's need. In addition, customer loves to have a project team with skills and specific certifications requested in RFP. The delivery project team should have the necessary qualifications or experiences that are specifically relevant to client's requirements.

(iii) Having a clear roles and responsibilities of the project team further enhances their respect.

(iv) Submit a well-written proposal. All client dislike generic approach in the proposal. They also do not appreciate sloppy, unedited proposals which are produced by copying from several other proposals. Any inconsistency in style or content due to lack of collaboration amongst the proposal writing team or lack of proof reading will lower the esteem of the IT service provider team.

(v) When customer invites IT Service provider team to explain the proposal, the most experienced and articulate person must lead the presentation. Oral presentations are very important in the IT Services selling cycle. Care should be taken to make a sound professional presentation with impeccable editing both text and numbers. IT Services selling company must ensure that key personnel are present during the time of the presentation. The presentation should not have irrelevant content and staff experience.

(vi) Be careful while using a prepared (also called canned) sales presentation. These refer to a presentation that is not adapted to each individual customer. However, such presentations are used in the initial stages of the sales cycle and are appropriate when presenting to a large number of customers whose needs/wants are similar. This also allows sales function to apply a high degree of control and standardization amongst its sales team. However, this may not take full advantage of interactive capabilities of sales team.

When to adopt consultative selling approach

Consultative selling involves developing good understanding of customer's needs before trying to propose as solution or close a sale. This is so named because ITSE firms must behave as an advisor to their customers to identify their problems and help solve problems. Sales representative along with pre-sales consultant initially make a brief statement of general benefits and then asks questions and listens carefully to understand the customer's needs. After the customer describes needs, they show how their solution or services meets those needs and attempts to close the sale. This is a collaborative problem-solving approach (also called need-satisfaction approach) is very appropriate because in IT Services, every customer requirement is different. This is a recommended approach for IT Services sales process for strategic and complex requirements.

Briefly, consultative selling steps are as follows:

(i) Understand customer requirement by asking right questions

(ii) Understand the decision making process and key decision makers

(iii) Analyze and research the problem, conduct fact finding study

(iv) Design solution

(v) Arrive at cost benefits of the proposed solution

(vi) Educate customer, manage objections and present the solution

(vii) Conclude services sale and develop jointly the implementation plan

(viii) Ensure customer engagement to achieve continued satisfaction

When to adopt formula selling approach

In this approach, the sales process starts with a pre-conceived presentation/outline to arouse customer interest. This way the customer can see broad outline of solution, which will help in clarifying his needs. Once, the customer engages into discussion, the proposal is further modified according to the customer needs. This approach shortens the sales cycle and most suitable in situations where customer is aware of the likely solutions broadly. During the presentation, the salesperson explains the solution and takes note of questions/objections by the customer and modifies the solution proposal accordingly.

7.4.4 Close Sales

This is the toughest part when a salesperson asks the customer for a purchase order and starting of the services delivery. In many IT Services situation the selling process involves in-depth education to the customer. This sometimes gives customer a feeling that with such understanding they can execute the services using other low cost options. But the smart IT Services sales person makes sure that such wishful thinking is curbed in the minds of the customer by showing potential risk, opportunity cost and the services provider unmatched capabilities.

The foundation of sales closing or conclusion is to know the customer's decision criteria, decision making process and decision makers. We have discussed about the roles played by various people in the IT Services decision, including influencers. The closing of the sales requires a clear understanding how emotionally as well as rationally the decision makers arrive at the purchasing the decision. Once those hot-spots (criteria for decision making) are captured, the decision can be obtained in the favour of the IT Services provider. Speaking the language of the customer industry, not using technological jargons, focusing on the business benefits and stakeholders interest, always makes positive influence at this crucial stage. IT Services sales person with deep insight of customer industry can create a sense of urgency to act, in the minds of the decision makers.

For example, while talking to the client CFO, the sales person must explain how the proposed IT Services and solution will improve profits, reduce cost and increase inventory turnover (if applicable). Alternatively while discussing with VP (Operations), the examples of reduced cycle time, improved quality, lower cost per person, etc. should be highlighted. A sales person must know the key success factors that drive the CEO's performance and should be able to draw its relevance to the proposed IT Services and solution. There would be no reason why the CEO would not support such investments in IT. In case the sales people are not conversant in client business terminology, financial terms then a proper training must be given.

All CEO and CFO want a business problem to be solved and that too at lower cost and shorter time. They are not enamored by the technology jargons or beauty of the power point charts. They want to know whether you

   (i) have understood their problem,

  (ii) have a method or proposal to solve them,

 (iii) have people and skills to do it, and

 (iv) have prior satisfied client base for similar exercise.

It is important therefore to state the value in financial and business performance terms. In order to be better than the competition in the sales situation, the sales team must communicate the value of their proposal properly and effectively. The proposal must clearly articulate the business problem it will solve and how it impacts key business drivers. The vendor must customize its value proposition for each decision maker and his constituency. It is advisable that one should never assume that the customer will see and understand the value of your product, service or solution unless it is clearly articulated and presented to them. In most business-to-business consultative sales, the selling is to be done to multiple people at different stages in the sales process.

IT Services value proposition should make a lasting impact. It is necessary that the value proposition and justifications presented is so strong that the client is able to move through the decision process with the proposal. This can only be done if the value proposition echo's the customer business drivers used, not in abstract terms such as saving, ROI, revenue growth, etc. and the customer agrees. The customer must have the issues and needs about which the proposal has been put forward.

7.4.5 Kick off the Services

The role of ITS sales team does not end as soon as the customer releases the purchase order for services. ITS Sales person must facilitate the Kick off (i.e. starting) of the IT services. Since most of the discussion would have happened with the sales team, it is important that the finer points and unstated expectations must be conveyed to the ITS Delivery team. The presence of Sales team in the kick off meeting is essential where the delivery team makes presentation of their approach of IT services. It is the ITS Sales team's responsibility to coach and support the ITS Delivery team leader about customer expectations, any promises made by them and finer points about the various stake holders in the customer organization. Post the initial kick off meeting, the ITS Sales team is expected to keep a close watch of the progress of ITS delivery and address any customer concerns. In addition they are the one who can use their influence to solve any delivery team issues encountered during the ITS delivery.

7.5 Monitoring and Managing Sales Pipeline

Monitoring sales pipeline or sales funnel is crucial task that the ITSE sales manager does. ITSE sales team will have several prospective opportunities at different stages of discussion while following the sales process as shown in Table 7.1. These stages can be classified as:

  (i) **Suspect:** Opportunities at the very initial stage when sales person is trying to gather more detail clarification.

 (ii) **Prospect** are those opportunities which customer has confirmed requirement but have not obtained budgetary approvals.

(iii) **Qualified lead** are customer requirement with approved budget. This also means that these customer requirements and expectations can be met by the ITS firm capabilities.

 (iv) **Confirmed lead** are attributed to those opportunities which customer has firm plan for seeking a IT service provider and has obtained management sanction for budget and engaging an external IT service provider.

  (v) **RFP released/Requirements discussed** by the customer. At this stage the customer has already documented and published their requirements and started to engage with potential ITS vendors.

 (vi) **Proposals submitted to Customer:** This refers to those opportunities against which the ITS firm has submitted its technical as well as commercial proposal. At this stage the sales team proclaims that "customer is likely to buy".

(vii) **Committed by the sales person:** These are opportunities according to sales team, are likely to be awarded to their firm. At this stage sales person gives a target date to his/her management of the likely date by which the customer will give order. This stage is also known as "customer is about to buy" stage. Such commitment of date helps the ITS delivery team to plan for resources.

(viii) **Confirmed by customer:** At this stage customer issues a formal letter of intent (called LOI) indicating its preference to award the ITS contract to the ITS vendor though it may not have given a firm order. This stage is characterized by the sentence "customer is confirmed to buy". Customers issues letter of intent to facilitate the ITS delivery team to plan for resources while the final terms of the ITS contract is being worked out.

(ix) **Converted into order or lost order:** This is the last stage of the sales process where the confirmed order is received by the IT service provider. In case of competitive bidding this situation may end up with lost order where the order may be awarded to some other firm.

It may be noted that the entire cycle from suspect (i) to Converted into order (ix) may take months depending on the client internal decision making cycle time. The sales manager reviews the progress of each and every opportunity at all these stages and monitors their movement. The understanding of the progress must also be conveyed to the delivery team for them to plan for resources and build capacity for delivery. The sales manager evaluates performance of his team and that of the sales process by the strength of the sales funnel. The term sales funnel is used to describe all opportunities at various stages by attaching a relative probability raging from 0 for suspects and 100 for confirmed order. Table 7.1 gives sample sales funnel of typical ITSE. Please note that probability % is notional and depends on the assessment made by the sales team.

Table 7.1   Sample sales funnel table

Opportunity serial number	Stage	Opportunity description	Estimated order value (in lacs)	Probability %	Notional pipeline strength (lacs)
Op10	Suspect	Customer A ERP implementation	100	0	0
Op8	Prospect	Customer B Onsite resources	20	5	1
Op7	Confirmed	Customer C IT Consulting	50	20	10
Op6	RFP released/ Requirements discussed	Customer A Data centre management	80	30	24
Op5	Proposals submitted	Customer E Service Desk	20	40	8
Op4	Committed	Customer D Project management	40	80	32
Op3	Confirmed	Customer F Network Implementation	60	90	54
Op1	Converted into order or lost order	Customer B Program management	70 or 0 in case of lost order	100	70
			Estimated Sales pipeline strength (sum of last column)		199 lacs

We have also discussed the target setting for sales team in Chapter 10.

7.5.1 Prepare Sales Staff

IT Services sales team should have deep business understanding of client industry over and above the knowledge of their own firm's services capabilities. They must also be equipped with knowledge about the client business processes as well. All services sales team must be taught how to conduct pre-sales research about the client industry and about the client firm. For every sales call they should be coached in advanced before the call, and thereafter, de-briefed when the sales call has been made. At times, the senior sales person does a role play exercise to build confidence amongst the new entrants. Over a period, efforts are needed to build sales culture within the enterprise. Investment in building the skills of sales staff (or that of the services partners) is one of the most important investments and can give greatest return, if done correctly.

Finally, the right price is the key of the conclusion of IT Services sales. Pricing is always an important differentiator in services proposal and must meet customer expectations.

7.5.2 Appropriate Conduct during the Sales Call

The conduct of the IT Services sales team during customer interaction is key factor that can make or mar the customer impression. In IT Services sales, polite and subtle approach of selling is the best. Aggressive sales persons who have low listening abilities are not found to be welcomed by the clients. As trusted advisor, IT sales person should not present himself or herself as "know all" individual who dominates in all discussion. Try not only to focus on a few people, but cover as large territory as possible. Finally, avoid surprises and refrain from making over promises during the engagement as lack of delivery will erode away the chance of repeat work.

7.5.3 Pre-define and Pre-assign Role during Sales Call

In situation where more than one person from the sales team are meeting the client, (a situating that normally arises), the team must assign and play different roles. Cutting the thoughts of each other, making contradictory statements or making unauthorized commitments must be avoided. Roles must be pre-defined and pre-assigned about who will explain the proposal, who will answer objections and who will address the pricing questions, etc. Not only this presents a cohesive team image in front of the client, but it also help the team to buy sometime in case the customer puts a query, asks for discount or any other additional scope.

7.5.4 How to Upsell/Cross Sell to the Existing Client

In order to sell some more services to the same clients in the current organization or its other divisions, one must ensure that the client is absolutely satisfied with the services so far. Only when you have delivered good quality, on time and within budget and have built a relationship of trust then only the next services should be proposed. In fact, satisfied clients informally act as an advocate for the future sales. They can give recommendations and referrals which can be used in other client situation. In IT Services business it is the word of mouth publicity which is the best. It is always recommended to build relationships for mutual success with the clients on a long term basis.

Remember the CIO would like to be seen in good light after having awarded you the first time contract for services. Once this has been ensured only then approach for more work of similar nature from other parts of the organization or new work from the same organization.

7.6   Best Practices for Successful IT Services Sales

Best practices[4] are those methods or technique that has consistently shown results superior to those achieved with other means, and that is used as a benchmark. In this section, we will consider some of the best practices for ITS sales situation for increasing the conversion rate into successful sales as follows:

(i) Mark Hordes[5] a noted sales expert opines that "Getting to yes" has not always been easy, even for the strong-of-heart and most dedicated services professional. This is a situation when the client agrees to take the services from a vendor. His advice is to build the services on "best day, everyday basis" and focus on doing the right things for services selling that is different than product selling. A salesperson should transforms into a highly competent and successful consultant who takes a total solution approach to solve a client's problem and in the process positions IT Services and consulting offerings in the best possible manners.

(ii) ITS selling requires a multitude of factors to culminate into sale. Some of the important one being capabilities and trust of the sales team, ITS firm's market reputation and quality of solution proposed and mix of team capabilities.

(iii) In any ITS selling situation the sales person have to structure the situation and make sure who will play what role to answer what all anticipated questions form the client. They have to take control of the selling environment and, quickly jell with the client demonstrating understating of client issues, and conveying forcefully their solution. They must carry a professional image to create a good first impression with the client.

(iv) Before any sales call, the team must conduct deep research about the client products, services and offerings, and their industry issues so that when confronted they can talk sensibly and present themselves as knowledgeable about the client environment.

(v) If the IT Services proposed is complex in nature, involves many skills and components as part of the solution, then it will require longer sales cycles. This situation is disliked by most salespersons as the longer closing cycle delays their commissions. In most cases such complex services and solution purchasing decisions are made by higher ups in clients' hierarchy. Many salespersons may not be equipped to discuss the proposal with senior executives of the client organization.

(vi) Sales team must understand the culture of the client company and behave accordingly. A young upstart company in technology space would be different than a matured market leader or public sector leader. Sales person should need to appropriately present themselves suited to these cultures.

---

4.   http://www.businessdictionary.com/definition/best-practice.html

5.   Best Day, Every Day: Rules of the Road for "Getting to Yes" in Professional Services Selling, January 2001 AFSM International 47, January 2001, *The Professional Journal*

(vii)   When you make presentation it should be a good tight story with visuals that the proposed offerings will address. It should not be just about how great the ITSE firm is. The proposed services and solution may include benchmark or matrix that will be improved after the said solution is implemented.

(viii) IT Services selling is developing a relationship experience right from the first meeting to the closure of sales. IT Services selling is about helping the client to explore solution of their problem. Like physiotherapist, the ITS sales person helps the client to loosen the stiff joints or alleviate pains but also at the same time keeps checking if the approach is working well with them or not. The sales person must ascertain and confirm the issue confronted by the client and the environment in which they operate.

(ix)   By engaging discussion with client team will help building a quick rapport. Client would be comfortable to see that the ITS firm has understating of client's industry, and hence, more qualified to take up the assignment.

(x)   Besides researching the industry and about the client, it is always good to share success stories. Giving examples from similar client situation where the ITSE has worked earlier without disclosing much detail helps in establishing credential.

(xi)   Proposal turnaround time is important for a progressing in IT Services sales cycle. A week is always the outer limit though 3–4 days is good target to achieve. Large proposal do take time, but the smartness is to gather the team and make them work together and ensure that client interest does not get deflected in any other direction just because the IT Services team has taken too long to respond to the client's request with their proposal.

(xii)   As discussed earlier, in any sales situation, the client organization will have several decision makers and influencers involved in the buying decision process. The IT Services team must figure them out early in sales cycle who they are and what are their objectives with respect to the proposed services and solution. Many will have their biases and mind set due to past history. The role of the IT Services sales team is to address them by proactively engaging them with. Since they would represent different constituency (i.e. functional discipline) their need and apprehensions would vary. For example, the CFO would like to have the least cost solution, but the customer marketing team may like to have the best in class solution. Even convincing them would need different style, some with cost effectiveness chart and some with user experience and some with the other client's feedback. Remember each one of them is may throw spanner at the critical time of the sales cycle. A good way to meet these people individually and ask them "what are their concerns and objectives" and also "what do we do next?" to seek their participation. Asking questions to the decision makers such as "what is the budget", "when do we start" etc. will always help to create a sense of urgency.

(xiii) The final proposal must ensure that the content is properly balanced to cover most of the questions and objections of decision makers and influencers. Use of words or phrases which are strong and hurting should be avoided, even if it may be true. The proposal must cover the client issues, the IT Services firm's view of the problem and suggested solution or approach, detailing out the stages of the solution build up or services delivered. At the end of every stage of the services or solution delivery, the team must articulate the outputs which will be achieved. If these deliverables are in the form of documents, say so or if they are in terms of measures or metrics then also clearly state them.

(xiv) As a general rule, charts and graphs should be used but in simple manner and not too many in the same page. With computer awareness growing in the client organization, playing gimmicks with jazzy charts should be avoided. Presentation content must include a chart on the IT Services firm's differentiators. All charts must have the title that summarizes the essence of the content of the chart. A chart must also be included that covers experience and team's credentials at the end of the presentation.

(xv) Successful IT Services selling will not happen by assembling few smart and articulate people but through rigorous planning and skill building. While some people may be inherent sales oriented, their numbers will be far and few and does not help in the long term for the organization unless a good pyramid of sales team is also created. For example, in a movie only hero or heroine is not enough, you have to have other characters, technical staff, people who work behind the camera etc to make the movie successful. All this requires skill building on the part of the organization to their sales team.

7.6.1 Building Trust is Important

IT Services selling is much different than other forms of sealing. Here the people who sell are also responsible for the delivery. Unlike most sales people who are usually extrovert, risk taker, pushing and details oriented, an IT Services selling person will be precise, risk averse, cautious and to the point in his statements. In IT Services selling, while the proposal presentation describes the task at hand, the buyer continuously evaluates the person and his/her capabilities. Famous author Charles H. Green[6] mentions that it is trust factor that helps in professional services selling situation that matters the most to finalize the sale. The factors that help build trust is summarized by Charles in the word CRIS representing credibility, reliability, intimacy, self-orientation (refers to focus towards the client, not towards themselves).

7.6.2 Entering a New Account/New Market

IT Services Enterprise face much challenge while initiating services to the new territories, new customers or in new industries. Lack of past credential or experience can go against them in the initial stages. Some small and mid size firm go with the basic services such as man-power staffing to gain entry and foot hold with the customer. Some other use the partnership approach to work with established players who could act as a complementor to their services. Such complementors could be the hardware manufacturers or software vendors.

However, despite this, a good sales team with deep knowledge of the subject can create winning opportunities albeit a small one without having past experience within the industry, region or with the customer. Here, the consultative selling approach is very useful along with the brand building exercise that the marketing and business development teams would have done already. Remember, services selling is done by the people who have adequate experience

---

6. http://trustedadvisor.com/public/File/pdf/articles/2001_Selling_Professional_Services.pdf accessed 23092011

in services delivery as well and can use their experience to demonstrate that they are a worthy candidate to be tried out at least first time.

7.6.3 Managing Internal Competition

In some cases, the selling team may be competing against an internal team who may be having home grown solution or method to meet the requirement. Several ERP services ran into rough weather as the internal home grown applications with customized combination (XLS worksheets) and reporting was considered good enough and the new ERP solution was not seen as adding anything new. In such situation the role of approvers and leader of IT Services (CIO) becomes very critical. The ITS sales team must articulate how the new solution will benefit the client in the long term as they may not be able to perceive benefits in immediate terms. Advantages such as flexibility, enhanced ability, quality of the IT system etc. needs to be conveyed. In addition, the internal team who is acting as a competition should also be addressed as to how the new scenario will overall benefit them as well the organization.

7.6.4 Managing Continuous Sales Relationship

Unlike products, IT Services selling relationship should be maintained throughout the services delivery life cycle. This relationship is the seed through which the issues and risk during the process of execution is managed. Remember selling has to be considered in a wider perspective here, which covers convincing the customer with your approach. This will need establishing relationships at various levels of the client organization, covering CEO/CIO down to the actual users.

While the process of sales continues, the IT Services sales team must ensure the role of communication of the progress as an essential feature. Seasoned sales person meet prospects even when they have no immediate business to do, but through these meetings the relationship remains warm and new opportunities pour in times to come.

IT Services selling is about instilling confidence about the ITSE Services expertise and people performance. This, if conveyed properly, will lead to new opportunities generation. Finally, the sales person has to develop his/her unique relationship style to jell quickly with the client team.

7.7 Pitfalls to be Avoided during Selling IT Services

Some of the pitfalls to be avoided and precaution to be taken are as follows:

Ensure healthy and transparent communication

ITS sales consultants should ensure no communication gap like not keeping the client informed of current situation and so on. This is considered as one of the most serious problem.

Ensure quality of deliverables

The other major pitfall(s) are less than acceptable quality of service or inconsistency in deliverables and missing deadlines. ITS delivery team should never request additional hours or remuneration to deliver already agreed to scope.

Ensure stability in team

Frequent project team turnover and always focusing on selling rather than performing should also be controlled. Deploying unqualified consultants just because they are available or baiting and switching of key personnel gives a very bad reputation.

Be polite and flexible

Lack of politeness in communications, inflexibility in deliverables and arrogance in behaviour should be avoided at all cost. Many IT Services firms have suffered due to these generic defects in their conduct.

7.8 Summary

We started the chapter with examining the process of IT Services sales in detail by addressing the following concepts:

(i) Buying process of IT Services in large organizations and various decision makers and influencers who participate in the buying decision process. We surmised that every company and CIO have to be treated uniquely by understanding their needs and buying orientation. By understanding these hidden behaviours and a clear understanding of their needs we can take the first step of IT Services selling.

(ii) We then looked at a brief summary of IT Services offerings covering services such as manpower augmentation or resources staffing, fixed price and finally complete outsourcing.

We then presented detailed steps for IT Services selling as follows:

(i) Identifying and qualifying the prospective customer

(ii) Ascertaining their requirements

(iii) Preparing a response and proposal presentation

(iv) Closing the deal

(v) Kick off the services

We presented various stages of sales cycle called sales funnel and how the sales team manages the sales opportunities progress over these stages using the probability concept. We then discussed some of the approaches of IT Services selling such as consultative selling and formula selling approach.

The chapter also discussed some of the best practices for proposal preparation, submission and presentation. Tips for upselling and cross selling to the existing client were also discussed.

We also underlined that building trust is very important in IT Services selling as it will lay the foundations of long term relationship. This chapter also dealt with necessary concepts useful while entering a new account or new markets. Managing internal competition is an important part of IT Services sales process, this subject was also given a brief treatment.

In addition, we discussed how managing continuous sales relationship through communication will help getting to new opportunities. All sales people have to develop a unique relationship style of their own to jell quickly with the client team.

Finally, we concluded the chapter by listing some of the pitfalls to be avoided during selling IT Services.

Review Questions

7.1 Describe the process of IT Services sales in detail. Draw necessary diagram to explain it comprehensively.

7.2 What are the three typical IT Services offerings? Do they require same or different approach of selling? Explain.

7.3 What precautions will you take to write a winning IT Services sales proposal?

7.4 When will you adopt consultative selling approach and when will you follow formula selling approach?

7.5 What are the suggested approaches for upselling or cross selling to the existing client?

7.6 Name and explain some of the important best practices for successful IT Services sales?

7.7 Write short notes on:
  (a) Need for building trust in IT Services selling
  (b) Managing internal competition
  (c) Entering a new account/new market
  (d) Managing continuous sales relationship

7.8 Explain some of the prominent pitfalls to be avoided during selling IT Services.

Suggested Further Reading

Reiss, Tony, *How to Sell Professional Services*, Managing Partner Magazine February, 2000.

Green, Charles H., *Selling Professional Services*, 2001, www.TrustedAdvisor.com. accessed 29112012

Chapter 8

Delivery Management of
IT Services

We enjoy the process far more than the proceeds
—Warren Buffett

8.1 Introduction

The revenue generating engine of any IT Services Enterprise is the delivery wing of the firm. Delivery team is like the kitchen of a restaurant which can make or mar the success of the food business. You can attract a customer by façade of the restaurant and smart advertising, and also make them order a dish, but once the customer tastes the food and does not like it, he will never return! Such a customer, in addition, will also give a negative publicity. Even in best of restaurants or food chain, one minor error (for example, if a customer falls ill after eating food) can lead to disastrous situation. Similarly, the IT Services Enterprise has to depend on impeccable delivery capabilities for sustained revenues through happy customers.

In this chapter, we will discuss various processes in the delivery organization in an IT Services firms. Depending on the type of service offerings some of these processes may or may not be needed, but on generic basis most of them would be applicable in all types of IT Services.

8.2 Delivery Management Processes Overview

Broadly, the delivery management function in IT Services Enterprise has to manage the process akin to order fulfillment in any manufacturing enterprise. Based on the customer requirements as stipulated in the services contract, the delivery management processes ensure its fulfillment leading to collection of payments.

The four major process groups of delivery management are delivery planning, execution, governance and improvement. Figure 8.1 gives an overview of delivery management processes. We will now expand each of and improvement these processes which are grouped as follows:

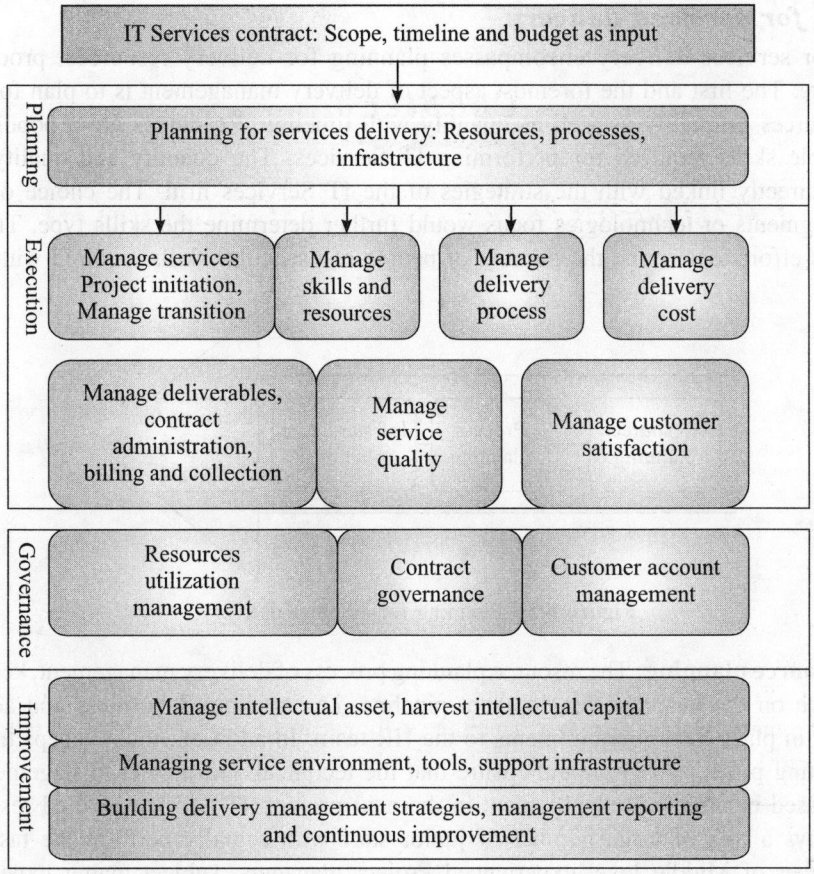

Figure 8.1 Delivery management processes overview.

8.3 Delivery Planning

The processes under planning group enable IT Services Enterprise create capabilities for services delivery. It also includes those processes that are invoked when the customer contract is signed and some of them are run across multiple processes on contractual basis. For example much before any services contract is signed the IT Services firm starts building skills by employing and training suitable individuals.

As discussed earlier, delivery planning processes are for building delivery capabilities of the IT Services firm. It is like preparing the menu, buying raw material, kitchen equipment, hiring trained cook, and so on before opening up a restaurant. Delivery planning processes in the similar manner lay foundation of the firm's delivery capabilities.

We have seen in Chapters 1 and 2 that IT Services landscape is vast and complex. This necessitates that requisite capabilities are built in advance to meet customer expectation and competitive challenges. Capabilities required to deliver different IT Services are usually different and there are finer issues that require to be tackled to keep the delivery processes efficient and effective. We will describe each of the sub processes shown in Figure 8.2 in the following sections.

Planning for services delivery

Planning for services delivery encompasses planning for delivery resources, processes and infrastructure. The first and the foremost aspect of delivery management is to plan for requisite skilled resources in quality as well as quantity with timeline. Resources are a popular way to denote people skills required for performing IT Services. The quantity and quality of skills demand is directly linked with the strategies of the IT Services firm. The choice of projects, customer segments or technologies focus would further determine the skills type. The success rate of sales efforts determine the number of people of particular skills required with timeline.

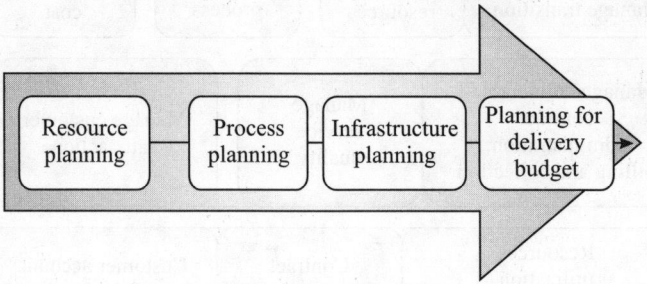

Figure 8.2   Planning for services delivery.

(i) **Resource planning:** The resource planning process of delivery management, keeps a close watch on the business development pipeline, i.e. anticipated business and accordingly puts in place hiring requirements to the HR team. In addition, it also keeps track of the existing project progress and ensure that the technical and project management staff is released in time for redeployment in the next project. IT Services skilled resources are always a mix of large number of junior staff who actually perform the task, smaller number of Middle level experienced Project managers, subject matter experts (called SME) and very few senior level general management individuals. Predictably, hiring complexity increases and availability decrease as the experienced level increases. The entry level junior resources though available in large numbers require training and skill building time to be productive. This entry level resources also have highest turn over in the industry which makes the importance of continuous training necessary. Given all these considerations, resource planning process is of utmost importance in any IT Services firm.

(ii) **Process planning:** It defines steps following which the IT Services will be delivered to meet customer expectations. Unless suitable process for services delivery is well-defined, it will be very difficult to ensure uniformity and consistency all across the team. Services quality, repeatability and efficiency can only be achieved by ensuring all members of the IT Services team follow a set of pre-defined steps to achieve a desired outcome. Whether the services required are of consulting/advisory nature or developing software as per the requirement specifications of the client, all need a well-articulated processes. While clients of IT Services, value deep capabilities and experience of the delivery team, in reality such level of experience and capabilities may not be available in adequate numbers always. The risk associated with not having adequately trained and experienced skilled resources is addressed through strong process framework and its adherence by the entire team. Delivery processes defined are expected to be well-document for performing certain services[1] with detailed steps so that there is less ambiguity. Remember, all IT Services firm have to develop their own processes which may be at variances with others. Standards like ITIL, COBIT, CMM can be adopted to define firm's specific delivery processes or these processes can be further innovated/customized by the ITS enterprise process design team to suit specific customer needs.

(iii) **Infrastructure planning:** Infrastructure planning is a capital intensive process where the IT Services firm is expected to plan for physical and IT infrastructure for the services to perform. Most outsourcing IT Services providers have to build huge campus or infrastructure to house their team and supporting infrastructure. All these offices should be conveniently located for staff members to reach and should be cost-effective as well. For many, these physical and technology infrastructures are showcase to give confidence to the prospective customers. It is a well known fact that cost of real estate in most cities across the world is exorbitant and is rising everyday. Managing such physical infrastructure also require overhead expenditure such as security, uninterrupted power supply and amenities such as parking space, cafeteria services and safeguard against flood, monsoon, man made disturbances such as public rallies, etc. All this requires a long drawn process to look for suitable infrastructure centers for deliveries, which will be time consuming and costly.

(iv) **Planning for delivery budget:** Given these above requirements finally the delivery management has to plan for delivery budget and seek necessary release of funds from the corporate finance group. The investment in infrastructure is considered to be strategic and is done in advance, but the investment in hiring is done while keeping a close watch on the expected business pipeline.

The delivery budget carries all types of expenses required for the services delivery such as: Manpower, capital expenses for office infrastructure and IT including voice, and video, operating budget for infrastructure upkeep, travel budget for customer interaction or project implementation, research and development budget, employee welfare budget for social occasions, birthday, anniversary gifts, long service awards, performance awards, etc. and training budget.

8.4 Delivery Execution

These processes are deployed while performing IT Services projects for the client. Its sub processes are:

   (i) Manage services project overall management; task and timeline
  (ii) Manage project initiation and or services transition
 (iii) Manage skills and resources
 (iv) Manage delivery process
  (v) Manage delivery cost

---

1. For IT Service management processes read *IT Strategy and Management,* PHI Learning and for Business and IT consulting processes read *BIT Consulting; Concepts and Cases,* TMH, both by Sanjiva Shankar Dubey.

  (vi) Manage deliverables, contract administration, billing and collection

 (vii) Manage service quality

(viii) Manage customer satisfaction

These processes are used while executing IT Services projects for customers. These are the processes that customer views hence make or mar the impact. The various sub processes are described as follows (Refer Figure 8.1):

Manage services project initiation

When the services contract is awarded, the delivery management has to plan for starting the project and accordingly staff necessary team. While the resource planning process was concerned about the number and duration at a broader level, this process will detail out to individual project levels. All services projects are constituted as close knit unit led by a team leader. The designation of the team leader can be project manager, project executive or project director, depending on the size of the project. Project initiation process ensures selection and deployment of these project leaders who in turn select and appoint other team members. This process briefs the project leadership of the outcome expected as per the contract.

At this time the business development team starts handing over the client background information and other understanding to the delivery team. Some IT Services firm call this process as contract initiation process where the delivery project organization takes over from the business development (or sales) team and starts building rapport with the client counterparts.

Manage services transition

In most cases whenever a new IT Services contract is awarded it is quite likely that these services would have been performed by an existing service provider. The existing services may have been rendered by a group of people hired by the client or an existing vendor. The new IT Service provider has to take charge of the these services and start delivering then services as per the new contract.

Services transition is generally not applicable to advisory or planning services such as Consulting, Strategic IT planning, etc. It is also not a norm in new development and build services (e.g. software development) unless the contract with earlier service provider is terminated or changed due to non performance or any other issues.

However, this process is an integral part of perform services which includes application maintenance, infrastructure maintenance, process delivery, call centre services, etc. Remember the client has awarded these services to a new firm to meet certain services objectives which may be over and above what it was getting in the past. This objective may be to improve current service quality, reduce overall cost of services or develop entirely new services. Just because a new contract has been awarded, the existing contract is never terminated abruptly. There should be a planned and gradual sunset of the existing services introduction of the new services.

This process is called managing services transition.

Service transition process is invoked during the initial days of signing the services contract. It may be re-invoked, if the services contract scope is enhanced and more services are added to the existing ones. Services transition process included several stages as described in the Figure 8.3.

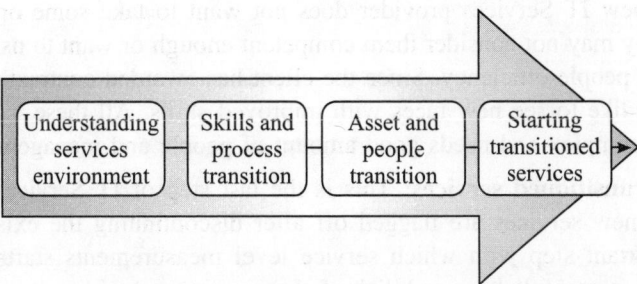

Figure 8.3 Managing services transition.

The broad process sub-steps of IT Services transition process are as follows:

(i) **Understanding customer services environment:** This step is conducted wherein the outgoing service provider explains various components of services, their outcome and challenges to the new team. This exercise is done in a joint workshop where the client is also present as facilitator to ensure that the outgoing team shares all details to the incumbent team. Usually, this exercise is conducted over a few weeks depending on the size and complexity of the services contract.

(ii) **Skills and process transition:** This is a stage when the work being performed by the existing team is handed over to the new team. The new team starts taking over the services in a gradual manner without disrupting the exiting operations. This process steps also takes over entire services delivery process, budgets, unfinished tasks, management reporting and also emergency processes for services which may be required only occasionally. If the new service provider is experienced enough in contracted services, the transition process is conducted smoothly, otherwise it requires verification and constant check on behalf of the client team.

(iii) **Asset and people transition:** All services contract will require that during transition phase all knowledge assets are transitioned to the new service provider. It means data, existing process charts; past history of services performed, management reports, collaborative repositories for knowledge and history of customer's complaints' etc., are properly explained and transitioned the new team. If the new service provider is going to use its own IT infrastructure environment then these entire knowledge asset are transferred and converted into the new environment. This is a tricky step in reality because the outgoing service provider may not be too willing to share their knowledge base to the new service provider.

It is always the contractual responsibility of the client to facilitate this process and the moral responsibility of the outgoing service provider to cooperate with the new service provider in the overall interest of the client keeping the future relationship in mind.

In many services contract even the people are transitioned to the new service provider. It may happen in cases when the new IT Service provider also buys out the existing provider or the service currently being rendered by the in-house team is transitioned to new team. This is by far the trickiest affair which concerns people, their aspiration and apprehension in the new arrangement. This step requires close support of HR team from the client, outgoing and incoming organization. The situation becomes more complex when the new IT Services provider does not want to take some or all of the existing team as they may not consider them competent enough or want to use different methods to improve people efficiency. Since the client has awarded contract to a new vendor, it would also like to see new faces with improved skills. All these issues make this step extremely complex and needs good amount of people and management skills.

(iv) **Starting transitioned services:** This is the last step of IT Services transition process where the new services are flagged off after discontinuing the existing services. This is an important step with which service level measurements starts. The new service provider assumes full responsibility of the services, providing management reporting and adheres to the standards of services promised in the contract.

Manage skills and resources

Once the delivery project is kicked off the project team has to continuously manage and maintain the desired levels of skills for delivering the requisite services. IT Services project will require both long term and permanent resources as well short term resources to perform specific tasks. Availability of good resources is always a challenge for IT Services firms and it impacts the services delivery quality regularly and repeatedly. Every IT Services project makes sure that they plan for backup resources, the need of which arises due to attrition or short term absenteeism due to employee's personal circumstances. This is an important process for IT Services delivery.

Manage service delivery process

Depending on the services offerings the services team would have to create, implement and measure a suitable services process to meet the service objectives stipulated in the contract. Typically, the process of perform services follow a phased transition approach where the processes are improved gradually in stages without disrupting the exiting services operations. In case of build services (i.e. Software or product development) the new projects are expected to adhere to the established processes. Any modification is done under a strict supervision of process experts to meet the current client requirement.

However, in planning and envisioning services (e.g. consulting , IT strategy and planning) only the over all delivery process is defined in broad terms and the delivery team is allowed to innovate and try out new ways to meet the project objectives.

Manage services delivery cost

Ultimately the IT Services business requires a meticulous management of delivery cost. We all know that in services business any man-hours lost cannot be recovered or cannot be stored for future use. Accordingly, a close planning of the skills on-boarding (i.e. induction) in the project and de-boarding (release) from the project is needed. Other costs such as infrastructure, travel, cost of software and tools in use, are also meticulously planned and managed to keep them to minimum.

Manage deliverables, contract administration, billing and collection

All services contract will have a stipulated deliverable such as reports, service level attainment, transition of people, launch of improved services, benchmarking with best practices at a repeated/stipulated intervals, etc. All this has to be planned and achieved otherwise there would be financial conditions such as stoppage of payments, or imposition of penalty, etc. by the client.

Typically, the delivery team reviews the contract very minutely and arrives at the contract deliverables. A deliverable calendar for the entire contract duration is prepared covering when and what is to be delivered to the client, every quarter, and month or in some cases every week. After preparing the contract calendar the project office[2] of the project team takes over to regularly follow up with the delivery team to submit contract deliverables for onward submission to client.

Contract administration refers to those process steps which ensure that the services are delivered as per the contract clauses. This includes management of contract scope, boundary of services, time, working hours, etc. and also keeps in check the new scope. Even splitting the services location or relocation of offices need to be carefully studied to find the impact of the cost and performance of the services. This step also ensures the IT Services firms adherence of service levels, based on which they can claim bonus or pay penalty as applicable.

This process also takes care of the billing aspect of the contract. Services billing can be at times complex based on scope, service levels, numbers of applications, calls or processes under taken or it can be as simple as % of contract value based on certain milestones. In both cases requisite data has to be presented by producing the bill to the client, a task which only the delivery team can do and assist the finance and accounts team to present the bill for the payment to the customer.

Manage service quality

This process relates to managing servcies quality which is always a major differentiator for any IT Servcies firm. We have discussed this process in detail and its impact on business development in *Chapter 9* **IT Services Quality Assurance**.

Manage customer satisfaction

Finally, all services must lead to a satisfied customer, a measure that needs to be established in the initial stages of the contract to prevent any dispute at later stages.

Managing customer satisfaction process has several steps and is an important process for client and service provider relationship point of view. The sub steps of this process is shown in Figure 8.4.

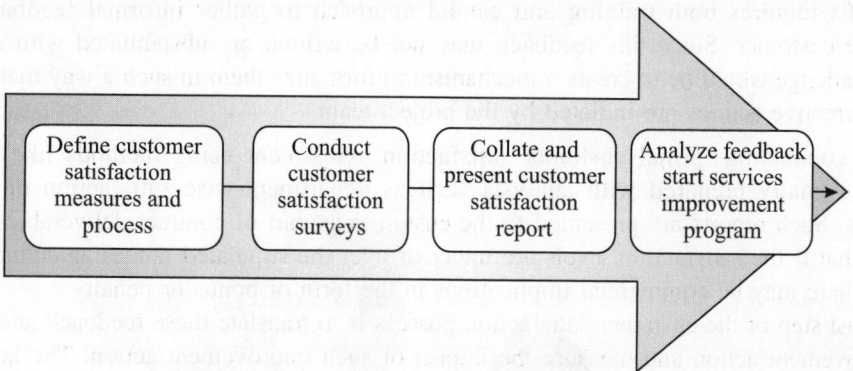

Figure 8.4 Managing customer satisfaction.

---

2. A small group within the Project team that manage all project and contract management task.

The first step of the customer satisfaction management process is to define and agree with the customer the satisfaction measurement parameters and the process by which these parameters will be measured. Typically, the client looks up to the IT Services provider to define the measurement process and performance measures which it agrees or suggest modifications. The customer satisfaction can be ascertained through the following:

(i) Periodic user survey of end users in customer organization

(ii) Formal feedback from responsible customer executives

(iii) Informal feedback called from various customer interactions by the account management team.

We will discuss each one of them in detail.

(i) **Periodic user survey:** Customer satisfaction can be measured by certain hard facts (e.g. number of complaints in a month, average time of resolution, etc.) as well as measures by conducting periodic user surveys. These surveys can be conducted half yearly or annually as agreed in the contract. These may be targeted towards various user groups for example, end users, client's customer, senior managers, etc. Usually these surveys are anonymous in nature where the respondents are asked to give point wise rating on pre-designed questions and also write their comments. These feedback forms the basis of identifying the reasons for customer dissatisfaction and initiating improvement actions

(ii) **Formal executive feedback:** The second form of measuring customer satisfaction is to seek a formal feedback from the responsible executive from within the customers organization. Such feedback is taken usually by the IT Services provider by deputing an independent agency specialized in conducting customer feedback. In certain cases if the customer agrees it can also be conducted by another manager who is not connected with the current customer. Typically, this feedback is sought during face to face (or tele calling) interview to maintain client confidentiality and objectivity.

(iii) **Informal sensing of customer satisfaction:** By far, the most difficult but the most useful method is to get a sense of customer satisfaction informally and regularly. This is done through the regular interaction of the project team members with the customers. This requires both training and candid approach to gather informal feedback from the customer. Since this feedback may not be written or substantiated with data, the challenge would be to create a mechanism to formalize them in such a way that suitable corrective actions are initiated by the project team.

After conducting formal customer satisfaction assessment using methods like surveys, a report is finally prepared with analysis such as department-wise satisfaction on various parameters. Such reports are presented to the customer as part of contract deliverables. It may be noted that if the satisfaction levels are under or over the stipulated ranges as defined in the contract, there may be commercial implications in the form of bonus or penalty.

The last step of the customer satisfaction process is to translate these feedback and surveys into improvement action and measure the impact of such improvement action. The last one is a continuous process that the IT Services Enterprise must do to improve its service.

8.5   Delivery Governance

These processes ensure that services projects are delivered as per the satisfaction of the client meeting contract specifications. Its various sub processes are as follows (refer Figure 8.1):

   (i) Manage contract governance

  (ii) Resources utilization management

 (iii) Customer account management

 (iv) Manage intellectual asset, harvest intellectual capital

  (v) Managing service technology environment including tools

 (vi) Managing services support infrastructure

(vii) Knowledge management

(viii) Building delivery management strategies

 (ix) Management reporting

  (x) Continuous improvement

Governance processes play an important role in the success of any IT Services enterprise. The term Governance[3] describes the mechanisms to ensure that established processes and policies are adhered to by the organization. Governance processes ensure oversight and accountability to ensure compliance with processes and policies. These ultimately help in arriving at any corrective action in case of any deviations intentional or otherwise due to changing conditions. The sub processes of delivery governance processes are described in detail in the subsequent section.

Manage contract governance

Contract governance is the first and the most important process of delivery management of IT Services. Poorly executed contract governance process leads to loss of money and causes customer dissatisfaction at the end.

IT Services contract is a document of promise between the IT Services provider and the client. It also sets the expectations and the scope for all the services that the customer has contracted for delivery. Contract governance process ensures that the contract is honoured and executed as stipulated.

The content of contract may not be known to all the people in either side of the services delivery relationship, customer and vendor. Due to absence of widespread knowledge of contract terms and conditions, expectations and assumptions may vary. Contract governance processes bridges this gap. It gives visibility, control points and performance management parameters to executives from both sides.

While the contract governance process usually is a part of the delivery cycle, the process starts much earlier when the sales efforts are undertaken. Drafting a contract that does not become a nightmare for the delivery team is one of the key criteria for the IT Services success.

---

3.   http://www.looselycoupled.com/glossary/governance access 21082011. Also Webster's Third New International Dictionary (1986:982) defines as "the act or process of governing, specifically authoritative direction and control".

All established IT Services firms make sure that all services contracts are also subjected to delivery team review before it is submitted to the client. By ensuring delivery team buy-in, the success of services delivery becomes certain. The delivery team understanding of contract clause leads to advance actions such as provisions for adequate resources, tools and processes to meet the stipulated requirements.

Figure 8.5 gives a representation of the contract governance process.

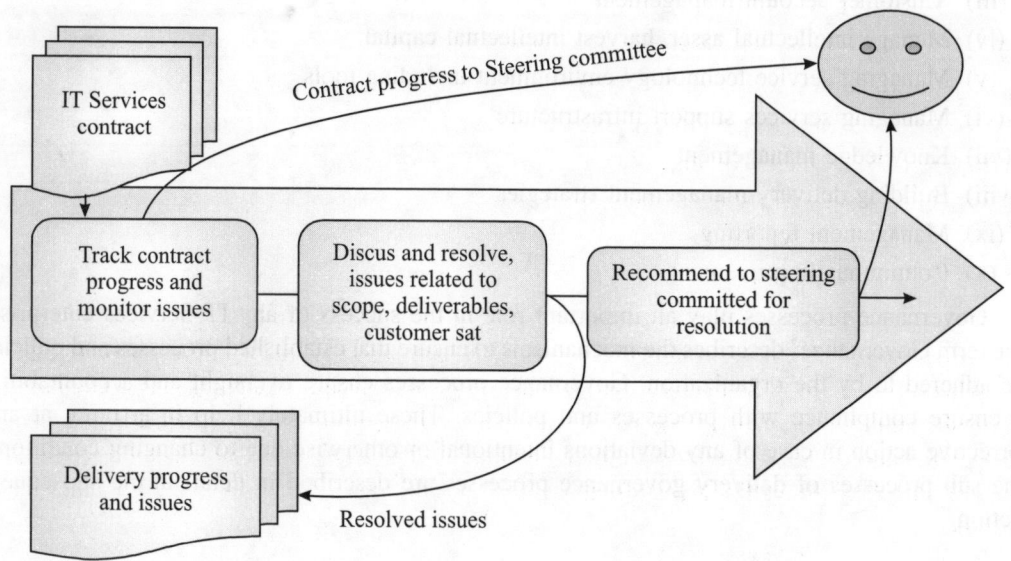

Figure 8.5   Contract governance process at a glance.

Contract governance process ensures that there is a single point responsibility to track various aspects of the contract and all stakeholders are kept informed at pre-defined intervals. Such updates are done during contract governance meetings (monthly or quarterly) covering to check whether all contract deliverables, payments for services, customer satisfaction measurement, etc. are placed for record and review. This process also addresses scope issues, non-performance of any services, new additions of services or changes arising out of the business conditions. Contract governance team works with their counter part in the client organization. Together they prepare updates and bring out recommendations to the services project steering committee comprising of executives from customer and IT Services provider.

In case of any dispute, the solution is sought as per the provisions made in the contract. The contract governance process ensures that the matter is amicably resolved for the benefit of both client as well as the IT Services provider. Poor contract governance process impacts the credibility of the IT Services organization. It leads to loss of revenue for the customer and additional cost to the IT Services provider for doing things which may not be a part of the contract. In the era of outsourcing of IT Services, the contract governance process can help both sides equally well and keep the disputes at minimum.

Resources utilization management

Resource utilization management process ensures that the resources availability matches the demand. Depending on the type of services being offered, maturity level of the IT Services and the general resource availability in the market, this process aims to achieve higher utilization level in the team. The utilization percentage refers to the team's time billed to the customer. Not all hours can be billed to the customer as the employee will take leave, undergo training programs or work on un-billable activities such as proposal development.

Utilization also varies for every level of the resources, higher the experience level lower is likely to be utilization as the senior people will have to work on business development and administrative responsibilities such as team mentoring, salary reviews, etc.

Having a well-designed resource utilization management process gives several benefits to the organization as follows:

(i) Faster decision-making between planning and delivery.

(ii) Consistent and continuous review leading to reduced risk of either lack of resources or large bench strength[4]. This will reduce the delivery risk of project delays and business risk of not able to undertake a project for want of lack of adequate resources.

(iii) Concise reporting of IT resource helps identify underutilized IT resources that can be repositioned

(iv) Reduce costs through better utilization of resources.

(v) Resource utilization management process allows delivery managers to uncover bottlenecks and address causes of poor service delivery.

(vi) Optimum level of resources helps in reducing unnecessary expenditure on infrastructure.

(vii) Improved efficiencies in project planning and staffing.

Resource utilization management process in large IT Services firm is a complex task that requires fair amount of automation and use of tools to manage resources. With multi-country and multi-city operations within the same country this process cannot be implemented by using worksheets or line-of-sight management.

Several resource management tools[5] give features such as:

(i) Locating resource within a location or across locations using a search engine to fit availability, client and project requirements.

(ii) Complete information about an individual travel preferences, contact information, skills, certifications, department and location information.

(iii) Search and schedule based on multiple selection criteria such as job role, skill, certification, travel preferences, location, and availability.

(iv) Reports covering bench strengths, resource utilization, and utilization forecast.

---

4. Bench strength; refers to unutilized people who are not assigned to any projects. Typically they will be new recruits waiting for projects or individuals who have been released after a project completion. The later category would be experienced and senior staff with a higher salary.

5. http://www.quickarrow.com/ accessed 29112011

These tools also allow the services firm to customize utilization rules covering standard work hours per week; work days per week; company and department holiday schedule. It also helps to tailor utilization goals to individual resources so that the a realistic resource planning can be done.

Resource monitoring facilities of these tools give insight of:

(i) Unstaffed projects for assignment

(ii) Ascertaining requirement by looking a sales pipeline project opportunities

(iii) Project completion schedules to give upcoming resource availability.

Most IT Services companies seek resources from business partner and subcontractors as well. Their resources also need to be managed using such tools where their resources database can also be maintained. By integrating partners and suppliers resource, the resource planning can be further streamlined.

Customer account management

The expansion of any IT Services business is though the existing projects and accounts. By doing the good job the IT Services firm can lay its claim for more and more services, and also enhance their capabilities by expanding their knowledge. The processes of account growth, managing customer satisfaction, contract management, etc. are led by account management team. Account management is a holistic process that comprises of steps that protect and growing account. Byrnes[6] advocated that account management process must include the following:

(i) Profitability management covering aspects of contracted value vs. cost being incurred

(ii) Account relationship maintaining good relationship to achieve customer satisfaction

(iii) Product (or services) migration planning: After a few years all IT Services would require to be replaced by new services or environment customer account management must initiate this activity well in advance.

(iv) Account planning for growing the existing level of services, increasing profitability, adding a new scope of services.

Figure 8.6 shows the various sub processes of an Account management process.

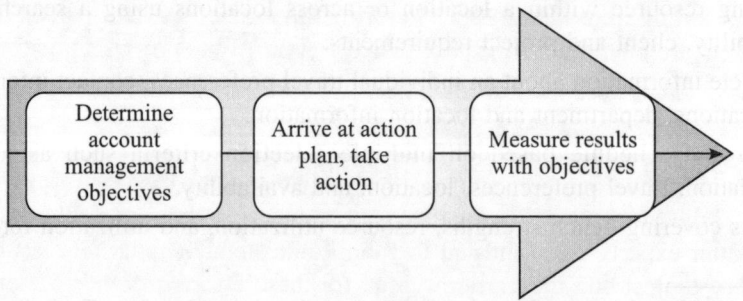

Figure 8.6   Account management process.

---

6. http://hbswk.hbs.edu/archive/4296.html accessed 22082011. Jonathan Byrnes is a Senior Lecturer at MIT.

Account management process encompasses the following steps:

(i) **Determine account management objectives:** This step ensures to establish the account management objectives. Typically, IT Services account focus on monitoring service levels, cost and customer satisfaction. In addition to it growing the account size, adding more revenue are also objectives for the account management team.

(ii) **Arrive at actions:** Based on the objectives account management team ascertains action plan in each of these areas and takes actions accordingly. For example, if the objective is to reduce cost, account management action would be automating the services as much as possible to reduce dependence on individuals.

(iii) **Measure the results with objectives:** Finally, all these actions will lead to the results that need to be compared with the objectives set. This is done periodically preferably on the monthly basis.

Account management process is like the navigational process for the entire account where it helps the delivery manager to compare results with objectives.

8.6   Delivery Improvement

Delivery improvement processes includes those processes that help build and enhance capabilities of the ITS delivery organization. Most of the time ITS delivery takes place by making project teams which get assembled when the customer signs a contract and gets disbands when the contract terminates. However, across project these delivery support processes ensure that learning from each projects are captured in the form of intellectual assets for later re-use, use standard tools and environment during execution and take long term strategic actions for improving delivery.

8.6.1   Manage Intellectual Asset, Harvest Intellectual Capital

This process ensures that the services performed by the team lead to retained and enhanced experience through systematic capture of best practices, delivery tools, templates, etc. All this leads to faster learning, repeatability and lowering the cost of services delivery. For example, if similar projects are being performed the lessons learnt from one should be transferred to the other and vice versa. A good management of intellectual asset leads to new services offerings besides reuse of these assets.

The challenge is to encourage the delivery team and reward them to submit intellectual assets which need to be codified, sanitized[7] and made available for the rest of the team. This process step is called harvesting the intellectual capital. In certain cases, the Project managers and subject matter experts are mandated to submit intellectual capital artifacts (documents) at the end of every project and they are rewarded for these efforts too. In addition, anyone who has developed any useful tool or template that can be a candidate of reuse can also submit it to the knowledge base and get due recognition.

---

7. Sanitization; in IT Services this means removal of client references and confidential data from reports, presentation and other documents for reuse/education.

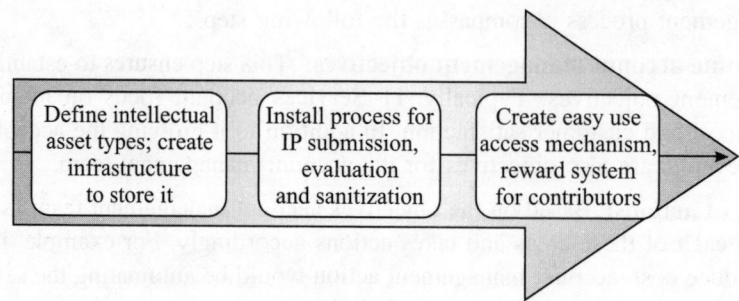

Figure 8.7   Manage intellectual asset, harvest intellectual capital.

As shown in Figure 8.7 this process includes:

(i) Defining intellectual asset types, for example, statement of work, presentations, reports, report format, etc.

(ii) Creating infrastructure to store it

(iii) Installing process for IP submission, evaluation and sanitization: defining when who and what format the intellectual capital can be submitted and who will assign the code, review it for client confidentiality etc.

(iv) Creating easy use access mechanism, may a times if the intellectual capital is not easily accessible its use diminishes. Having a good search mechanism give impetus for team to use and reuse the already available intellectual capita.

(v) Reward system for contributors, which should also give incentives for those who are active in contributing to intellectual capital.

Managing service environment, tools and support infrastructure

Delivery management also requires establishing the delivery environment and facilitating increased use of tools of automating the services task. Failure to do this will lead to increased cost, duplication of efforts and loss of productivity of the services delivery team.

For example, use of wiki or team rooms for facilitating collaboration requires servers and IT infrastructure. Software development tools, facilitating version control, testing requirement tracing, etc. are a few examples that are facilitated by this process.

The process owner creates an environment and tools required and makes them available whenever any project starts. In certain cases training, evangelization and support is also included as a part of this process. Figure 8.8 summarizes the process steps.

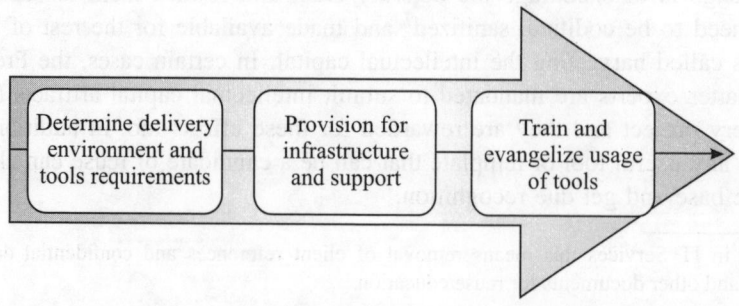

Figure 8.8   Managing service environment, tools and support infrastructure process.

Building delivery management strategies, management reporting and continuous improvement

Managing delivery is an exercise of continuous learning. Good delivery management team ensures that they have a long term vision of the way they would like to deliver their services and ensure a continuous improvement action leading towards of their goals.

This is an enveloping process that takes strategies development for improved services and establishes measurement and reporting processes.

Typically, this process is carried out by select experienced delivery members who create a strategic plan for delivery and measure the progress after actions are taken.

8.7 Summary

In this chapter, we examined the entire gamut of IT Services delivery management processes. Delivery management processes are not only revenue generating, but also have to be impeccable, flawless and efficient. Broadly, the delivery management processes in IT Services enterprise have four major process groups and their subgroups as:

1. Delivery planning which includes
   (i) Resources planning
   (ii) Processes planning
   (iii) Infrastructure planning
   (iv) Planning for delivery budget
2. Delivery execution includes
   (i) Services project management
   (ii) Initiation and or services transition
   (iii) Skills and resources management
   (iv) Delivery process management
   (v) Delivery cost management
   (vi) Deliverables, contract administration, billing and collection management
   (vii) Service quality management
3. Delivery governance includes
   (i) Manage contract governance
   (ii) Resources utilization management
   (iii) Customer account management
4. Delivery improvement includes
   (i) Manage intellectual asset, harvest intellectual capital
   (ii) Managing service technology environment including tools and
   (iii) Services support infrastructure
   (iv) Building delivery management strategies, management reporting and continuous improvement

Each of these sub processes were further detailed and explained with their importance and need for the overall success of the IT Services Enterprise.

Review Questions

8.1 What are the major processes and sub processes of IT Services delivery management? Explain with the help of a diagram.

8.2 Why delivery governance management is important in case of large and complex IT Services contract? Is it fair to say that proper delivery governance would help both client as well as the services provider? Explain with examples from the real life.

8.3 Your firm has recently been awarded a new service contract in a large bank. This bank already had an IT Services provider who was not selected for continuation. Which process would be the first process for successful delivery at the initial stages and why?

8.4 What is need of delivery process planning? Are there any standards which can be referred to adopt processes in your ITSE?

8.5 Which process ensures high utilization of the delivery team? Name and explain.

Suggested Further Readings

Good practice contract management framework, Office of Government Commerce (OGC), London.

Contract Life-Cycle Management—Ashif Mawji, Contract Management/November 2005, pp. 38–43.

Davanport, Thomas H., "The Benefits of Business Process Standards", *Harvard Business Review*, Vol. 83, No. 6, June 2005.

Davanport, Thomas H., "The Coming Commoditization of Processes," *Harvard Business Review*, Vol. 83, No. 6, June 2005.

Websites

http://www.purdue.edu/SPS/index.html

www.itgovernance.co.uk/catalog/cobit

www.itil.co.uk

www.sei.cmu.edu/cmmi

Chapter 9

IT Services
Quality Assurance

Perhaps the most important reason for pursuing quality is that quality pays
—Deming

9.1 Introduction

We will discuss in this chapter the challenges and issues of maintaining IT Services quality by relating it with principles of services quality and prevalent research. IT systems and services have become the lifeline of any business in the modern times. Its success and failure impacts that of the business that it serves directly or indirectly. While Service Quality of mundane and routine IT Services can be easily defined and measured the problem comes for those upper end IT Services that have newness either of technology, business needs or business model which require high degree of creativity. Such services have many new things to incorporate, explore and unravel. No sooner we perfect an IT Services based on a particular technology, a newer technology or business model emerges in the horizon and makes the process of building and measuring services quality difficult.

We will discuss the recent concepts, established processes and widely acclaimed best practices of establishing, measuring and ensuring quality for IT Services in this chapter.

9.2 IT Services Quality is a Competitive Differentiator

Delivering quality IT Services is a new competitive differentiator and the most powerful competitive weapon. The leading IT Services providers do claim to have perfected this art through superior process. Yet we witness failures of IT systems occasionally in the recent past that have impacted major operations of banks[1], airlines, airports[2] and many others. Customers are quite vocal and increasingly critical about quality of IT Service they experience and demand proactive strategies to address the quality issues.

---

1. http://ibnlive.in.com/news/sbi-link-fails-banks-open-today/189446-60-119.html accessed 03102011.
2. http://articles.timesofindia.indiatimes.com/2010-01-14/delhi/28123000_1_flight-operations-igi-airport-air-navigation accessed 03102011.

In the arena of IT Services, continuous innovation and creativity is needed to bring in newer features to keep the competitive gap wider. While for routine IT Services, the process may have achieved sufficient levels of maturity, the innovative and cutting edge services may yet not been tested and tried out. This brings in the new dimension of the problem as all newer services would have to be perfected to the desired service level, a level not yet established. While the service provider may themselves be learning on multiple aspects of services element and the technology, the client may be unaware of the ways to measure and evaluate services quality.

Take the case of new services that Apple, a newer range of i-products, offer. The end users are unlikely to know what are the best way to measure and monitor them! While a few customers speak highly about the innovativeness, many other complain and crib about its features, consistency and so on[3]. The service provider may blame it to the other players in the services delivery chain leading to loss of revenue, time or opportunity to the ultimate customer. For several decades, newer applications services like ERP, CRM and many others have gone through the series of problems with multiple customers. There are several research paper and books[4] published on the aspects of enterprise implementation and failures, where a new IT Services quality was less than desired at the initial stages.

IT Service firm have to use the superior quality of service plank to be able to differentiate from generic commodity services suppliers. Once the client is able to witness this difference with respect to other firms, it is very likely to continue or seek more services from the same firm a phenomenon we describe as Service stickiness. Many organizations have realized that maintaining excellence on a consistent basis is required if they have to gain customer loyalty and maintain organization's growth and survival.

9.3   IT Service Quality Makes Business Sense

Parasuraman[5] in his seminal article quotes that delivering superior service by maintaining high quality is a prerequisite for success, leading to gaining customer loyalty. In fact in order to succeed in the long term in any market ITS firms have to build large sticky customer base which can not be created unless the services quality is of superior standard and also cost-effective. This is the only tool that prompts customers to seek more and more services (stickiness) with the IT service provider, and thus, lowers down the cost of sales. Maintaining services quality is a business sense.

In this chapter we will draw a relationship between services quality and its impact of ITS sales. As we have discussed in the earlier chapters, the delivery of services has an important impact on growth of services and solution sales. ITS being result oriented services are required to be monitored for its quality and reliability.

---

3. http://www.zdnet.com/blog/hardware/updated-at-t-customers-speak-out-over-poor-service/5330

4. Davenport, H. Mission critical: Realizing the promise of enterprise systems, *Harvard Business Press*, 2000

5. Parasuraman, A., Zeithaml, V.A. & Berry, L.L. (1988) Servqual: A multiple-item scale for measuring consumer perceptions of service quality. *Journal of Retailing*, 64, pp. 12–40.

9.4 Services Quality

The definition several researchers[6] have concluded that service quality as evaluated by the customer is a comparison between their expectation and actual performance by the service provider.

Lewis and Booms[7] (1983), define service quality as a measure of the degree to which the service delivered matches customer expectations. Not only it needs conformance with customer expectations, but is required on consistent basis.

Service quality consists of service attributes, quality dimensions, measurement methods and models. The two service actors, i.e. The service provider and client have to work together. In the case of former service quality means conforming to specifications and requirements as delivered service quality[8] and perform to specifications and requirements that satisfy external customers and meet their expectations. The measurement of services quality requires several parameters[9] such as:

(i) Reliability—Perform promised service, dependably and accurately

(ii) Responsiveness—Willingness/readiness to provide prompt service

(iii) Competence—Possess knowledge and skill to perform the service

(iv) Access—Approachability and ease of contact of service personnel

(v) Courtesy—Politeness, consideration, and friendliness of service personnel

(vi) Communication—Keeping customers informed; listening to customers

(vii) Credibility—Trustworthy, believable, honest

(viii) Security—Freedom from danger, risk, or doubt

(ix) Understanding/knowing customer—Knowing customer's needs

(x) Tangibles—Physical evidence of service

9.5 IT Services Gap, Expectation vs Reality

Like many other services there will be situation where the customer expectation and the services delivered would not match each other. In this context the use of SERQUAL model given by Parasuraman[10] and its application in IT Services context is worth examining. Taking a cue from this research we have translated these principles to IT Services scenario, choosing a slightly different nomenclature. It has also been represented in Figure 9.1 for ease of appreciation for our readers.

---

6. Gronroos, 1982; Lehtinen & Lehtinen, 1982; Lewis & Booms, 1983; Lindqvist, 1987; Parasuraman et al.,1985; Zeithaml et al., 1988

7. Lewis, R.C. and Booms, B.H. (1983); The marketing aspects of service quality. In: L. Berry et al. (Eds.), *Emerging Perspectives on Services Marketing*, New York, AMA.

8. Yasser Ahmed Al Tayeb, (Parasuraman et al.1985;) quoted in The Effects of National Culture on Service Quality.

9. Parasuraman, A. Zeithaml, V., and Berry, L. (1985).

10. As above

Customer expectation gap

IT Services in many cases would be a new beginning by most organization. The reasons may be new technology or new way of doing things. Customer would not be well-equipped to explain his requirements. At the same time IT Services business development team often finds it difficult to understand and translate customer expectations and management perception. Customer at this stage requires lot of coaching and training to bring out the relevant requirements in as much detail as possible so that the services design can be done better to meet them. Many a times, the person explaining the requirement (e.g. IT team) may themselves be far away from the actual business users requirements.

Services design gap

The IT Services provider requirement gathering team at times is unable to translate customer requirements into precise service quality specifications or performance standards. Similarly the IT Services design team may not be well-versed with the nuances of the customer business and may fail to incorporate them into design.

Services delivery gap

Parasuraman calls it as implementation gap existing between the services delivered with the services quality specification. Most IT Services delivery processes may look good on PowerPoint charts, but in the actual work they may fail to confirm to the expectations of the standards. This is largely due to the skills issues in IT Services firms which gets accentuated as multiple layers of outsourcing is done. The attrition of the team, not able to understand the big picture and leadership of the delivery team further adds to this gap.

Services perception gap

The absence of IT Services like many other utility is felt far more strongly than its uninterrupted presence. This is not only a factor of continuous communication but also due to a mismatch of reality vs expectations. Business users typically get over-hyped expectations from a particular IT Services without realizing that the much touted examples of success would have required lot of efforts that may have been missing in their case. The role and responsibility of the services seeker in the case of IT Services is far more important than any other services. Their participation in requirement gathering, design and implementation, if ignored, would lead to a huge gap at this stage when the services are finally delivered and it will fail to meet the perceived requirements. For example, users may base their perception of IT Services on peak time performance (where huge transaction load may be coming up for example during month end) and the requirement specifications or services design may be based on average transaction. If the user has not stated this requirement or the design team has not visualized it then this will lead to perception gap.

Services value realization gap

This gap is very specific to IT Services as most IT Services has an implicit need to facilitate a business outcome. For example using a cloud-based sales force automation services is expected to increase sales effectiveness and growth. The role of business users and leaders becomes very important to take advantage of the information provided by the IT system, the absence of which may lead to a gap which is termed as value realization gap. We have discussed in other chapters that unless the target value is defined right from the beginning of IT Services and solution planning, it will be hard to quantify and realize. If the first four gaps are addressed from the beginning then this last gap will be much easier to tackle.

Figure 9.1 shows theses gaps in pictorial form which also symbolizes that the gaps at the initial stages will lead to larger gaps at the subsequent stages.

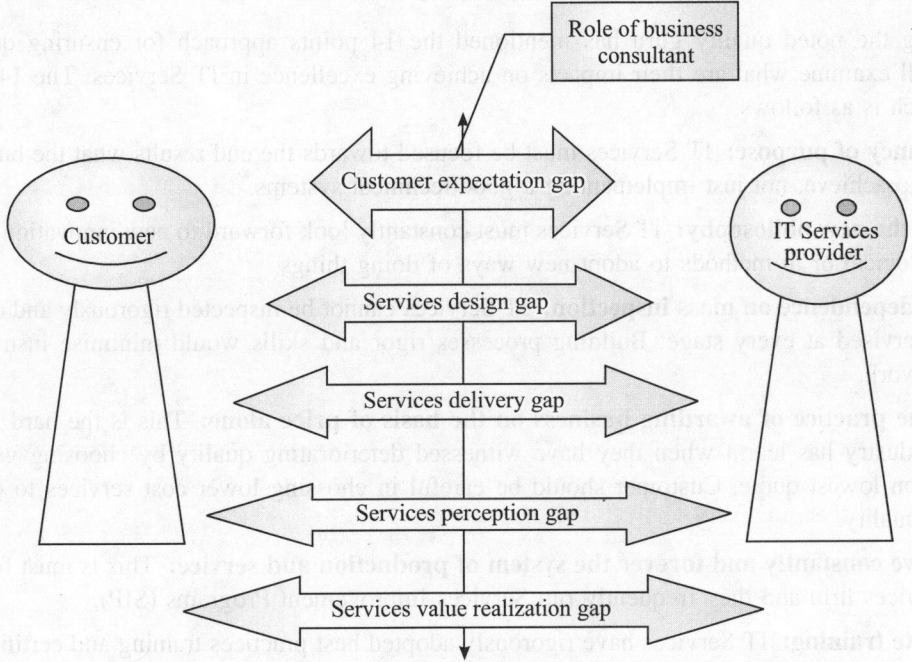

Figure 9.1   Gaps at different stages of IT Services delivery life cycle.

Role of a business consultant in minimizing these gaps: There is also an arrow shown vertically that goes across all these gaps. This is to define the role of business consultants in minimizing the IT Services gap.

As we have seen these generic gaps would be much larger if the services are new either for the services seeker (which may be the case most of the time) or by the services provider. In case of routine IT Services these gaps are likely to be less as compared to complex and innovative services that are being built for the future requirements.

In order to minimize this gap, most leading IT Services provider lead the requirement and business development phase through Business Consulting professionals. These professionals are able to elicit the requirements far more thoroughly than a pure services sales person. Business consultant would bring the focus to ultimate value to be achieved from the services being planned and help the services users in educating and coaching in the process. By his continued involvement through the IT Services planning and delivery life cycle, these gaps would not creep or will be addressed well in time. Several hand offs between requirement definition, design, delivery and outsourcing team can be minimized if the Business Consulting team is involved at every stage of the services delivery life cycle.[11] It is like the central stick that holds various layers of burger together or like the rod used while cooking of *seekh kabab*[12] which Indians are so fond off.

9.6 Examining Deming's Philosophy to Achieve IT Services Quality

Deming the noted quality guru has mentioned the 14 points approach for ensuring quality. We will examine what are their impacts on achieving excellence in IT Services. The 14-point approach is as follows:

Constancy of purpose: IT Services must be focused towards the end results what the business wants to achieve, not just implementing a good technical systems.

Adopt the new philosophy: IT Services must constantly look forward to new innovation either technological or in methods to adopt new ways of doing things.

Cease dependence on mass inspection: IT Services cannot be inspected rigorously and cannot be supervised at every stage. Building processes rigor and skills would minimise instruction and rework.

End the practice of awarding business on the basis of price alone: This is the hard lesson user industry has learnt when they have witnessed deteriorating quality by choosing vendors based on lowest quote. Customer should be careful in chossing lower cost services to ensure better quality.

Improve constantly and forever the system of production and service: This is must for any IT Services firm and they frequently run Services Improvement Programs (SIP).

Institute training: IT Services have rigorously adopted best practices training and certification on frameworks like ITIL, CoBit, CMM and PCMM to train the work force.

Institute leadership: IT Services quality can only be achieved if the leaders a IT Services are held responsible for the quality of service. In most leading IT Services firm the senior managers bonus and incentives are dependent on quality rating of their project.

Drive out fear: Leading companies from IT Services industry ensure that lack of quality is pointed out without fear by any one at any level in the organization.

Breakdown barriers among staff: IT Services firms are known for flat organization culture that helps building quality and teaming across organization breaking organizational boundary.

Eliminate slogans, exhortations and targets: Very rarely the IT Services firm publicize and goad people in this direction. It is assumed and inculcated as organizational practice and way of doing work.

Eliminate work quotas: While targets are defined for achieving certain mile stones, hourly and daily supervisions are discouraged.

---

11. Sanjiva Shankar Dubey, Business and IT Consulting: Concepts, processes practices, Tata McGraw-Hill, 2012.
12. http://steakout.com.au/burger-sticks.html and http://en.wikipedia.org/wiki/List_of_kebabs accessed 06102011

Remove barriers to pride of workmanship: IT Services team takes pride in solving complex issues and IT Services firm encourage such ownership through awards and recognition to such individuals.

Institute a vigorous program of education and self-Improvement: Most IT Services firm have rigorous skill building programs that helps building service quality.

Put everyone to work on the transformation: This is very evident in the IT Services firms that pursue excellence in service.

We will notice that IT Services firms who pursue excellence religiously confirm the Deming's principles.

9.7 Achieving IT Services Quality with Profit

It has been proved beyond doubt that pursuing quality objective is not at cross purpose to achieve profit objectives. In fact, the former enhances the later through increased customer satisfaction and repeat business. Some researchers[13] give an integrated view of services quality leading to enhanced profit of the firm. The concept of service profit chain is proposed by Heskette, et al., who consider that the internal service quality of the service provider firm is the starting point for building any successful profitable services organization. Good internal service quality leads to employee satisfaction leading to their motivation and retention, leading to increased learning and experience about the services being offered to the customer. All this leads to attainment of external service quality and value leading to customer satisfaction, loyalty and ultimately more revenue and profit for the firm. We are describing some of the best practices for acheiveing IT Services quality with profit.

Start with listening to customers

Listening to customer is of utmost importance in achieving IT Services quality. This will help getting customer's perceptions to choose a right service strategy. Bring these customer concerns and match with the ability of the IT Services firm and see where it can be made better with respect to Industry prevailing standards to arrive at the right service quality point. However, one can choose different services quality strategies for different offerings although each one of them may come from same firm. The right positioning on services quality continuum (see Figure 9.3) is typically a senior management decision.

Build a right service strategy for excellence

It is important to choose the right point in the delight to disappointment continuum (Figure 9.3) for the IT Services firm to build their services quality. It is also a factor of brand image and the type of customers and the projects the firm is serving or has in its portfolio. This is also dependent on the prevailing environment and rest-of-the industry approach. For example, a delight-oriented services like Business and IT consulting can not be accepted if any new entrant is promising cost effective minimalistic services quality. Similarly, a new firm joining BPO or call centre industry typically driven by lower cost has to adher to minimum services quality as practiced by the rest of the industry.

---

13. Heskett, Sasser, and Schlesinger (1997). The service profit chain. New York: Free Press.

Focus on business results

IT Services should focus on the quality of business results derived out of the IT services or solution. Just having IT systems with good technical quality (covering both software and hardware) which may be giving good performance, is not enough. It must also have better Information Quality, i.e. the output produced by the system. This output Information quality is however, a factor of quality and timeliness of data entered by the business users of the customer. Good IT service providers ensure end user training and motivation is also addressed so that the new IT system leads to better customer's business results. This will not only ensure enhanced customer satisfaction but better profit for the IT Service provider through extra business.

Building service quality through people

Following this best practice, leading IT Services firm give a lot of importance in building satisfaction through good internal processes. This leads to lower employee turnover thereby increasing skills and learnings which help in delivering better quality. All client organizations are concerned about the employee turnover rate of the prospective IT Services provider firm. A higher attrition means higher percentage of new employees, many of them would be untrained on the processes and systems of the IT Services firm. However, employee turnover is still very high in IT Services industry for variety of reasons prominent amongst them being the growing economy and increasing demand. A typical attrition of 10–15% is considered healthy which goes as high as 35% in BPO services. At the bottom of the skills pyramid attrition also helps to maintain the cost better.[14] By implementing good employee training, skill building and HR practices, IT Services firm can enhance its quality of delivery.

Employees skills, involvement can bridge the quality gap

Jay Kandampully[15], a noted researcher, mentions that when a firm's service employees develop the emotional connection with customers then only an exceptional service with ability to exceed customer expectations can take place. IT Services will always have newer technology that may have important bearing on the services quality. Many a times, the technology is rather new or being tried for the first time in the client situation that makes the unpredictability of the services quality factor too high. If the service provider employees have the right levels of skills and motivation, the gap arising out of newness of service can be reduced.

Figure 9.2 summarizes the approach on a diagrammatical form.

Balance customer delight and services cost

How much efforts should one make to delight a customer or how much one should optimize to avoid customer disappointment? Call centre industry is one example where faster speed to answer does not automatically get converted into customer satisfaction. As long as the customer is getting his grievances addressed after a reasonable wait, properly, politely and perfectly, he/she is happy to wait a little longer. But not too long so that he get dejected and hangs up.

---

14. http://articles.economictimes.indiatimes.com/2011–08–09/news/29867188_1_attrition-employee-ites-companies

15. Service quality to service loyalty: A relationship which goes beyond customer services Jay Kandampully Commerce Division, Lincoln University, Canterbur y, New Zealand, Total Quality Management, Vol. 9, No. 6, 1998, 431–443

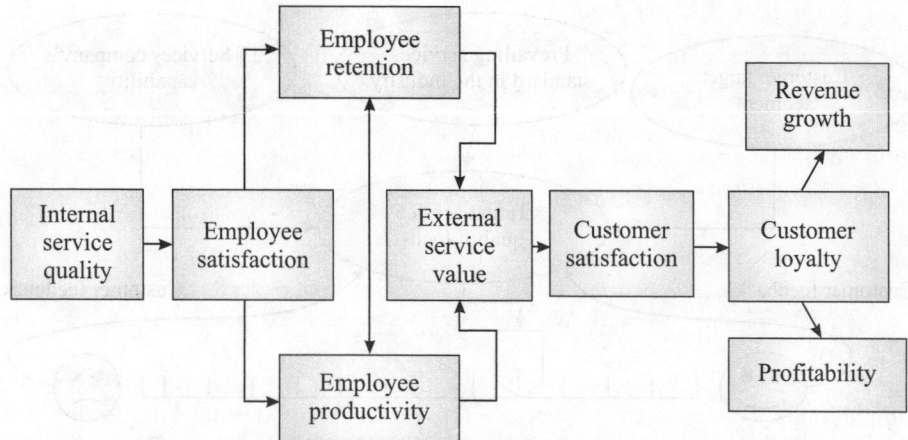

Figure 9.2 IT Services quality profit chain.

Similarly, in other ITS how much detail should one work on to delight the customer or how to simplify the work will require a delicate balance. So going back to the earlier example, a study[16] found that while less than 9 seconds of average hold time was a delight to the customer, any wait of more than 45 seconds were disliked by the customer. However, the wait period in between was almost neutral for the customer. This proves the point that one need to be aware to strike the right point to decide how much quality to be built in the services. Cormac[17] says that one cannot delight the customer in every transaction as it will call for quick decision, more empowerment of sales force and at times compromising the processes that may eventually lead to more breakdown. However, an experienced account manager would sense early emerging dissatisfactions and try to address them before it becomes an expensive complaint.

In order to define services quality the IT Services firm has to choose a customer focus. One can choose between delighting the customer at any cost (typically done by consulting forms) to become cost-effective and prevent escalation for dissatisfaction (outsourcing services). This is quite a wide range to choose from and the ITS firm can position itself appropriately as compared to its competitors as shown in Figure 9.3.

Figure 9.3 also shows some interesting understanding about the cost of service and its relationship with customer stickiness. Customer stickiness (like customer loyalty in product selling) is a factor of customer delight, yet it does not change proportionately. Customer stickiness goes up as we improve the services towards delight and goes down as the services deteriorate leading to customer disappointment.

Cost of service will go up on either side of this continuum. In case of delight the cost of service goes up due to extra efforts required to give better quality and predictability of the services quality. In contrast, in the poor services quality area this cost goes up due to higher cost of rework, paying service penalty and increased sales efforts to solicit new customers.

---

16. http://www.yakpact.com/whitepapers/White-Paper-sales-thru-service.pdf Cormac Murphy: Selling through service accessed 0212011

17. As above

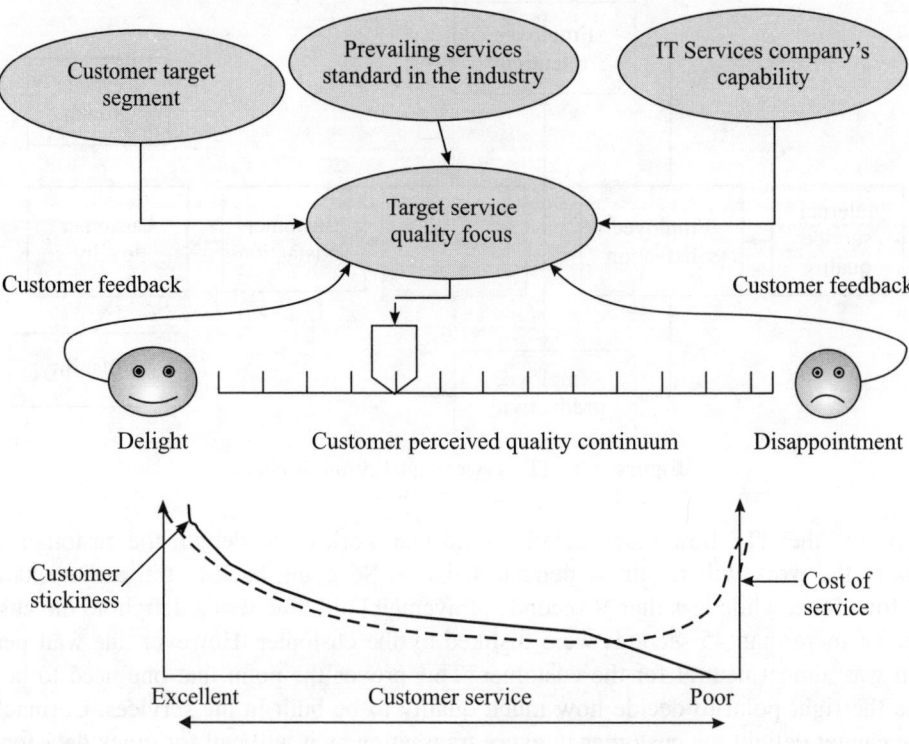

Figure 9.3   Defining the IT Services quality focus.

9.8 Summary

It is evident that for innovative IT Services design of services requires a careful planning and execution. Quality of IT Services is of prime importance for the success of any modern day enterprise most of them now increasingly depend on IT.

Delivering quality IT Services is a new competitive differentiator and the most powerful competitive weapon. While for routine IT Services the process may have achieved sufficient levels of maturity, the innovative and cutting edge services may yet not been tested and tried out. We started with a premise that delivering superior service by maintaining high quality is a prerequisite for success, leading to gaining customer loyalty. In this process service provider and client have to work together which is most true for innovative IT Services The framework of SERQUAL and Deming's led us to understand the role of quality in IT Services delivery. While a good service leads to profit, in IT the skills and capabilities of the team is most important. It is only the employee's skills, involvement that can bridge the quality gap. We argued that IT Services is about achieving end results, and therefore, one must consider the business outcome before designing the appropriate IT Services. While doing this a proper balancing of customer delight and services cost is also needed.

Incorporating experience of innovative Bharti Airtel IT outsourcing project, it was mentioned that starting form outcome down to design and co-creation of services design together with client is recommended. The team must focus on objective not on contract and select a suitable team mix comprising of visualizers, planners and perfect implementers to deliver the services.

Continued innovation is a hallmark of not only for exceptional service quality but also will help competitive differentiation of the firm. IT Services excellence not only enhances the firm's competitiveness and efficiency but also increases its revenue and profits.

CASE STUDY
Ensuring services quality for new innovative IT Services

In the year 2004, Bharti Airtel entered into a first of its kind outsourcing services contract with world IT leader IBM. Not only the contract was comprehensive covering all aspects of IT Services that a telecom operators would need but also revolutionary as the contract was outcome based. The service provider in this case IBM was to be paid based on the fraction of revenue generated by Bharti Airtel. This was not only a unique idea but also help revolutionizing the telecom operations that always needed huge capital investment and uncertainty of the subscriber growth. By ensuring the service provider "skin in the game"[18] the end result of this unique innovative IT Services model is not only the subject of several HBR studies[19] and numerous awards, but carved out a new way of delivering IT Services followed by many others subsequently. This first of its kind IT Services model also led to the following conclusions:

(i) *Start form outcome down to design of services:* This means that before designing any IT Services one should understand and visualize the business outcome to be produced out of this. Based on this visualization the necessary services and technology solution should be designed. For example, the majority of pre-paid recharge happens between 5–8 in the evening therefore necessary capacity of IT solution must be made available during that period and uninterruptedly.

(ii) *Co-create the services, design together with client:* In many innovative areas the knowledge of the future many not just lies with the service provider. Even if the IT Services provider may have the prior technology experience it will need depth of localized business needs and expectations to design these services. A joint team between business users, IT and IT Services provider proved to be the most successful and useful.

(iii) *Focus on objective not on contract:* The unique outcome based payment gave enough room and guideline to focus on objectives and not just technological best, but on relevant solution.

(iv) *Select a suitable team mix:* The team should comprise of visualizers, planners and perfect implementers. This issue has been discussed earlier as well and is again re-emphasized that for any new innovative services such a mix of skills are required for ensuring services quality from the day one.

Review Questions

9.1 Why do we ensure IT Services quality? Does it conflict with the profit objectives of the firm?

9.2 Explain various gaps that creep in during IT Services delivery life cycle and how it can be minimized.

---

18. Prahalad, C.K. and Mashelkar, R.A., Innovation's Holy Grail, *Harvard Business Review*, July–August 2010, p. 5

19. See references 7 and 8 for these HBR case studies

9.3 Explain how continued presence of Business consultant can ensure good IT Services quality.

9.4 How will you balance between the customer delight and cost of service? Explain with a diagram.

9.5 Which one is not true according to Deming philosophy applied for IT Services?

   (i) Constancy of purpose

   (ii) Cease dependence on mass inspection

   (iii) Institute catchy slogans, exhortations and targets

   (iv) End the practice of awarding business on the basis of price alone

9.6 How will you achieve IT Services quality with profit? Mention the best practices with examples.

9.7 How will you explain the statement "IT Services quality needs a careful balance between twin objectives of improved profit and reduced cost?

Suggested Further Reading

Gronroos, C., *Strategic Management and Marketing in the Service Sector*, London, Chartwell Bratt, 1982.

Lehtinen, U. and Lehtinen, J.R., "Service quality: A study of quality dimensions", Unpublished working paper, *Service Management Institute*, Helsinki, 1982.

Lewis, R.C. & Booms, B.H., "The marketing aspects of service quality". L. Berry et al. (Eds.), *Emerging Perspectives on Services Marketing*, New York, AMA, 1983.

Lidqvist, J.L., Quality and service value in the consumer services. C. Surprenant (Ed.), Value to your Service, New York, AMA, 1987.

Parasuraman, A., Zeithaml, V.A. & Berry, L.L., "A conceptual implications for future research". *Journal of Marketing*, 49, 1985, pp. 41–50.

Zeithaml, V.A., Berry, L.L. & Parasuraman, A., "Communication of service quality". *Journal of Marketing*, 52, 1988, pp. 35–48.

Martinez-Jerez, F. Asis, Narayanan, V.G., Jurgens, Michele, HBS Premier Case Collection, 2006.

Martinez-Jerez, F. Asis, Narayanan, V.G., Jurgens, Michele, Strategic Outsourcing at Bharti Airtel Ltd. One Year Later, *Harvard Business School*, 2006.

Chapter 10

IT Services Enterprise: Measurement and Driving Performance

If you can't describe what you are doing as a process, you don't know what you are doing.
—Dr. Edward Deming

10.1 Introduction

Managing IT Services Enterprise effectively and successfully cannot happen unless it adopts a rigorous process of measurement of performance and driving it towards perfection. This chapter is devoted towards deep-researched concepts for IT Services Enterprise performance drivers and some of the proven and practical approaches, adopting which any ITSE can derive superior results. For professional working in ITSE this chapter would be of immense benefit as using the concepts and processes they can properly measure and improve their team, department and individual performances.

We would attempt the theme of measuring and driving performance in this chapter from a philosophical approach, i.e. what is the ideal and leave our readers to pick up what they consider practical and useful in their situation. These theory and practices are not a musing of an armchair researcher, but have been tested and deployed in complex situation leading to successes enhancing value to several ITS Enterprise.

We will attempt to answer the following questions in this chapter:

  (i) What are good parameters for IT Service measurements?

  (ii) How do we measure IT Service effectiveness?

  (iii) How do we measure how good we are in the eyes of the customer?

10.2 Challenges in Measuring and Driving IT Services Performance

Measurement of IT Services Enterprise performance is tough. There is always a tight rope walking between client satisfaction (whereby do more for less) and being efficient (do less for

137

more)! This dilemma is captured by the terms the fight between efficiency and effectiveness. IT Services add some more complexity in terms to changing technology, thereby putting a continuous pressure on skills upgradation. Further the client themselves may not have all the ideas of what they need, therefore defining their expectation levels is like shooting a moving target. The endeavour in this chapter is to present framework to measure IT Services Enterprise performance in such a way that ensures both internal (efficiency) and external (effectiveness) perspective.

If measuring the performance is tough, driving the performance is tougher by any yardstick. IT Service is a people led business that has vagaries of economic events impacting other industries, and thus, creating a headwind to the IT Services industry. There is a choice of how and what to offer service and a lot depends on the team that you have. Small companies bring flexibility and customer sensitivity, but cannot hold their good skills for long, because they cannot pay good salaries. Big IT Services Enterprise are driven by structure and rules where individual brilliance is subservient to the organization's objective.

The question to think about is how can we motivate the same person for stellar performance when he/she is a part of small team with freedom to innovate at a lower salary or when he joins a big corporate where he/she gets good salary, but have to do exactly what he is told to, nothing less or more.

Tombaugh and McKants[1] opine that performance measurement metrics effectively enable management to drive continuous performance improvement by translating organizational missions into objective, outcome-oriented goals, disseminate and clarify these goals throughout the respective organization. This helps in aligning actions, resources, and initiatives with those goals. However, they can become effective only when used systematically in evaluating, selecting, and implementing improvement initiatives. Too many companies use the performance measurement system as a post-facto reporting, and not use them as a dashboard to drive performance. The effectiveness of any measurement system would be justified if they are continuously used to navigate the performance through the uncharted waters of the future!

10.3   Performance Management

According to Armstrong and Baron performance management is a strategic and integrated approach of delivering sustained success to organizations by improving performance of people who work in them, and by developing the capabilities of teams and individual contributors[2]. It is a combination or strategies, policies, processes and initiatives to empower and encourage people to act to meet the organization goals to meet customer services objectives. This also includes measurement of results, individual appraisal and rewarding people who perform better and reprimand those who are lacking in their performance.

10.3.1   Challenges of Performance Management

Any customer would like to seek services from the best service provider at a reasonable cost. The

1. Driving Enterprise Performance through Metrics Phil Tombaugh and Erin McCants, 2008.
2. www.nwpg.gov.za/.../Performance%20Management%20for%20Success.ppt accessed 09092011

same is true for IT Services as well. These enterprises will need to measure their performance and drive to achieve better levels all the time.

The purpose of any performance measure is to show how much away we are from our goal. Like a ship sailing in high sea must always know how much its speed is, what the direction is and the resistance forms the winds to exactly locate where the ship is and how far it is from its destination. Unlike the land, the winds will push or pull the ship in its direction or opposite to it. Finally, the purpose of any measurement is force and focus us to take action, a topic that we will discuss in the section on driving performance.

Performance measures also enable communication of consistent performance expectations and can be used as a key tool for aligning organization units for common goals and objectives. Once the performance measure is clearly articulated and defined, it will facilitate decentralized decision making as everyone would not know what to achieve and how they will be measured giving enough room for innovation and flexibility. Performance measurement approach gives systems perspective of managing the IT Services organization and enables its growth.

Any effective measurement must observe the following criteria:

   (i) It should represent customer criteria

  (ii) It should be objective, correct, periodic, measurable and reliable

 (iii) Should represent the process (s) that produces it

  (iv) Should reflect the change

   (v) Induce improvement

Any IT Services Enterprise uses people to perform certain services and they follow certain processes. The success of service delivery is a combination of people (their skills and motivation) and how efficient the processes have been designed. The later part is also achieved through automation, continuous learning and liberal use of IT. This together will lead to meeting strategic objectives of achieving revenue or profit. Finally, all of these together must lead to a satisfied customer who is willing to take more and more services and acts as reference to other customers. A performance measure communicates the deviation from important goals and drives performance in that direction. A well-defined measure will be like a compass and help the firm to remain on course. However, if this is not done, improper measures can have a negative impact, and can divert resources and focus in the wrong direction.

The study conducted by Neely[3] looked at the best practices for setting up the performance measure. The top 5 out of 22 of this list are worth examining:

   (i) Performance measures should be derived from strategy

  (ii) Performance measures should be simple to understand

 (iii) Performance measures should provide timely and accurate feedback

  (iv) Performance measures should be based on quantities that can be influenced, or controlled, by the user alone or in co-operation with others

   (v) Performance measures should reflect the business process, i.e. both the supplier and customer should be involved in the definition of the measure

---

3. Designing performance measures: A structured approach Andy Neely, Huw Richards, John Mills, Ken Platts and Mike Bourne, University of Cambridge, Cambridge, UK, (1997) *International Journal of Operations & Production Management* 17, 1131–1152.

10.3.2 Using Balanced Score Card Approach for Performance Definition and Measurement

The balanced scorecard approach outlined by Robert Kaplan[4] combines the internal measures of service efficiency with external measures of service effectiveness to meet customer satisfaction.

Kaplan and Norton[5] proposed that measuring performance should be done by using multiple measures that cover the following:

(i) **Financial performance:** Relevant to investor and shareholders which shows profits and losses and revenue, its growth, etc

(ii) **Customer satisfaction:** The way our customers perceive our services

(iii) **Internal business process:** How efficient we are, covering aspects of cost

(iv) **Employee and organization innovation and learning:** How do we continuously improve, bring new services and add value to our customers.

Table 10.1 shows a typical balance score card for an IT Services company. Given all these performance measures the company has to choose the best one reflecting their current state and can help taking them to future state.

Table 10.1   Balance score card for an IT Services company

BSC measures	Financial	Customer measure	Internal performance	Employee and organization innovation and learning
Typical indicators	Financial success in achieving strategic goals	Customer satisfaction	Efficiency, projects completion within time and budget	Employee utilization, satisfaction, attrition, innovations ideas gathered/employee
Measurement index	Revenue, profit, EVA, unit revenue, new contract signed, order value or largest order, % of large orders, order back log for execution, lost order	Customer sat index (survey or feedback), repeat orders, growth of revenue from same customer, referenciability of the customer	Process benchmark On time project delivery, cost per employee, service quality, MTTR (mean time to restore)	New patent submitted, employee satisfaction index, attrition %, employee survey conducted by independent groups, employee skill levels/certification, Number of suggestions per employee, learning time for new employees

Note: These measures will be different at different stages of the organization growth and will also depend upon the size of the organization.

---

4. The Balanced scorecard Measures that Drive Performance by Robert S. Kaplan and David P. Norton, *Harvard Business Review*, January–February, 1992.

5. As above.

10.3.3 **Relationship between Various Performance Measure**

All these performance measures should not be seen in isolation, but they are interdependent and related. For each of these areas we will have to identify the measures that can be considered as Drivers (lead indicators) which influence Moderators (lag indicators) leading to outcomes. For example, if we are able to fulfill customer order in time and efficiently, (driver) it will lead to customer satisfaction (lag indicator) resulting into more customer order hence increased revenue and profitability. Similarly, employee satisfaction leads to better retention rate that will translate into growth in revenue for the enterprise. We will take this as our starting point for creating the performance measurement matrix for IT Services Enterprise, and detail out for every function.

10.3.4 **Aligning Performance Measurement in the Organization**

One of the important characteristic of any successful IT Services firm is that the performance measurement system is aligned across the organization from the top to bottom. If the company goal is to increase its profitability, every employee must know and work towards it. Accordingly, the performance measurement systems must be designed to cascade across the layers of the organization.

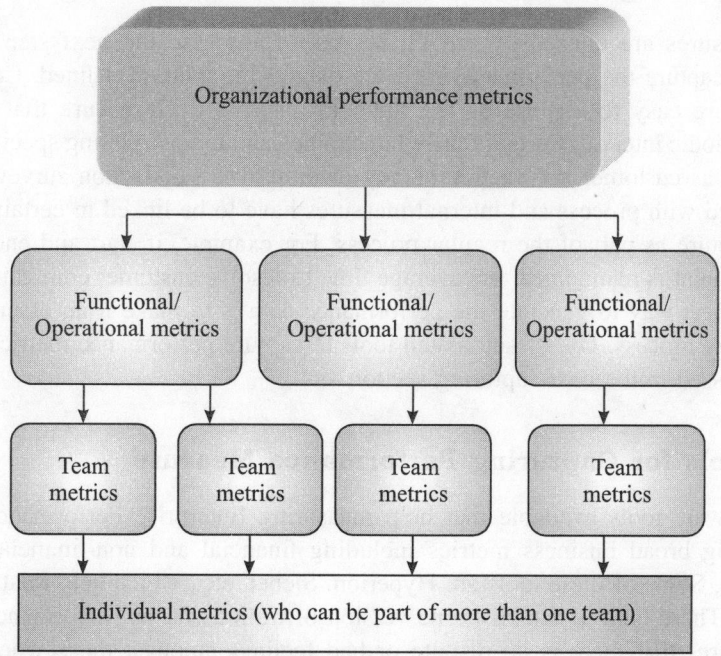

Figure 10.1 Alignment of metrics across the IT Services organization.

If we design the performance metrics bottoms up then there would be chances of lack of alignment and lack of focus towards the overall organizational goals. The problem with bottom up measurement is that it tends to emphasis on what can be measured against what should be measured. While strategic metrics define long term objectives, the operational metrics have to focus on short term objectives. For example, hiring fast may be an operational metric, but hiring the right quality and in time a strategic metrics. Alignment ensures that there is no interdepartmental disputes and no working of cross purpose to each other. Alignment is not just mathematical distribution of numbers amongst departments and functions, but deep thinking interpretation and proportional distribution between various metric levels.

As we have discussed earlier all metrics should be developed using a balance score card approach.

10.4 Measuring Performance

Once the performance measures are defined and aligned they need to be measured and monitored. The achievements must be compared against the target set. The measurement of performance must be translated to each and every processes being followed in the organization. In other chapters we have talked about the key processes for every functions and measurement of their effectiveness must be ensured. The next step would be to find how and where the data will come from at what frequency.

10.4.1 Capturing Performance Measures Results

Whatever measures are chosen by the IT Services Enterprise the next step is to devise a mechanism to capture the performance measure data at the interval defined. Certain measures like financial are easy to capture as the financial process cycle ensure that these data are available at periodic interval. Certain others have to be captured by running specifically designed processes such as customer satisfaction survey or employee satisfaction survey. Certain other measures related with process and internal measures have to be linked in certain way that they are easy to capture as part of the regular process. For example, if start and end time of every customer complaint is maintained, the average time to resolve customer complaint can be easily captured. The best way to generate the performance data is to make it an essential step of the services delivery process. Use of automated tools to capture performance metrics are advisable. They are discussed in the next capturing section.

10.4.2 Tools for Capturing Performance Measure

There are software tools available that help measuring Enterprise Performance Management (EPM) covering broad business metrics including financial and non-financial, tangible and intangible ones. Some of these tools are Hyperion, Siebel, etc., which help relating targets with achievements. These help to establish one version of truth as far as performance measurement goes, and ensures that there is no dispute or bad feelings amongst those who are measuring performance, and those who are being measured. Enterprise Performance Management Solution for SAP is one such solution that covers financial and commercial performance across the entire business. It has features such as data management, data analysis, reporting, tracking risk and compliance issues which help in planning, budgeting and forecasting.

With these tools ITSE companies can:

(i) translate strategic goals into tactical execution

(ii) better manage business risk

(iii) have a better ability to monitor strategies

(iv) enable more insightful, faster decision making

(v) drive greater connection between the finance and IT departments

(vi) conduct integrated planning and forecasting, tied to results

(vii) gain consistent definition and model of the key drivers of current and future value

10.5 Driving Performance

Good performance does not happen automatically for the leaders of the IT Services organization. Also, it is easy to preach than practice, and therefore, the leaders at any level of the organization must act as a role model to show that their acts are in consonance with the overall organization goals. The worst part of performance management is to stop at measuring and not driving the performance. Metrics can only inform what is going on, ultimately someone has to act. It is like installing CCTV camera at critical locations where terrorist may strike, but not able to watch the suspicious movement and act accordingly. For example, a post fact view is too painful[6], and costs dearly to the organization, individuals as well as to the nation!

Driving for performance is a journey from where the organization is and where it want to be. By far this is the most difficult part of the performance management program.

Importance of performance reviews

Leading ITSEs give a lot of emphasis on performance review of teams and monitoring progress. Whether it involves the review of sales pipeline or delivery performance of the IT Services delivery, reviews are a way of life where the team presents the progress, shares constraints and seeks support. IT Services team, as we have explained in earlier chapters, works at several location (including client offices) and at times, work from home. It is the regular and rigorous review that helps to keep the team know, what progress is taking place or what road block is being encountered. The cycle of the team review may vary from daily meeting to weekly, monthly, and quarterly reviews. The larger is the interval of review, higher the level at which the review meeting will take place, and larger would be the spread of the review and lesser detailed would be the content. For example, a small team may meet at the end of everyday to review the daily operational performance, whereas the entire business unit may be reviewed by the CEO one a month or by management board once a quarter.

We have described the content and need of dashboards that are used as a means to convey the progress in addition to customized presentation for senior management reviews.

Review meetings also help to enhance communication amongst all participants. Social networking sites deployed within the ITSE also help in sharing progress and becoming a key milestone without a formal meeting.

---

6. While writing this chapter a bomb blast in Central Delhi by unnamed terrorist group killed so many innocent lives and crippled many others. Lot of debate happened of non-existent/non-functional CCTV camera, but the real issue was, the question to think about, is there anyone watching them to prevent any such attack?

Most reviews in Global ITSEs happen on conference call or video calls which are expensive and are held at predetermined times, intervals and participant lists. Decisions taken are recorded and actions against individual are monitored at regular intervals.

10.5.1 Drivers and Blockers of Performance

This is matter of several researches to identify the factors that drive and those which block the performance. These are the softer factors of organization, culture and human behaviour that fall under this category.

Drivers of performance constitute several factors such as:

(i) **Customer orientation:** By far, the most important driver to enhance performance is to create a culture of customer orientation and sensitivity for any IT Services Enterprise to be successful.

(ii) **Ease of decision making:** In services situation lack of decision-making and delay is a sure recipe of underperformance

(iii) **Accountability and responsibility:** Unless there is clarity as to who is accountable and who is responsible for a particular activity, good performance cannot be achieved

(iv) **Team work:** Services is a team game which cannot succeed if the players are not supporting each other and come to rescue if one part of the team is in trouble.

(v) **Spirit of innovation:** It helps to make continuous improvement

(vi) **Taking calculated risk and ability to contain it:** In services situation, the growth requirements will demand tweaking the business model or imbibing new technology for which the delivery team may not be fully prepared. A noted entrepreneur of IT Industry in India would always throw challenge to the delivery team to perform and bring results under constraints and support them to take risks.

(vii) **Fairness of reward system:** One of the important reason to have good performance measurement system is to ensure the fairness of reward in the services team.

In comparison the list of blockers is pretty long. While the reverse of all the drivers will easily qualify to be the blockers the most prominent blockers are as follows:

(i) **Internal rivalries amongst departments and individuals:** Competition is encouraged in the organization, but it should not end up fighting internal teams or departments.

(ii) **Bureaucracy or dictatorship:** This relates to style of working and culture within the organization. As the IT Services company become large they tend to be bureaucratic. In small and mid-sized companies, the authority and decision-making is concentrated in a few people, this leads to dictatorial style of working.

(iii) **Lack of trust:** This is frequently sighted reason by non-performing companies. The trust flows from top and the lack of it is manifested when there is too much of supervision or micro management. In contrast with reposing trust comes responsibility that the employees should show. For example, if salary is deducted when someone comes late shows lack of trust by the employer, and making personal calls throughout the day using office phones or visiting social networking sites during office hours by the employees is sign of lack of responsibility. Both impair driving high performance culture.

(iv) **Lack of communication of vision:** Lack of communication of the firms vision and long-term goals is a major blocker for higher level of performance. Unless every individual is able to see and measure his/her contribution towards the overall organizational goals, superior performance will not come.

(v) **Culture of performance:** This relates to the organization culture built over several years. This also is a result of quality of people hired in the organization, reward and punishment system, openness to take risk and role models being played by the leaders.

10.5.2 Driving Individual Performance

Success of services enterprise depends on the success of the individuals. It is no wonder that individual performance is meticulously measured in IT Service Enterprise, and key performers are rewarded. Ulrich[7], in his seminal article mentions about Individual *Dignity Entitlement* developed by Motorola which uses a set of six areas that drives the individual performance. A brief summary of these drivers are as follows:

(i) Meaningfulness of job contributing towards success of the enterprise

(ii) Behaviour and knowledge to be successful

(iii) Training available to upgrade skills

(iv) Having a detailed career plan that is under action

(v) Regular feedback to improve performance

(vi) Care for the employees preferences

Milnor[8] opines that while 80% of the human capital metrics are standard, the remaining 20% should be customized to suit the organization type and culture. The standards human capital matrices fall under the heading attraction, retention, development and motivation where as the customized one should focus on measuring those initiatives that the organization takes for a particular purpose. All these metrics should be related with the organization goals and strategy and should be detailed and cascaded down to the people who are performing these activities. For example, if an organization has taken an initiative of talent acquisition then it must be detailed out to the levels of how many offers were made to a particular B-school (or any other place) and how many of those were accepted or rejected.

10.6 Use of Templates and Dashboards

Templates and dashboards serve the unique purpose to document and present the performance measures. In Table 10.2, a sample performance measure template and in Table 10.3 a management

---

7. Ulrich, D. (1997). Measuring human resources: An overview of practice and a prescription for results. Human Resource Management, Fall 1997, Vol. 36, No. 3, pp. 321–335 Q 1997 John Wiley & Sons, Inc.

8. Numbers That Count: Driving Enterprise Performance Through Human Capital Metrics, By RJ Milnor, June 2, 2011, Human Capital Management, White Papers & Research.

reporting dashboard of performance measure are shown. While there will one dashboard for the entire organization (or its units), every function or project team can have its own dashboard.

There will be several measurement templates, all of which will be feeding the data into the dashboard. The automation tools as described in 10.4.2 if used in the IT Services Enterprise, will be able to capture the template as well as produce the dashboard as desired.

Table 10.2 Performance measurement metrics template

Name of the metrics: New order booking	**Responsibility:** Sales manager	**Reviewer:** VP sales
Target set by: CEO	**Target:** 3 million/year	**Last review:** 30 June 20xx
Reasons of measurement: Every sales manager is required to carry a sales target		
Measurement definition: The value of order booked by the sales manager, if more than one sales manager is involved then the value will be proportionally divided based on the efforts.		
Progress or gap Analysis: Achieved 1 million in first six months, balance 2 million		**Source of data:** Monthly sales report
Tracking/Reporting responsibility: Sales operations analyst	**Review frequency:** Weekly	**Unit of measure:** Rupees

Table 10.3 Performance measure dash board as on date

Area	Process	Measure	Current results	Target	Gap	Steps for improvement
Financial	New order booking	Total orders value	1 million	3 million	2 million	Improve lead conversion process
Customer	Delivery of service	Number of repeat orders	1	10	9	Improve customer service
Internal	Employee provisioning	Overhead cost per employee	10 K	7 K	3 K	Improve process efficiency
Innovation	Innovation management process	Number of suggestions submitted/per employee	0.2	2	1.8	Training and cross-functional teaming

10.6.1 Review of Dashboards

The review of dashboard is an important activity for the management to drive performance. These reviews should be conducted as frequently, atleast once in a month. The dashboard review helps to educate a team about current effectiveness of the efforts being made and identify areas for improvements. Dashboards and their review helps build credibility amongst the team and everyone is able to clearly see where they stand. It also helps to allocate resources, provide incentives, rewards and reprimands to non-performers.

10.6.2 Visual Display of Achievements

IT Services Enterprise use automated tools to capture performance data and variance against the target. However, using visual display of achievements gives more visibility and charges up people for action. These targets and performance measure can be make part of intranet site pages.

10.6.3 Mathematics of Target Setting

We have discussed in the earlier section of how performance measures should be driven top down and aligned across the organization, right upto every individual as far as possible. The word *as far as possible* is used to make the performance management system practical and simple. In certain job roles where the output is easy to define and the output is routine in nature it should be left at that. The effort to define, link and measure will too complicate and will cost too much without any significant benefits. For example lines of code per day by a software coding programmer or no of function points in case software development have become standard measures which can be straight away adopted by development services team.

But most other roles, especially that in the business management functions, like marketing and sales, delivery management and providing services to the customer, targets must be defined in such a way that every individual knows how he/she will be measured and what is the mechanism by which the targets can be achieved. The following example for defining the sales team target and then breaking it into monthly and weekly target will help understand the process:

(a) An IT Services company wants to achieve ₹30 million of revenue in a particular year. This is the strategic target.

(b) Assumption 1: In the past the company was able to bag orders with average size of ₹3 million.

(c) Number of orders required in a year: $\frac{a}{b}$ i.e. $\frac{30}{3}$ = 10 orders

(d) Assumption 2: The past experience shows that lost order percentage was about 50%, i.e. for every two proposals submitted for IT Services the company could convert only one.

(e) Number of proposals to be submitted in a year for achieving the target: c/d, i.e. 10/0.5 = 20 proposals to be submitted

(f) In the past customers purchase used to be in the ratio of 20, 20, 25, 35% in quarter 1, 2, 3 and 4 respectively.

Hence, number of proposals to be submitted every quarter would be

Quarter 1 = 0.2 × e = 4, Quarter 2 = 0.2 × e = 4,
Quarter 3 = 0.25 × e = 5, Quarter 4 = 0.35 × e = 7, Total 20 proposals

(g) Suppose the past data of the company tells that out of every 2 customer requirements only one was found to be a qualified lead of customer requirement where ultimately the proposal of services were asked for. So using this assumption one can calculate number of leads as follows: i.e. Qualified leads = f × 2

Quarter 1 = 4 × 2 = 8, Quarter 2 = 4 × 2 = 8,
Quarter 3 = 5 × 2 = 10, Quarter 4 = 7 × 2 = 14

Total 40 qualified leads are required to be worked by the sales team in a year.

(h) Keeping scope for errors and assumptions: If the sales team has to achieve its target and exceed, it must keep scope for errors and assumptions. So considering 25% as the margin of errors the number of qualified leads required in the year becomes $1.25 \times g = 1.25 \times 40 = 50$ leads. Giving 2 weeks in a year as holidays this means the team must generate one lead per week and one order per month.

(i) So the target would be
  (i) Number of leads/week: 1,
  (ii) Number of order per month: 1
  (iii) Average order value: 3 Million Rupees

In case the order value is small or large the target will be accordingly adjusted.

So, if a sales person is not able to generate one qualified lead per week or four qualified leads per month he is unlikely to achieve his sales target.

This is a simple mechanism to show how yearly objectives can be further broken into weekly or monthly targets for ease of measurement. Similar approach can be taken for any other function or process. In the interest of compactness of the book we have not taken other examples.

10.7   Reasons of Failure to Drive Performance

One must consider some points of failure while executing performance management system and driving performance. Some of the salient points must be considered as follows:

  (i) Lack of alignment and cascading of organization goals with every department, function and individual performance.
  (ii) Lack of communication and understanding of the goals by the employees.
  (iii) Complex process of goals and measurement. Confusion about why such a goal has been assigned. Too many or too little individual goals.
  (iv) Lack of ability, resources assignment for performing task.
  (v) Inadequate monitoring and measurement. Either too little that brings slackness or too much when the employees are only going from one review, to other review, and busy preparing performance reports!
  (vi) Faulty reward and recognition. Not rewarding those who do a good job and not punishing those whose performance is lagging.
  (vii) Obstacles if any, arising in performance is not identified and eliminated. If these obstacles are beyond control, a work around needs to be found out or target revised.
  (viii) Absence, delayed or inadequacy of feedback given on performance.
  (ix) Performance management not been ingrained in day-to-day management of people.
  (x) Culture of employee empowerment and care is lacking, therefore employees are unwilling to give their best.

10.8   Summary

We started our discussion of measurement of IT Services Enterprise performance with a comment that this is the tough part of management of ITSE. There are several measures that contradict and seem like cross purpose. For example, adding more value by doing extra work may seem opposite to its cost as well as efficiency. We presented in this chapter a framework to measure IT Services Enterprise performance that ensures both internal (efficiency) and external (effectiveness) perspective.

Apart from measuring, the chapter shows that driving the performance is a complex task. The following questions were answered:

(i) What are good IT Service measurements?

(ii) How do we measure IT Service effectiveness?

(iii) How to measure the effectiveness in the eyes of the customer?

The Performance Management and its challenges are also defined. Balanced score card approach for performance definition and measurement were used and a typical balance score card for an IT Services company has also been presented. We also drew relationship between various performance measures. The ways to align performance measurement in the organization has also been presented.

Then the ways to measure performance and the ways to capture performance measures were discussed using some prominently used tools. These tools help in translate strategic goals into tactical execution, managing business risk and monitor strategies.

The steps for driving performance are then discussed. Drivers and blockers of performance in any ITSE are also discussed, in detail.

Driving performance in ITSE firm has large bearing on individual performance. Success of services enterprise depends on the success of the individuals and we used individual dignity entitlement developed by Motorola to explain it further.

The chapter underlines that templates and dashboards serve the unique purpose to document and present the performance measures. For this purpose a sample performance measure template was presented. These dashboards must be reviewed periodically. Making the team and high performance achievements visual, encourages more and more people to aspire for better performance.

In a unique effort, the mathematics of target setting was discussed with an example. Finally we brought out reasons of failure to drive performance and what actions should be taken to prevent them.

Review Questions

10.1 Why it is tough to measure performance of an ITSE?

10.2 Why does the author say that driving the performance is a complex task?

10.3 What are good IT Service measurements?

10.4 How do we measure IT Service effectiveness?

10.5 How do we measure how good we are in the eyes of the customer?

10.6 Define performance management and its challenges. What method will you use for ITSE performance measurement?

10.7 Translate a balanced score card approach for an IT Services company measurement.

10.8 How do we capture performance measures results? What are some prominently used tools and what benefits they give?

10.9 What are the drivers and blockers of performance in any ITSE?

10.10 What is the need of templates and dashboards in measuring and monitoring performance of an ITSE?

10.11 Define mathematics of an ITSE performance target setting. Set targets of a firm that wants to make a revenue of 10 million dollars for average deal size of 500,000 and success rate of 1:10 (initial leads to confirmed order). Make other suitable assumptions for the ITSE firm.

10.12 What are the reasons of failure to drive performance and what actions should be taken to prevent them?

Suggested Further Reading

Kaplan, R. and Norton, D., "The balanced scorecard—Measures that drive performance." *Harvard Business Review*, January–February, 1992, p. 71–29.

McCunn, P., The Balanced Scorecard: The Eleventh Commandment, *Management Accounting*, 1998, p. 34–36.

Neely, A., Richards, H., Mills, J., Platts, K. and Bourne, M. (1997) Designing Performance Measures: A Structured Approach, *International Journal of Operations & Production Management*, Vol. 17, Issue II, p. 1131–1152.

Dresner, Howard, *The Performance Management Revolution: Business Results Through Insight and Action*, 2007.

Adding Value Through Human Resources: Reorienting Human Resource Measurement to Drive Business Performance, Yeung, Arthur K. and Berman, Bob, *Human Resource Management*, Fall 1997, Vol. 36, No. 3, pp. 321–335 Q 1997 John Wiley & Sons, Inc.

Davenport, Thomas H. and Beck, J.C., The Attention Economy—Understanding the New Currency of Business, *Harvard Business School Press*, Boston, 2001.

Chapter 11

Creating a Winning
IT Services Team

*Teamwork is the ability to work together toward a common vision. The ability to direct
individual accomplishments toward organizational objectives. It is the fuel that allows
common people to attain uncommon results.*

—Andrew Carnegie

11.1 Introduction

No IT Services book is complete without the discussion on the characteristics of a winning
team. Services that too related with IT is delivered through teams. They come in various shapes
and sizes, have different characteristics and require meticulous preparation, development and
management. Being constituted across land boundaries, languages and cultures these challenges
become much more interesting as well as enriching to face. IT Services team comprise of
large number of knowledge workers (in fact all of them), all of them are ambitious, smart and
intelligent variety. Yet they are also human beings who are driven by needs for making their
life healthy, desire accolades and praise and need to be told when they run astray.

We have devoted this chapter to define characteristics of winning teams in IT Services
Enterprises. Granted that these teams will also be bound by the culture of the organization
and the policies thereof, yet it is necessary to build unique abilities and synergies in sub teams
across the organization. We would like to underline the precautions required and endeavour to
be made to give the right environment so that these teams may flourish and bring laurels to the
enterprise.

Competitive games and sports is one example where the teams bring success to the
organization they represent. It could be a club, sports body, company or a state. While the team
performs on the ground, their performance is largely dependent on the policies and the practices
of their owning body, something that affects before or after the game. It may start from the
selection process, environment for their training and development, and finally, the reward and
recognition they bring. If their performance on the ground has been good or bad, the impact of
all these external factors cannot be undermined.

So is the case of IT Services team. They typically work closer to the customer, and at
times, the customer may be more aware of their capabilities than their managers sitting at the
corporate headquarters. Their focus is towards the current problem that the customer is facing

151

and the least they should worry about whether their salary cheque is getting credited on time or not! The IT Service teams command and control structure is totally different than a typical functional command and control structure. In addition there will be people (and such people will be many) who would work on multiple teams throughout the year because their skills are required by different groups at different points in time. In this chapter we will discuss the issues like

 (i) What would motivate these individual contributors?

 (ii) How can the organization take care of their aspirations?

 (iii) How can we get all teams to work for the common organizational goals?

These are a few questions that this chapter will attempt to answer by simply underlining what are the types of team and what are their winning characteristics.

This chapter is not intended to be a treatise on team building theory or extensive discussion on human motivation aspects. These are the subjects well-discussed in thousands of books and described endlessly. Our attempt is to pick up some of the key ideas and interpret them for teams for IT Services Enterprise. These ideas would not be just based on secondary research but also on first hand experience of building and developing various types of successful teams for variety of IT Services organization. This is an interesting subject which can go on forever, but we will resist our temptation and limit our discussion to this chapter.

11.2   What is a Team?

As defined by Cohen and Bailey[1], a team is a collection of individuals who are interdependent in their task, who share responsibilities for an outcome and see themselves as well as by others as an entity within larger body like organization unit, or a corporation. The team is defined by several characteristics that make it successful. However, it also has to perform within the boundary of the firm hence must get directed and influenced by the larger approach and culture of the firm.

11.2.1   Type of Teams in a IT Services Enterprise

Most IT Services Enterprise are global in nature and comprise of multi-location team. They possess varied technical skills and work on wide ranging projects for diverse customers. Unlike the manufacturing or physical services (like logistics, healthcare or hospitality, etc.) their customers and partners can come from many nationalities, located in different time zones and with cultural differences. To run a successful ITSE and becoming successful in such enterprise one must know what types of team they may be part of, what are the unique characteristics and how to bring the best out of each of them.

For the simplicity's sake we have categorised the ITSE teams into four major internal teams and two external teams. The four internal teams are:

---

1. What makes Teams work: Group effectiveness Research from the shop floor to the executive suite, Susan G Cohen, Diane E Bailey , University of southern California, Journal of Management 1997, Vol 23, No. 3, 239–290.

(i) **Client facing team:** Includes sales, marketing, business development, account management or engagement management.

(ii) **Support team:** This includes support teams that enable operations of the ITSE. These are typically addressed by the functions such as Human Resources, recruitment, finance (including cost and pricing), quality management, infrastructure management (including IT infrastructure), research and development and others.

(iii) **Delivery team:** They are like the production unit of the manufacturing firms and undertake services task for the customer.

(iv) **Management team:** The team comprising of managers who are closer to planning and strategy formulation, especially the senior managers. They also have to work as a team for the common objectives of the enterprise and ensure that conflicts, if any, between various sub-teams are resolved.

The external teams generally fall under two categories:

(i) *Subcontractor teams:* ITSE engages large number of full or part time contractors to work on projects and assignments of various natures. In front of the customer they ultimately they have to be seen and working like the ITSE team in all respect though their payroll may be coming from the subcontractor firm. A winning team combination includes a significant role from the subcontractor firms. We have discussed some aspects of such team later in Section 11.2.2.

(ii) *Client/Customer IT team:* IT Services are delivered in tandem by partnering the client or customer IT team. Not only they provide the client business knowledge, but are also the bridge between the actual users and the ITSE team. Typically, these people may come from the CIO organization of the client or IT champions that are part of the business units.

A winning ITSE team has to consider all these teams to work towards a common goals and objectives as shown in Figure 11.1.

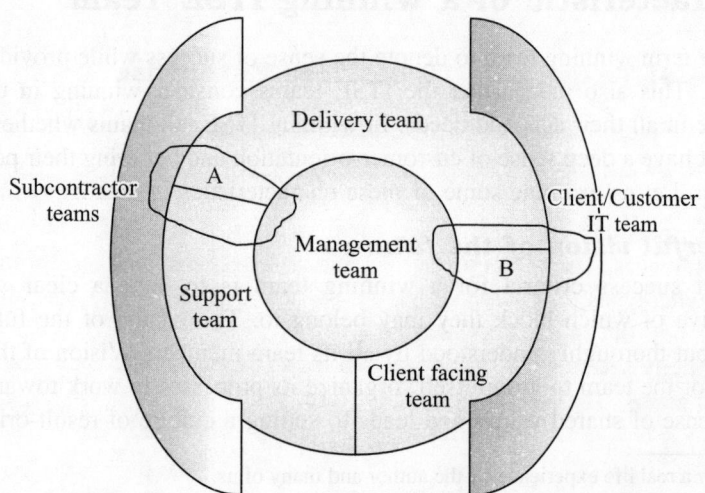

Figure 11.1 Various teams in an IT Services Enterprise.

A and B are interface zone that requires more care as explained in the next section.

11.2.2 Managing Interface Zones

These are the zones were people from various organization have to get together towards the common objective of the end customer. There may be a differences of opinion, issues that may have commercial compulsions or clash of ego. Remember the way manufacturing enterprise have long realised that the competition is not between the two front running brands, but the entire supply chain, in the similar manner for IT Services the entire service delivery chain has to work towards the end objective of the end consumer for which the services are being provided for. For example, a mobile phone user calls for activating his/her new 3G services to the call centre of prominent telecom operator. The call centre may be outsourced to one of the BPO company, who in turn may have dedicated their IT infrastructure to yet another hardware and networking company. The people sitting on the call centre desk may belong to another manpower staffing company. Given all these multiple layers of IT services chain (and it is most common these days), if each member of the delivery chain is enthused, empowered and interested in resolving the customer problem, the customer satisfaction would automatically come. However, if persons from the services delivery chain, hide under contractual boundaries, limit their efforts to routine processes and pass the problem to other department or unit, the customer satisfaction and care will suffer[2].

World class ITSE ensure that the colour or logo of their employee or sub contractor badge does not come in the way of end-customer service. They frequently resort to team building exercise, brainstorming sessions, process benchmarking across the services delivery chain, and ensure that the end customer services are not compromised. In case a person or team is found to be doing excellent work they are recognized and rewarded as if they are a part of the front ending organization[3].

11.3 Characteristic of a Winning ITSE Team

We are using the term winning team to denote the sense of success while providing the services to the customer. This also means that the ITSE teams consider winning in the market as a necessary feature in all their acts and deeds. In winning ITSE, all teams whether they are client facing or support have a deep sense of customer-orientation and bettering their performance than their competition. Let us examine some of these characteristics in detail:

Have a powerful vision of the future

One of the first success criteria for a winning team is to have a clear vision for their future, irrespective of which block they may belong to. This vision of the future is not only communicated, but thoroughly understood by all its team members. Vision of the future acts as a driving force for the team to group itself; organize its processes to work towards achieving it. It imbibes the sense of shared values and leads to setting a culture of result-orientation.

---

2. It is incidentally a real life experience by the author and many of us.
3. This too is a real-life experience, the name of the companies are not shared here but their services are well known.

The role of the leader is precisely to create a vision and lead people towards achieving it. Leaders have larger responsibility to also create the team's focus towards the client success. Their task of delegating, empowering, coaching and supporting team remains. The leader should encourage team to capitalize on their strengths rather than micro manage them. By creating a positive working environment based on trust, transparency, and with genuine efforts towards work-life balance, the leader can instil a sense of shared values around what is important for the organization and usher a work culture that ultimately leads to superior results.

Define roles and responsibilities and measurement system

In order to work towards achieving the vision, each member of the team must know what he/she is expected to do, and how his/her performance will be measured. It need not be sometimes individual measurements and can be a team measurement, through the former is always better to have and can also eliminate ambiguity.

Adequate resources, relevant training and necessary tools to perform

A winning team is always adequately staffed, not more not less, has all the capabilities and preparation to perform the task and tools.

Has a culture of services and cooperation between them

This takes to build over time and a consequence of investment leaders make right from the beginning of the team formation. A poor culture is difficult to correct and good one always is contagious in nature. When a new person joins the team he/she starts behaving like one already in practice.

A deep study by Chatman on industry and organization culture confluence suggested that culture of a firm is influenced by the industry culture. In IT Services industry, direct supervision is more difficult as many people will work independently at the off site locations with the client organization. (Magnet, 1993; Normann, 1984). IT Services sector relies heavily on social control mechanisms, such as cultural values, to direct members' actions (O'Reilly, 1989).

The elements of organizational culture range from fundamental assumptions through values and behavioural norms to actual patterns of behaviour (Rousseau, 1990). Values typically act as the defining elements of a culture, and norms, symbols, rituals, and other cultural activities revolve around them (Enz, 1988). When the members of a social unit share values, an organizational culture or value system can be said to exist (Weiner, 1988). Chatman further define elements of organization culture by seven dimensions: innovation, stability, and respect for people, outcome orientation, detail orientation, team orientation, and aggressiveness ITSE leaders must take advantages of there concepts while creating a suitable culture in their organization.

Promote continuous learning

One of the important characteristics of Successful IT Services team is that they learn as they go along the path of growth. Learning organization is a term credited to Peter Senge in his widely read book called Fifth Discipline (1990). A learning organization increases its values, and derives competitive advantage from, continuing learning, both individual and at team/organization level. This is achieved through systems thinking, personal mastery, mental models, shared vision, and team learning. All these characteristics demonstrate their relevance to IT Services Enterprise that has to incessantly improve and innovate their services. In addition, before the team transform into a learning team, every individual has to go through a personal transformation process.

The theory of double-loop learning proposed by Chris Argyris is also useful to ingrain the learning by questioning and testing rigorously. By the process of double loop learning, managers can constantly challenge employees to think creatively about the needs of the organization. More concepts and discussion about managing learning and promoting knowledge management is dealt in Chapter 11.

Drive team for performance

A necessary characteristic of a winning team is their drive for performance. Be it sales or delivery they have to be focussed to achieve their objectives in the stipulated time.

Give opportunities and impetus for growth for team members

ITSE teams typically comprise of large number of young professionals. In the early part of their life they want to build their future and grow. So a team (or ITSE) that does not provide opportunities and impetus to grow will not be able to hold such budding professionals for long, and thereafter, the team will suffer.

Team must have energy and resilience

They should also create a team that has high energy and resilience to deal with deadlines and customer demands. Most high performer want to take extra work that enthuses them, enables them to be creative and display their talent. They want to run an extra mile to please the customer and the team leader must encourage creating such an environment with the team. Most strong teams become stronger when faced with problems or adversity.

Empower the team

In the context of IT Services virtual working is becoming an increasing norm (thanks to the technology). In such situation unless the team member is empowered, enthused and acts responsibly, the results would not come. So, it is all the more necessary to teach them how to do things rather than directing every step. By allowing clear cut responsibilities providing the necessary resources and discretion the team can be a self-directed team. Such an empowered and self-directed team develops a clear, explicit and mutually agreed-upon approach. They also repeatedly examine the mechanics whether it is working well. When they find areas of improvement, they just work towards it.

Spread the positivity all around

More often, the services team will face tough situations when the customer will demand more and the team will find lacking. By creating a positive team atmosphere where trust and openness is granted will help. This will increase commitment and involvements from the team. When there is positivity then creativity, risk taking, supporting each other comes naturally. Make sure that the atmosphere breeds trust which is the most important ingredient as without which nothing will ever work in ITSE. There should be informal, comfortable, relaxed atmosphere where the fun and laughter sustains them without any obvious tensions.

11.4 Managing People in Services Organizations

It is a well-known fact that a manager success depends on his people or team. He cannot be successful unless he develops superior people management practices. Lacking this ability will lead to project failure. ITSE is full of intelligent and smart people, but many of them lack the ability of managing people. Most of them would have spend years in technical roles, and suddenly, they become team leader at relatively young age as compared to other industries. In such a situation, their lack of preparation for managing people impacts team performance. Many organizations, therefore bifurcate the technical task management and people management responsibilities and assign the later to slightly more matured managers. Yet the problem remains as ITSE needs more and more good people managers as their size is growing.

All prospective people managers must read several books[4], articles and case studies related with human aspects of management and imbibe best practices in their profile. Understanding of human psychology, some of the proven framework[5] must be used in people management situation. In managing ITSE Enterprise, the soft skills are required in much greater proportion

Given the fact that most ITSE team would have members from varied background, high gender diversity and cultural orientation, the role of people management becomes very important. Working with people from different countries needs some more understanding and preparation. Despite temptation to write more on this subject, we will just summarize here some of the best practices of people management relevant to ITSE, and encourage readers to dig deeper in this fascinating subject by going through the classical literature on this topic.

Some of the people management best practices are as follows:

(i) While managing IT Services team it is proven that use of fewer and better people is much better than having large team. In the case of former you may have to pay more salaries to good people, but that is the price you pay for superior performance.

(ii) While assigning the work, if we consider individual capabilities and motivations the results would be far more superior.

(iii) In any high performing team, there are star performers and some team players. The most intelligent ones sometimes are too critical and self-centred. These people should be either corrected or avoided. The team should be balanced.

(iv) Good managers show a consistency of behaviour, respect to individuals, involve everyone in the decision-making, and honestly tell what is going right or wrong in the team[6].

(v) A good people manager follows a simple principle, motivate, educate, facilitate and eliminate. Motivate to those who are capable and independent, educate the newcomers, facilitate the doers with resources and eliminate who are not falling in line with the team goals.

(vi) Finally, get rid of people who do not work well with the team, without delay. Read and contemplate SALT 11.1 to understand what needs to be done if a team has undesired characteristics.

SALT 11.1: The Undesired characteristics of team member.

(i) Tommy is the most intelligent guy of the group. Put him in any situation and he will come back with a good answer. Customers like him and superiors like him the most. But when he is in a meeting no one else would speak, as he will always cut them short with a better answer.

---

4. Such as "How to win friends and influence people" by Dale Carnegie

5. *Situational Leadership Theory*, Paul Hersey and Ken Blanchard Hersey, P. (1985). The situational leader, New York, NY: Warner Books

6. Sommerville, Ian, Software Engineering, Chapter 25, Addison Wesley; 9th ed., 2006.

(ii) Johnny is the critique of the team, the idea shooter who is great in finding fault and rightfully so as most of his observations and bang on the point. Bring him in the team discussion and the atmosphere will get degenerated.

(iii) Monny is the darling of the group. She always performs a given task without a murmur. She also stays late, comes early and skips lunch many days in a month to finish the urgent and pressing task given by her superiors and peers.

(iv) Sonny is the bully of the team. Recently promoted as deputy team leader has all the ingredient of becoming the next Dictator of Middle East kingdom. But he gets the work done fast and with quality. His mangers like him and want him to be promoted as a full fledged leader.

(v) Bonny is the go-getter, always cheerful, cracking jokes and making the team environment lively. He is the connoisseur of team get together. Because of his good relationship he gets his work done by others and becomes part of success easily.

(vi) Nommy feels that knowledge is power. So she hordes them and in abundance. Only shares them with boss and only when it is absolutely necessary. She is most valuable and during her absence people run helter shelter as no one would have any information to perform the task.

There are the characteristics that the team leader must closely observe amongst the team members and apply corrective measures.

11.5 Develop Skills, Certification Performance Enhancement

Winning team is known for their abilities because that is the most important feature for their survival. The ITSE spend multiple initiatives to build capabilities of their team. By building skills and capabilities the ITSE team can carry out task efficiently and effectively. Since information technology is an ever changing field, some of these capabilities requires continuous refresh and rejuvenation. In addition to it, ITSE works on projects of different business domains that need to be understood by its people to be able to effectively appreciate customers' issues. In this section we will give a framework of developing and managing skills.

In short, the ITSE Enterprise has to have a three type of skills/capabilities in all its team members.

Technology skills

Specifically refers to the skills required for services being provided or supervised by the individual. It covers the IT related skills such as software development, Consulting, IT Architecture, and so on.

Business domain skills

All IT Services have be performed for customers who come from various businesses such as manufacturing, retail, health care, telecom etc. The generic skills of IT Services are tailored to suit specific requirements of these business domains.

Soft and other generic skills

It refers to those skills which are beyond technology and business domain, but refer to people management, team management, communication, program management, etc., and are generic in nature.

In fact, any individual has to move along all these dimensions over time as he/she is getting more and more experience as shown in Figure 11.2.

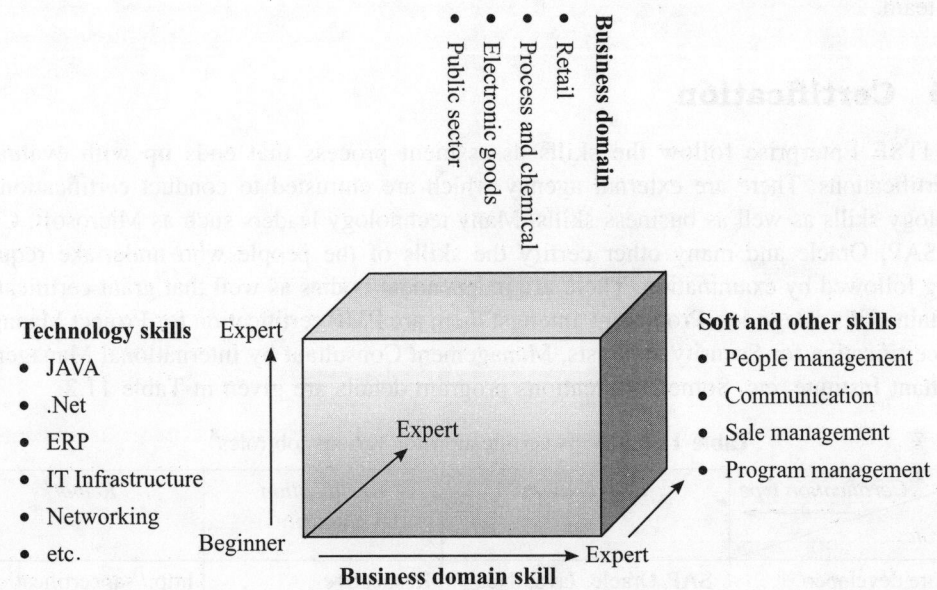

Figure 11.2 Skill/capabilities cube.

Depending on the role being performed by an individual the skills/capabilities require may be different and with different combinations. Table 11.1 gives some ideas of various job roles and desired skills and capabilities levels falling under these categories. For example, a Project manager may have medium capability in a particular technology, but must have high skill level on soft skills such as team management, process management and so on. On the other

Table 11.1 Skills and expertise levels summary for various job roles[7]

Skills type → Job roles in ITSE ↓	Technical	Domain	Soft skills
Software developer	High	Low	Low
Project manager	Medium	Medium	High
Sales and marketing	Medium	High	High
Delivery managers	High	Medium	High
Business managers	Low	Medium	High
Support team	High in their areas such as HR, Finance etc	Low	High and medium depending upon their function
Business consultants	High	High	Medium as they have to work with clients

7. Abridged list.

hand, a Business Consultant has to be very high on domain as well as the technology he is advocating, but may be medium on soft skills as consultants are normally individual contributors in the team.

11.6   Certification

Many ITSE Enterprise follow the skills assessment process that ends up with evaluation and certifications. There are external agency which are entrusted to conduct certifications on technology skills as well as business skills. Many technology leaders such as Microsoft, Cisco, IBM, SAP, Oracle and many other certify the skills of the people who undertake requisite training followed by examination. There are independent bodies as well that grant certifications for certain skills categories. Prominent amongst them are PMP certification for Project Managers, CISA certification for Security Analysts, Management Consultant by International Management Consultant Institute, etc. Some certifications program details are given in Table 11.2.

Table 11.2   Skills certification for various job roles[8]

Certification type / Job roles	Certification	Certification authority	Remarks
Software developer/ Technical specialist	SAP, Oracle, Java, .Net, CCNA, CISA, Cisco Certified Architect	Respective companies	http://sapcertification. info/news.php http://www.cisco.com http://education.oracle. com
Project manager	Certified associate in Project management (CAPM)® Project management professional (PMP)® Program management professional (PgMP)® New — PMI Agile Certified Practitioner (PMI-ACP)SM PMI Risk Management Professional (PMI-RMP)® PMI Scheduling Professional (PMI-SP)®	PMI institute	http://www.pmi.org/ Certification.aspx
Sales and marketing	Sales School certification	Various	
Service delivery managers	ITIL: Foundation, Intermediate, Expert and Master	United Kingdom's Office of Government Commerce (OGC)	http://www.itil-officialsite.com/home/ home.aspx
Business consultants	Certified management consultant	IMCI	http://www.icmci.org/

---

8. Abridged list

The important part of these certification programs is the support and encouragement provided by the organization to their staff members. All of them require devotion of additional hours, preparation and reasonable amount of examination fee which many cannot afford. If proper incentives are provided and is also used as necessary criteria for granting further progression then only the ITSE capabilities will increase through well-orchestrated certification programs. In addition, many leading ITSE firm develop their own certification program that is cost-effective as well as more tailored to suit its requirement better.

11.6.1 Maturity Assessment of People Practices

As software industry grew in last 30 years the processes of software development were standardised and capabilities were assessed by a Capability Maturity Model (CMM) proposed by leading universities and researchers.

In the same order, the people processes were also proposed to be assesses for its maturity levels by People CMM processes assessment model. People Capability Maturity Model (People CMM) is a proven set of human capital management practices that provides an organizational change model through an evolutionary framework based on a system of workforce practices[9]. People Capability Maturity Model (PCMM[10]) helps track evolutionary path of people process maturity into the stages of ad hoc, managed, defined, predictable, and optimized stages.

The People Capability Maturity Model (People CMM) framework enables ITSE firms to chart out a development course in people area. The details of these process is available in the widely read book by Curtis, Hefley and Miller.

Many leading ITSE firm success is largely due to the superior people practices. IBM, Infosys, Wipro, TCS, Cognizant and many other ISTE firms are known for people orientation and perhaps this is the reason of their resounding success. Many have adopted to get them assessed on PCMM levels and proudly display their levels in their company website.

11.7 Work Place Environment

Most IT Services companies have very large percentage of young employee population. Primarily due to the growing need and also because the younger minds are more amenable to pick up newer technology faster. Many ITSE have therefore created a campus like work place environment where there are places for recreation and fun along with work. Google is one such company that encourages several off-beat approach to create an environment that does not resemble stereotype offices with big halls and covered with standard small cubical or workstations. While creating the work place that looks informal is one such initiatives, ITSE firms have to think beyond this. The issues of diversity, small and nuclear families with small kids or aging parents, time wasted on long commutes and working at odd hours to address global customer requirements have taken a toll on the work-life balance issue of many employees in the ITSE firms. While most of the initiatives to manage their personal life have to come from

---

9. People Capability Maturity Model (P-CMM), 2nd ed.: Bill Curtis, Bill Hefley, Sally Miller, July 2009.

10. Further details can be obtained from PCMM official website http://www.sei.cmu.edu/cmmi/solutions/pcmm/

the employees themselves, supportive policies of working-from-home, maternity/paternity leave, short sabbaticals, part time working, free counselling on personal issues, etc., are some of the practices winning ITSE adopt with great results. ITSE firms who are oriented towards this ethos regularly participate in third party surveys of their employees and seek benefits from the objective feedback after such survey and studies. They also imbibe some of the practices and policies of the peer group without any hesitation as this is in their best interest.

11.8 Summary

This chapter is devoted to define characteristics of winning teams in IT Services Enterprises. The stark differences of ITSE team are also highlighted as they have to closely work with customer and partners many would join for short period of time, and then move onto different projects. ITSE team also join work remotely at times away from their office premises and away from the line of sight of their managers. In these situations, the issues like motivation, aspiration and alignment towards organizational goal becomes very important. In this chapter the key ideas are picked up and interpreted for teams of IT Services Enterprise.

The chapter begins with defining what is team and what are the types found in a typical ITSE firms. Since these teams will come from various organizations and will have different aspirations and objectives, one must consider aspects of managing Interface Zones.

World class ITSE ensure team building across the services delivery chain to ensure that the end customer services are not compromised.

Our next stop was to define the characteristic of a winning ITSE team. Having a powerful vision clear roles and responsibilities and measurement system are a few characteristics that were discussed. In addition, adequate resources, relevant training and necessary tools to perform along with culture of services and cooperation amongst team members was found important.

The aspects of managing people in services organizations were also looked at, which are somewhat unique given the nature of the ITSE work.

Next, the processes to develop skills, certification and ensuring performance enhancement were also discussed. A skills growth cube and table for assessment was also presented.

ITSE organization continuously assesses the maturity of their people practices. Use of People CMM processes assessment model was discussed.

Finally, the chapter argues whether ITSE should strive to make their organization the best place to work and ensure work life balance. The practices adopted by some of the winning ITSE in this respect was also discussed.

Review Questions

11.1 What are the characteristics of winning teams in IT Services Enterprises?

11.2 How ITSE teams are different than teams of other industries?

11.3 What are your prescriptions to manage Interface Zones of various team in a typical ITSE? Explain with a diagram and example.

11.4 What are your recommendations for managing people in IT Services organizations which are somewhat unique?

11.5 Describe the process of developing skills, certification and ensuring performance enhancement in an ITSE. Draw skill planning and management cube.

11.6 How does ITSE organization assesses the maturity of their people practices? What are your recommendations? Give examples from ITSE firms who have adopted this assessment and what results they have obtained.

11.7 How can ITSE strive to make their organization the best place to work and ensure work life balance? Do you think it is important and if yes for what end results?

Suggested Further Reading

Douglas MacGregor, *The Wisdom of Teams*, Kaztenbach and Smith

Magnet, M., Good news for the service economy, *Fortune*, 127(9), 1993, pp. 46–52.

Normann, R., *Service Management: Strategy and Leadership in Service Businesses*, New York: Wiley, 1984.

O'Reilly, C., Corporations, culture, and commitment: Motivation and social control in organizations, *California Management Review*, Vol. **31**, 1989, pp. 9–25.

Rousseau, D., Quantitative Assessment of Organizational Culture: The Case for Multiple Measures, B. Schneider (Ed.), Frontiers in industrial and organizational psychology, Vol. **3**, 1990, pp. 153–192, San Francisco: Jossey Bass.

Weiner, Y., Forms of Value System: A Focus on Organizational Effectiveness and Cultural Change and Maintenance, *Academy of Management Review*, Vol. **13**, 1988, pp. 534–545.

Enz, C., The Role of Value Congruity in Intraorganizational Power, *Administrative Science Quarterly*, Vol. **33**, 1982, pp. 284–304, Freeman, J.

Senge, P., *The Fifth Discipline*, New York, Doubleday, 1990.

Chapter 12

Managing Knowledge, Innovation and Creating a Learning Organization

> *Business has only two functions—marketing and innovation*
> —Milan Kundera

12.1 Introduction

ITSE firms growth and survival depends on continuous innovation and managing the re-use of the intellectual capital through a robust process of knowledge management. In this chapter, we will discuss why this is an important aspect of the ITSE Enterprise for its management.

12.2 ITSE is an Adaptive Organization

ITSE must be an adaptive organization, which continuously senses changes in the Business environment and assesses internal developments to mould itself accordingly. Adaptive organization is subject of deep research and our endeavour in this section is to examine some of its key principles form ITSE perspective. In this context, ITSE have to incessantly strive to learn new abilities, new technologies and new way of service the newer expectations of the customer. Can we accept any banking services without their ATM being available or any enterprise without a well-contented website? Tomorrow, the expectation will move to mobile computing and not too far in future, any device computing! All this requires ITSE to build processes and capabilities to manage new knowledge and assimilate it for action.

12.2.1 Learning Spiral for an ITSE Firm

ITSE firms is full of bright an intelligent individuals all rearing to share their learning with the rest of the organization. They want to experiment with newer technology and processes, and need an avenue that can help them achieve that. Nonaka & Takeuchi (1995)[1] proposed learning

---

1. The Knowledge-Creating Company: How Japanese Companies Create the Dynamics of Innovation, Ikujiro Nonaka (Author), Hirotaka Takeuchi (Author), Oxford University Press, USA (May 18, 1995).

spiral model after deep study of Japanese auto electronics industries that are wroth imbibing in ITSE context.

A learning organization goes through a learning spiral as a continuous learning process through four stages as given below. We will examine how these stages can be made relevant in ITSE context through simple examples.

Socialization

Internal tacit knowledge is shared by an individual as related with organization context. For example, a system administrator watches a typical behaviour just before the collapse of a server, either high utilization or activities. This is shared and confirmed with data and system logs with other member of this team.

Externalization

The next person(s) converts the shared knowledge into more meaningful articulated form. The observation is further examined in other context, simulated or data from past failure is collected to support that observation. Finally, leading to a conclusion and corrective action to be done before the server reaches that threshold.

Combination

Combining relevant knowledge, codification, summarizing, editing and propagating to make it more usable for rest of the organizations. Here the role IT is significant to speed up the process. So, the recommendations arising out of the observations and simulation in earlier example is converted in do-how and dont's for all systems administrators who are part of similar environment. It may necessitate a new code to be released to fix that behaviour, in certain cases. Using knowledge dissemination tools such as WIKI, Team rooms, etc. the entire organization can get to know about this problem.

Internalization

In this step, explicit knowledge becomes a tacit knowledge actionable by people. Such knowledge may end up in people behaviour, method of doing things or change in approach towards a problem. This is the last stop of every cycle of learning spiral when the organization learning gets internalized by individuals. So continuing over earlier example, these actions become a part of the routine checks and operating procedure of systems administrators of the data centers. The learning spiral then moves up to the next level of socialization as more and more tacit knowledge is externalized combined and internalized to reach to the next stage of learning. Figure 12.1 depicts this process in a pictorial form.

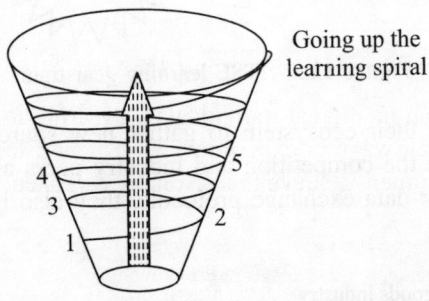

Figure 12.1 Learning spiral of an ITSE organization.

The net result of following the learning spiral model is that the key learning of key individual is converted in documented form and ingrained in new services products and processes of the ITSE.

12.2.2 Where will the New Learnings Come from to the ITSE?

All research and theories of *learning organization* have been far rooted in the manufacturing and brick and mortar[2] industry which are known for stable process, gradual customer preference change and near same technology for many decades. ITSE, on the other hand, have to serve other businesses processes and systems through software and services. Any change either driven due to customer, competition or regulation will trigger a need for new services and processes in the ITSE firms. In addition, the Information Technology itself is an evolving discipline that is changing everyday into new tools and discovery. So this model of learning generation, capture and dissemination by just focusing inwards may not be adequate. ITSE operates in far more dynamic industry ecosystem, because of its very nature of supporting other industries, and therefore, requires a additional layer for knowledge internalization for becoming a learning organization. This layer comprises of customers, partners and other stakeholders.

By tapping the interaction with the customer, partners, independent researchers and competition, ITSE can seek and reach out for new source of knowledge. In fact, we would like to show this interaction by series of gears enmeshed in the form of gear train to show this process of learning across the ITSE ecosystem.

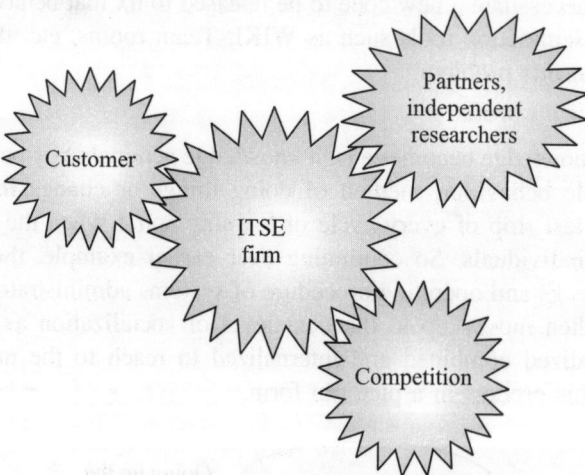

Figure 12.2   ITSE learning gear train.

ITSE firms have to tap their ecosystem to gather new sources of knowledge. At times, they have to keenly observe the competition and industry peers as well. In certain areas such as process standardization or data exchange protocols, they also have to work together in the spirit of cooperation.

---

2. A term attributed to physical goods industry

12.3 Enablers of Knowledge Creation

Knowledge management is not just collecting the documents in a database and giving facilities to query them. It is about process that is as distinct from capturing information. KM is strategic activity to enable the ITSE firm and its employees get right knowledge at right time so that they can use it to improve their response time and quality. The major challenge in going up the path of becoming learning organization is to enthuse and motivate the team to create capture and put to effective practice the knowledge already available. We know that people come and go in an organization, but as a collective team their performance can improve or deteriorate.

Several researchers[3] have identified and summarized some common key enablers that are necessary to create a learning culture within the organization. Noticeable amongst them are as follows:

(i) Have a long term vision of the organization learning

(ii) Develop a strategy of what knowledge the firm wants to capture

(iii) Create a healthy climate in the organization to implement learning and KM efforts through proper support and encouragement

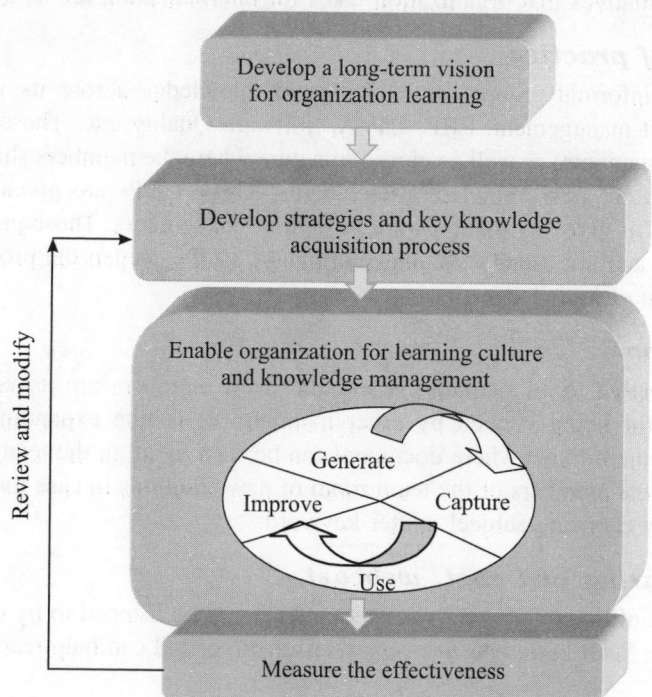

Figure 12.3 Learning and knowledge management process.

3. A. Measuring and Building a Learning Organization: A Systems Approach, Dr. Michael J. O'Brien ((513) 831–8042.) and Joan E. Bennett, Eighth IEEE-USA Careers Conference. B. Is Yours a Learning Organization? by David A. Garvin, Amy C. Edmondson, and Francesca Gino, hbr.org | March 2008 | *Harvard Business Review*, 109, permission@hbsp.harvard.edu

(iv) Process and structure to define how the learnings will be captured, evaluated, codified and disseminated

(v) Create a system to define process and technology that enable capture and dissemination of knowledge

(vi) Performance goals/feedback leading to rewards and recognition to KM contributors

These steps are shown in Figure 12.3.

12.3.1 Internalization of Knowledge into Practice

Many organization proudly announce their multi-million dollar investment in knowledge management systems and technology. They may have created systems and processes by which the intranet site has tera bites of presentations and copies of reports, and work in progress artifacts. Yet if this knowledge is not internalized and used by people to demonstrate better results than this investment will remain ornamental in nature. Internalization of knowledge remains a major challenge for learning organization. Capturing knowledge and making it easily available is only a battle half won.

Some of the initiatives that organization takes for internalization are as follows:

Communities of practice

ITSE firms create informal groups for exchange of knowledge across its various practices, for example, project management, ERP, JAVA, Software Quality, etc. These groups are open (allowing external members) as well as closed in nature where the members share achievements, ask questions and store new knowledge documents. These COPs are given small budget to promote any events or give any token award to highest contributors. These practices are led by few senior experts, and are usually voluntary in nature. COPs deepen the process participation and in-formalization of knowledge sharing.

WIKI, team rooms

These are collaborative tools available where the team members are asked to upload their knowledge assets for being viewed by other members. It is like expanding the concept of physical library on the intranet where document can be seen by all in the team. Such tools have facilities to inform the members of the team room of new additions in case they have registered their preferences by choosing subject matter keywords.

Knowledge sharing pod cast, webcast

These are online or offline talk given by experts which can be listened to by the team members using their desktop. Such initiatives are very cost-effective, and can help reaching out to larger number of people.

12.3.2 Learning and Knowledge Management Leads to Innovation

While the perspective of knowledge management and learning is to improve ITSE capabilities and efficiency, this is not enough for their long-term survival and growth. ITSE must attempt to capture what it learns while performing the services with its client and reuse it, modify it and improve it. This way the time spent on discovering every project can be reduced. Most

ITSE firm take this as an important activity, but this is not the sufficient condition though it is necessary to have such processes and practices in place for their day-to-day operations.

Innovation process is the step beyond that the ITSE firm adopt to keep pace with the market conditions and customer requirements. There is a lot of hype about innovation in the current times and our endeavour in this short section is to just bring out the salient aspects of the innovation process that progressive ITSE firms adopt. In this process, they not only promote internal collaboration, but external collaborations with academics, delivery partners and peer groups to work on new projects and technologies which might find favours with the customers.

While ITSE must encourage wide use of available knowledge and its sharing as well as its use, care must be taken that it does not act as speed breaker for innovation. ITSE firm must balance innovation with reuse of the intellectual capital/knowledge assets.

12.4   The Path of Innovation

Mohanty and Deshmukh[4], in their seminal article offer six generic and interactive forces that influence any business corporation to evolve into a learning organization, which are:

   (i) Customer power
  (ii) Information power
  (ii) Global investors power
 (iv) Global market power
  (v) Power of simplicity
 (vi) Power of the organization

According to Wheatley, organizations like ITSE are like a spider's web. Unlike a machine where replacing a dysfunctional part such as a bad manager or team or unprofitable service line will restart it. Wheatley[5] says that "if a web breaks and needs repair, the spider doesn't cut out a piece, terminate it, or alter the entire web apart and reorganize it. She reweaves it, using the silken relationships that are already there, creating stronger connections across the weakened spaces". So the IT Services Enterprise needs to be careful that it is much more networked organization, and therefore, requires a different treatment.

12.4.1   Need for an Innovation Process

A question may be asked that whether innovation can also be bound by the shackles of process. Innovation or creativity are supposed to be brilliance of ideas coming up occasionally in individuals or groups mind and how can ITSE force itself to be innovative by adopting a process!

The purpose of innovation process in any ITSE firm is to ensure that a mechanism exists to get the innovative ideas converted into reality. ITSE comprises of large number of bright and innovative individuals, who would like to contribute their ideas. If such innovation process

4. Mohanty, R.P. and Deshmukh, S.G., (1999), "Evaluating manufacturing strategy for a learning organization." *International Journal of Operations & Production Management*, 19(3), p. 308.
5. Wheatley, M.J. (1999). Leadership and the New Science. Berkeley, CA, Publishers Group West.

does not exist, any such ideas will never see the light of the day. We will take up the innovation process that is typically adopted in an ITSE firms for the understanding of our readers.

12.4.2 Typical Innovation Process

There are many innovation framework[6] and processes researched. In simple terms, the innovation process is called innovation funnel where ideas are collected and they are taken through the evaluation stages leading to selection of pilot, and if proved, useful for commercialization.

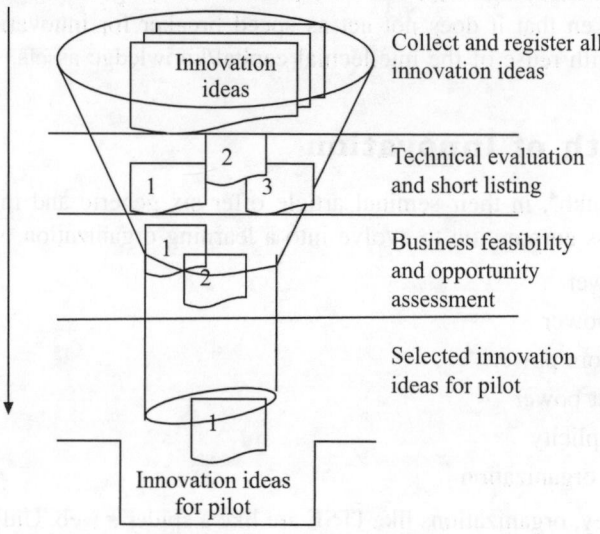

Figure 12.4 Innovation funnel.

Innovation in ITSE is not only limited to use of technology but in the services processes or business model as well. Instead of fixed price contracts or contracts based on number of people deployed, ITSE firms increasingly are embracing outcome based contract where the reward or revenue is based on the success of the services performed. For example, in outbound customer solicitation services run from various call centers, the payment is based in the number of successful customers not on the basis of number of outbound calls made. In the areas of business model innovation even the hardware and equipment deployment is being converted into operating expenses or pay for use increasingly.

Innovation in ITSE firms leads to more and more intellectual property developed by them. The intellectual property developed by the research and development helps in process re-engineering to bring better efficiency in the system.

12.4.3 Innovation Best Practices

Some of the good innovation practices are as follows:

---

6. Read Chapter 8, Managing Ideas, pp. 159–170, *Innovation with IT*, Sanjiva Shankar Dubey, Tata McGraw-Hill.

 (i) **Productizing service:** Instead of defining the services requirement everytime, and then proposing a statement if work, the approach is to upfront define what all services for what all duration or scope will be performed at what price. This way, the customer is clear as what ultimate is going to be charged for what services.

 (ii) **Servitizing products:** In this approach the software including associated hardware, storage and network is provided as service where the customer pays based on hours of use or number of users who can at a time use the application. Salesforce.com is one such example, where the salesforce automation application is available at a fee based on number of users, data volume, etc. with cloud computing gaining ground this innovation model is likely to gain more popularity in future.

 (iii) **Revenue sharing:** This innovation in business model has been practiced by leading telecom operators in India such as Airtel, Vodafone and Idea, where the entire IT Services provided by the service provider in this case IBM will be based on sharing a percentage of revenue of the customer. So if the customer revenue grows the ITSE gain or vice versa. Touted as one of the major business model innovation with two HBR articles written on Airtel project, this is a landmark innovation by any ITSE which is now being followed by others. However, this type of innovation requires great amount of thinking and greater amount of efforts by both ITSE and the client to make it a success.

 (iv) **Intellectual asset harvesting:** In any IT Services project the team may generate several new codes, documents, algorithms of processes which can be re-used in other subsequent projects. This is called intellectual asset harvesting which reduces time to do similar efforts in other projects, and can become part of the knowledge base.

 (v) **From selling labour to IP:** Software development services companies typically deploy their team to develop software for their clients. Instead, if they develop a ready to use software that can be deployed at many clients. In this way they will be selling the copies of the software code and small labour to install and maintain it. In this process, the ITSE would innovate from selling labour to Intellectual property.

 (vi) **Innovation jam:** Idea jamming made popular by John Kao[7] who uses the metaphor of jazz for creative improvisation in business situation[8]. In this process, ITSE firms organize discussion around some ideas which is subsequently voted or improved by other participating members. All this discussion is visible and read by everyone. Ultimately few ideas that receive highest vote are selected for further investment.

 (vii) **Creating innovation multi-disciplinary/multi-organization teams:** This can be achieved with academics and peer industries to wok on typical customer problems which can be beneficial to all participants.

12.5 How to Build a Learning Organization

Innovation and learning orientation will not happen in any ITSE overnight. This is slow and painstaking process that the organization and leadership have to implement. There will be

---

7. Jamming: The Art and Discipline of Business Creativity John Kao, Harper Paperbacks (March 28, 1997)
8. http://www.johnkao.com/jamming.html accessed 23092011

challenges of participation and openness of sharing of ideas and knowledge in the team. The effort is required to create an atmosphere of trust and support which will help the team to come out openly. Learning and innovation requires continuous reinforcement to make it established by suitably rewarding the participants.

Garvin[9] opines that learning organization develops approaches for the following:

    (i) Systematic Problem-solving

   (ii) Experimentation (new approaches)

  (iii) Learning from past experience

  (iv) Learning from best practices (of others)

   (v) Knowledge transference

Given these stages it is necessary that leaders of ITSE firms take keen interest in this process.

12.6 Summary

In this chapter we discussed an important aspect for ITSE firms growth and survival in this chapter, which is its ability to continuously innovate through a robust process of knowledge management. It presented a learning spiral framework for an ITSE firm quoting Nonaka & Takeuchi (1995)[10] which covers going up the stages of

    (i) Socialization

   (ii) Externalization

  (iii) Combination

  (iv) Internalization

The research question as to where the new learnings will come from the ITSE has been examined. It established that by tapping the interaction with the customer, partners, independent researchers and competition, ITSE can get new source of innovation.

The next discussion was on the enablers of knowledge creation noticeable amongst them are

    (i) Long-term vision of learning

   (ii) Develop a strategy

  (iii) Create a healthy climate

  (iv) Process and structure

   (v) Create a system

  (vi) Performance goals/feedback leading to rewards and recognition to KM contributors

The next step of this journey was to understand the process of internalization of knowledge into practice. The likely initiatives defined were:

---

9. "Building a Learning Organization" David A. Garvin, *Harvard Business Review*, Knowledge Management. Harvard Business School Press, 1998.

10. The Knowledge-Creating Company: How Japanese Companies Create the Dynamics of Innovation, Ikujiro Nonaka (Author), Hirotaka Takeuchi (Author), Oxford University Press, USA, (May 18, 1995).

(i) Communities of practice

(ii) WIKI, Team rooms

(iii) Knowledge sharing prod cast, webcast.

The chapter underlines that learning and knowledge management leads to innovation. Innovation process helps ITSE firm to keep pace with the market conditions and customer requirements. While ITSE must encourage wide use of available knowledge and its sharing as well as its use, care must be taken that it does not act as a speed breaker for innovation. ITSE firm must balance innovation with reuse of the intellectual capital/knowledge assets.

We also defined the path of innovation covered by six generic and interactive forces that influence any business corporation to evolve into a learning organization. These are as follows:

(i) Customer power

(ii) Information power

(iii) Global investors power

(iv) Global market power

(v) Power of simplicity

(vi) Power of the organization

The discussion was enlarged to reinforce the need for an innovation process which ensures innovative ideas are captured and converted into reality. The chapter defines a typical innovation process and its various stages that an ITSE can adopt.

We then presented some of the prevalent innovation practices followed by leading ITSE firms. Some salient ones discussed are:

(i) Productizing service

(ii) Servitizing products

(iii) Revenue sharing

(iv) Intellectual asset harvesting

(v) From selling labour to IP

(vi) Innovation jam

(vii) Creating innovation multi-disciplinary/multi-organization teams

Finally, we discussed the ways to build a learning organization quoting research studies.

Review Questions

12.1 Why it is important to have innovation and knowledge management processes for ITSE firm's growth and survival?

12.2 Using the framework of Nonaka & Takeuchi (1995) describe the concept of learning spiral.

12.3 What are the sources of new learnings and how will you tap them?

12.4 What are the enablers of knowledge creation? Describe each one of them briefly.

12.5 Describe the process of internalization of knowledge into practice. Give suitable examples from your work place or through secondary research.

12.6 How will you describe the path of innovation? What are the generic forces that shape the innovation path?

12.7 Describe need for an innovation process. Define a typical innovation process and its various stages that an ITSE can adopt.

12.8 Write short notes of the following Innovation practices:

    (a) Productizing service

    (b) Servitizing products

    (c) Revenue sharing

    (d) Intellectual asset harvesting

    (e) From selling labour to IP

    (f) Innovation jam

    (g) Creating innovation multi-disciplinary/multi-organization teams

12.9 What are the ways to build a learning organization? Quote relevant research studies to support your argument.

Suggested Further Reading

Garvin, D. A., Learning in Action: A Guide to Putting the Learning Organization to Work, Harvard Business School Press, Boston, MA, 2000.

Argyris, C., On Organizational Learning. 2nd ed. Oxford: Blackwell Publishing, 1999.

Amidon, Debra M., *Innovation Strategy for the Knowledge Economy*, Butterworth-Heinman, Newton, MA, 1997.

Tsang, E., Organizational learning and the learning organization: A dichotomy between descriptive and prescriptive research, *Human Relations*, Vol. 50 No. **1**, 1997, pp. 73–89.

Kofman, F. and Senge, P., "Communities of Commitment: The Heart of Learning Organizations", Organizational Dynamics, Vol. 22, No. **2** , 1993, pp. 5–23.

Chapter 13

Managing IT Services Enterprise Growth

The most difficult problems in the world do not have obvious solutions....
They require creativity and tenacity
—Anonymous

13.1 Introduction

IT Services companies have to grow to remain viable. Unlike their product counterpart this business is people-oriented business which necessitates that the people working in these companies also grow as the years progress, earn more and enrich themselves professionally. All this is only possible if the company grows, does business with more prestigious clients, projects that are complex in nature and large in terms of team. In addition, the cost of employee will always be increasing every year due to inflation and increased cost of living. In absence of a well-defined growth path the IT Services company would not be able to satisfy their employee needs as well as the needs of the stakeholders like investors, founders, suppliers and partners.

In this chapter we will discuss not only challenges but governing principles as well related to ITSE growth. Our approach would be to describe deep theoretical foundations that are applicable to ITSE firms giving examples of how successful ITSEs have managed their growth using some of these principles. . The chapter will discuss concepts, processes and best practices of managing growth of an IT Services enterprise.

13.2 Factors for Growth

In the enterprise growth framework[1] study carried out by a leading development agency on the behest of international Aid agency concludes that the growth of private enterprise is a based on following factors:

---

1. Enterprise Growth Initiatives: Strategic Directions and Options Handbook, Prepared for the U.S. Agency for International Development, Bureau of Economic Growth, Agriculture, and Trade, Authors: Ulrich Ernst, Marina Krivoshlykova, Donald R. Snodgrass, James Packard Winkler, July 2004, 7250 Woodmont Avenue, Suite 200, Bethesda, Maryland 20814, Development Alternatives Inc.

(i) Demand for services

This is always increasing due to increasing use of IT in all spheres of our work. So all ITSE are likely to grow.

(ii) Quality of the business environment

IT Services industry is always welcomed with open arms as it is low capital, clean in terms of environment and regulatory provisions, employment intensive and promotes entrepreneurial culture. A favourable business environment provides economic and political stability, offers low costs for business transactions, and allows for efficient business operations, which lead to greater innovation and creativity. ITSE have developed good capabilities for business development which is helping its growth.

(iii) Supply response of an enterprise

The supply response of an enterprise is to see whether it is able to provide the right services at right price to its customers. This factor is totally under the control of the enterprise though it will also depend on overall services ecosystem consisting of clusters of enterprises providing similar services or have value chain relationships. This means that the enterprise has to work with other enterprise for say hardware, software, infrastructure, skills, intellectual products, etc. For IT Services company, this ecosystem has now become global in nature.

Given this framework, it is apparent that while the first two are the influencing factors needed to be taken into account, the last factor is one that the enterprise has to focus (Figure 13.1).

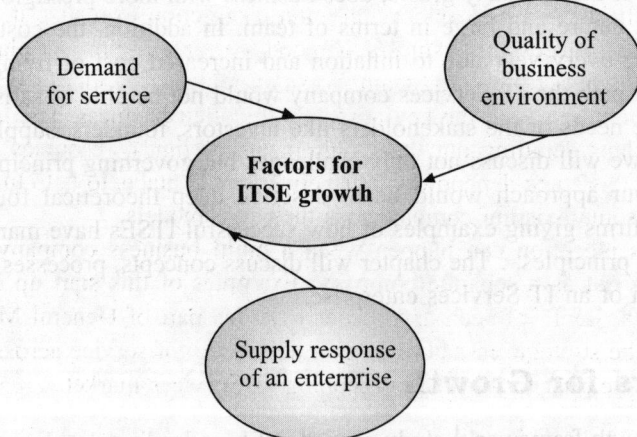

Figure 13.1 Factors of ITSE growth.

13.3 Stages of Growth

IT Services Enterprise go through an evolutionary cycle. As shown in Figure 13.2, it passes through different stages of the evolution leading to growth, mergers, acquisition or splitting as the case may be. We will discuss these stages in the subsequent paragraphs.

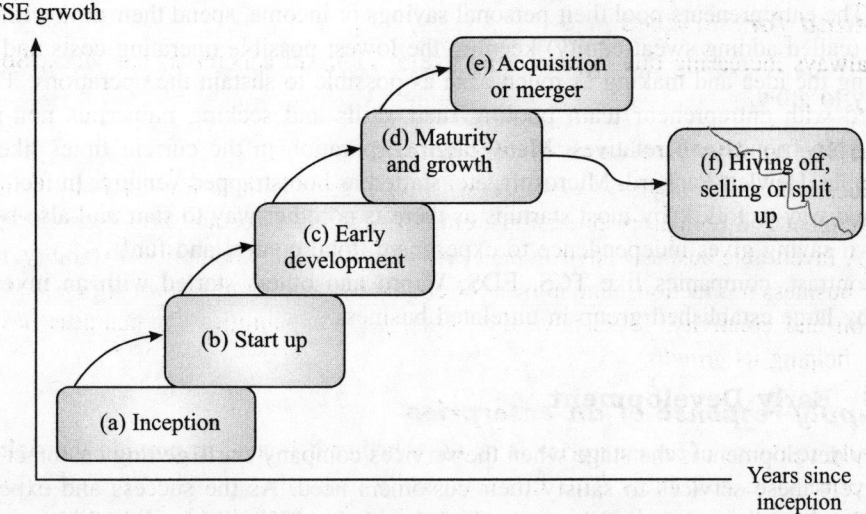

Figure 13.2 Stages of growth for an IT Services Enterprise.

13.3.1 Inception

Typically ITSE starts with an entrepreneurial idea when a person or group establishes a services venture. During this period the entrepreneur or the management team gains motivation to launch an IT Services business and assembles the necessary competence to take the idea further. These entrepreneurs identify the business opportunity and take action to realize it. Having great idea alone will not lead to a successful business. All good ideas require proper planning followed by execution. During this phase the initial team works on refining the idea, ascertaining its market potential, target customer set and the key attractors to solicit business. The inception team also prepares business plans detailing out the requirements of funds, resources and infrastructure. The entrepreneur at this stage depend on their network of contacts to help him with shaping up their ideas and use some existing companies as their role models.

Sometimes, this inception can happen when a multi business company with IT Services capability hives this out as a separate company. Examples of this start up can be seen in the names of 3i Infotech, L&T Infotech and earlier EDS (as part of General Motors). Motivation of doing this could be strategic in nature to gain uniformity of service across group companies or totally opportunistic, just to join the burgeoning IT Services market.

13.3.2 Start Up

Once the idea is firmed up, the company moves to the next phase called start-up phase. Unless the company is funded by an exiting business group who also pools all the existing IT resources as a part of new set up and hire management team to run it as subsidiary (or join venture), the start up happens with the entrepreneurial funds and resources. The later one is also called bootstrapping[2]. In the case of bootstrapping by entrepreneurs, the business is built from the

---

2. http://www.businessdictionary.com/definition/bootstrapping.html accessed 04092011

scratch. The entrepreneurs pool their personal savings or income, spend their time without being paid for (called adding sweat equity) keeping the lowest possible operating costs and focusing on proving the idea and making as much cash as possible to sustain the operations. This phase is marked with entrepreneur team pooling their skills and seeking numerous non-monetary support from friends and relatives. Many large corporation in the current times like Infosys, HCL, Apple, Hewlett-Packard, Microsoft, etc. started as bootstrapped venture. In fact, this is an established way to follow by most startups as there is no other way to start and also by pooling one's own saving gives independence to experiment, total control and fun!

In contrast, companies like TCS, EDS, Wipro and others started with an investor fund backed by large established group in unrelated business.

13.3.3 Early Development

The early development is the stage when the services company starts getting customer contracts and delivers these services to satisfy their customers need. As the success and experience of delivery happens irrespective of the type of services being offered the original ideas get proved or disproved and new one starts to take a shape. The focus at this stage is to execute the services contract well so that the initial successes can be claimed for new business. Stories[3] of personal involvement of the entrepreneurs in the execution of services contract are quoted in case studies which gives rise to successful execution and building customer relationship. Many customers have on record said that small and mid-sized companies have the flexibility and are not polluted by the low-quality customer service practices that become the market norm.[4] This is the phase when growth opportunities assessment and selection is done by the founder and close knit management team. Since the firm starts to expand they also find it difficult and challenging to hire good managers and ensuring quality of their output.

At this stage the IT Services firm requires investment to hire more delivery staff, project managers and support staff. They may also need to move to a suitable office space. The personal savings may prove to be inadequate and bank loans are difficult to solicit at this stage. They may like to seek small fund from venture capitalists, the initial one are also known as angel investors and the subsequent ones are called first round venture capitalist, second round VCs etc. All these incoming funds are traded for a portion of equity held by the founders. The later investors buy out the earlier investors at a premium leaving the founder entrepreneur as it is or taking their share as well. The value of equity is decided based on the companies business in hand, outlook, market conditions and the management team track record.

13.3.4 Maturity and Growth

After some time the services firm end up in phase when it is able to generate cash by delivering services, and build a pool of capital through profit accruals. Managing growth at the stage would come from prudent investment in business development, opening new delivery

---

3. Stanford Graduate School of Business, Case Study.
4. As above, Bill Price, an Amazon executive describing their choice of Daksh (later IBM Daskh) as BPO service provider in June 2002.

capabilities, bidding for larger services contract, etc. all this can be done at a pace dictated by the entrepreneurial appetite and prevailing market conditions. Venture capitalist who have made investment typically want to withdraw their funds at a suitable premium by selling their stakes to other equity partners or with founder's concurrence in open market by announcing IPO. Though the process of IPO is time-consuming and complex, the net result is win-win for everyone. The venture capitalist are able to sell their equity either in en-block or over time, at prevailing market rates and founders also start getting the reward of the all the hard work they have put in the form of market capitalization of the stock held in their name. Employees contribution are given stock options as part of their. Some prominent customers/partners who would have got stock in lieu of the business association also get benefited.

13.3.5 Acquisition or Merger

The next growth stage involves activities such as acquisition of smaller services companies or merger with equal size company to build further synergies. IT Services companies size determines their strength to undertake the volume of work. Growing inorganically though practiced largely by almost all ITSE, does take time. Many large companies want to enhance their delivery capabilities by this route, and believe that the combined entity will be far more attractive in the minds of the customer.

Acquisition and merger route of growth has its own challenges. Yet it is a popular method adopted by cash rich IT Services corporations. However, issues of cultural compatibility, focus with the type of services do crop up, which makes merger and acquisition a conplex method for ITSE growth.

13.3.6 Hiving off, Selling or Split Up

A corollary of acquisition and merger is hiving, selling or splitting the large IT Services firm into smaller one for better management and operations control. IT Services firm typically sell off those services which are no longer most profitable as part of their portfolio. Sometimes this is done to retain synergy within the corporation and leave that part of portfolio that is no longer relevant in new scheme things. IT Services firm typically shed business related with serving old technology, skills of which may be difficult to obtain, and thus, may create customer dissatisfaction at some point in time in future. These are also called developing exit strategies for the IT Services firm.

13.4 Process of Managing Growth

Managing growth is managing the strategies and their implementation for the firm. The purpose of any business including IT Services business is to bring revenue and profits for its shareholders, provide quality services at reasonable cost to the its customer and an opportunity of professional growth to their employees and partners. For the purpose of simplicity managing growth is divided into phases as shown in Figure 13.3.

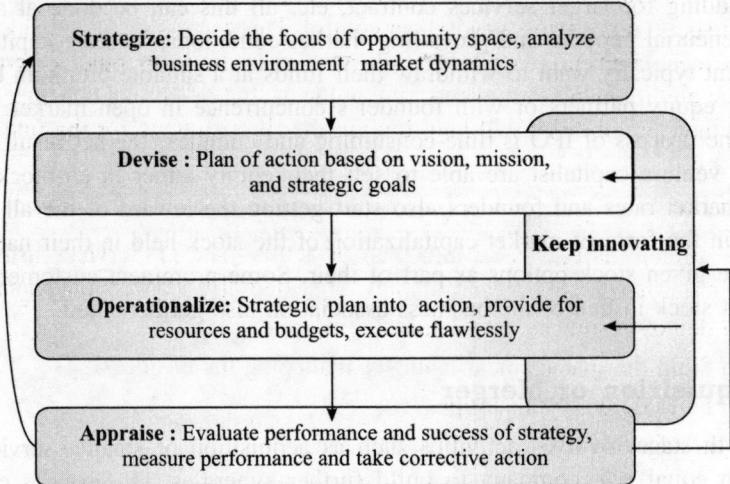

Figure 13.3   Process for management of IT Services Enterprise growth.

They are further elaborated in the subsequent sections.

13.4.1   Strategize

IT Services Enterprise must develop a strategic niche for itself. Most companies make mistake of doing everything that a successful multinational or large Indian IT Services companies do. Trying to blindly copy the working model of leading ITSE may not work in most of the cases.

This step is required to understand industry structure considering competitors and complementors and keep into account the market demand, trends and driving forces. By understanding the current level of industry-specific rules, regulations, and quality standards will help to establish what level of capabilities are required for being successful. This step also views market failures, constraints, and opportunities so that the best strategy can be formulated.

Some tools used for this purpose are as follows:

  (i) Sectoral analysis
 (ii) Value-chain analysis
(iii) Porter's Diamond and Porter's Five Forces
 (iv) SWOT analysis (both industry as well as for the firm)
  (v) Benchmarking
 (vi) Market segmentation
(vii) GAP analysis

Some of these may look too complex for the small IT Services firm, but must be adopted as a rigor as the organization grows.

This process step for strategizing involves analyzing business environment and global market dynamics specifically from IT Services perspective by the management team. They must brainstorm various opportunities and pick up the market, target services offering that gives them some unique advantage through their skills or capabilities. They may require vetting their approach with other industry experts who have far more depth of knowledge about the future trends. In order to extrapolate the future a technique scenario planning can be used. Scenario planning helps to determine factors beyond our control. This exercise helps considering significant factors such as recession, currency fluctuation, visa restrictions, or other external factors that shape the market environment. Past events may guide us, but by putting our imagination to work and reason out their possibilities will help finding the right strategy for the future[5].

13.4.2 Devise

In this step the strategy is converted into plan of action. The IT Services firms defines what services to offer at what price for what market. This step also answers questions such as

(i) How to deploy resources for business development?

(ii) How to build the management team for managing the business?

(iii) How to build delivery capabilities?

(iv) What type of customers and projects to solicit?

In this step, the IT Services firm must also consider its constraints, such as capability limitation, capacity constraints, resource constraint, quality standards, productivity and innovation ability while soliciting new business.

Some of tools used in the earlier steps would be useful though the focus now would be on building expertise within the firm. Tools like Swot analysis, benchmarking, GAP analysis (gap between the best in class and the current level of performance) are useful. The output of this step is to devise a set of prioritized strategic goals for over the next five years, detailed out in yearly and quarterly targets.

This step concludes as what is the IT Services firms[6]:

(i) Vision statement that answers the question, "*Where do we want to go?*" It is also considered as '*An Image of the future we seek to create*'. For example, world famous GE corporation in 1980 defined its vision as "*to become the number one or number two in every market we serve and revolutionize this company to have the strength of a big company combined with the leanness and agility of a small company.*"

(ii) Mission which represents clearly and precisely its purpose for existence, and how it will achieve the vision. For example, 3M mission statement is "*To solve unsolved problems innovatively*".

(iii) Strategic goals and objectives (used interchangeably) which means the ends toward which effort and action are directed or coordinated. These are more specific targets that the company wants to achieve in shorter time frame. Strategic objectives are externally focused measured that may be categorized into the following:

(i) Revenues, profits, market shares

(ii) New wins, innovation of new services

(iii) Team size, productivity

(iv) Community objectives such as employment generation potential, in the context of IT Services firms.

---

5. For details of ITSE strategy development read Ch. 6 Innovation with IT, Sanjiva Shankar Dubey, Tata McGraw-Hill education, 2008. For scenario planning Chapter 5 should be consulted.

6. These statements are quoted from various sources

13.4.3 Operationalize

This step involves strategic plan into action, estimates of resources and budgets, and efforts to execute flawlessly. This is the execution process where each function of the organization runs its activities as per the defined processes. [The processes for IT Services firms have already been discussed in Chapter 3 to 7].

13.4.4 Appraise

This step involves activities to evaluate performance and success of strategy, measure performance and take corrective action. This step ensures whether the actions planned have been delivered, targets defined have been met, and goals envisaged have been achieved. This process has been discussed in detail in Chapter 8.

13.4.5 Keep Innovating

One of the processes of ensuring IT Services growth is to keep innovating its services and processes to give a better and efficient services to the customer. IT Services deal with emerging IT discipline, and there will always be a scope of innovation on continuous basis. This process has been detailed out in Chapter 11.

13.5 Managing Growth Alternatives

IT Services firm grow in various ways and can choose from various alternatives. We give here the alternatives of growth using organic means, i.e. growing from within not by acquisition or merger. Basically, this process is the judicious mix of inter playing the four factors in such a way that it gives rise to more and more opportunities. Figure 13.4 gives a simple framework for choosing from growth alternatives.

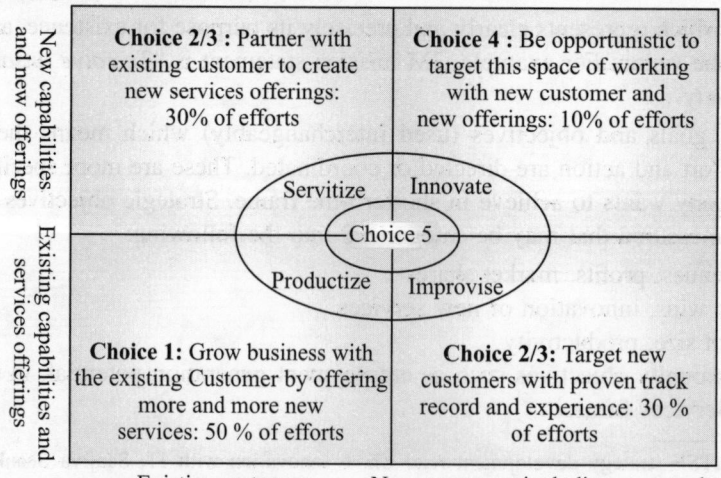

Figure 13.4   Organic growth alternatives for IT Services firm.

Let us describe each one of them in detail. The sum total may be more than 100 if you pool all your efforts. The idea is to give a broad recommendation and also to make 100 % of results one has to put in more than 100% of effort.

13.5.1 Choice 1

Grow business with the existing customer by offering more and more new services. This is by far, the most promising amongst all of the growth alternatives. Your firm may have delivered some services already and that too successfully, and now the same customer may be looking at some other services. If these services capabilities are already available, may be by having done services to other customer, they must be positioned and offered to the existing customer. This task is also sometimes referred as mining of the account. Alternatively, the scope of current services can be enhanced by deploying it to other divisions or other functions. Large IT Services firm which have multiple capabilities across consulting, outsourcing, BPO, system integration etc., routinely follow this model to expand their business. This approach is known as farming the account. Both these together constitute the process of growing the account base.

13.5.2 Choice 2

Partner with existing customer to create new services offerings. Existing customers are the best bet to develop your new offering capabilities. They would have already experienced the ITSE's services, and if they are happy, they are the most likely one to try out new services. Keeping the customer in the know of your new capability development efforts makes a good case for expanding the capability bases.

13.5.3 Choice 3

This approach demands targeting new customers with your success stories with services provided to other customers. By now the track record and experience get proven and most customers would like to work with a service provider who has experience of working in their industry and type of projects.

The choices 2 and 3 can interchange their places depending on the company's strategy, market conditions and opportunity in hand.

13.5.4 Choice 4

Be opportunistic to target this space of working with new customer and new offerings as and when the opportunity arises. This is an open space with some amount of risk but many companies have proven success in this area.

13.5.5 Choice 5

This is a disruptive, non-linear growth model[7]. In this approach new services models are used to attract customers based on the existing success, new IP based tools and new technology

---

7. http://www.business-standard.com/india/news/it-companies-may-take-time-for-non-linear-growth/366731/

developments. Here, the focus is not on increasing the head count for additional source of revenue. By increasing the number of value-added services which are intellectual property (IP) based and by following different business models such as SAS, Cloud computing etc., a growing IT Services firm can exercise this option.

There are four variants of this approach. They are as follows:

(i) **Productize it:** Here the service becomes a form of product. It may arise out of a situation where a software development project gives rise to a product that can be sold in multiple copies.

(ii) **Servitize[8] it:** There may be a IT product, some thing new and innovative but the customer in not willing to pay for its licensees or infrastructure. In such cases letting the product be used on hourly basis or any other service model can lead to attracting new customers and revenue.

(iii) **Improvise it:** This is true in cases when you are attempting to attract a new customer and they want to make some necessary changes to suit their needs. The firm must be ready to improvise it for the benefit of the customer.

(iv) **Innovate it:** Be innovative with new customer and new technology based on all the capabilities to find new growth opportunities. Here the approach will be to try something totally new and disruptive in nature following new technology wave such as SAS, Cloud computing, Mobile computing, etc. Fred Giron[9], Forrester researcher opines that IT Services industry now have to use a disruptive model which will challenge the existing labour-cost arbitrage liner model. His premise is based on the increasing clout of Cloud Computing and suggest that the future of IT Services growth that he names as IT Services Industrialization 2.0 will increasingly be led by the following:

- Sharing resources across many clients, one to many model also called pooling
- Increased automation through IP-based solution to increase efficiency
- Client self-service using automated provisioning following SAS models

13.6 Best Practices for Growth

Some of the best practices for growth include the following:

(i) Increased engagement with employee make them empowered to work in the best interest of client. This will increase customer focus, better delivery and new source of capturing opportunities.

(ii) Operations excellence and efficiency in all spheres of work must be ensured. The success of Infosys is largely credited for their operational excellence.

(iii) Build client relationship and often exceed the brief of the contract and mesmerize the customer with excellence service.

---

8. The term servitization was coined in 1988 by Vandermerwe and Rada, http://servitizer.com/servitization-defined.html

9. http://blogs.forrester.com/fred_giron/11-09-01-it_services_industrialization_20 access 05092011

(iv) Be passionate about customer success not just your revenue.

(v) Assign resources with priority; don't delay in the start of project as you will lose revenue.

(vi) Do not let the team sit idle, make them do some creative work for internal use, keep them motivated, always.

(vii) Always recruit best talent not only in technical capabilities but also for their ability to work in team and with client.

(viii) Strike a balance between candidate values and competencies to select the right candidate.

(ix) Try to enhance relationship with board level in the client organization with people who are responsible for making decisions.

13.7   Pitfalls to be Avoided during the Growth

At this stage, we must discuss some of the pitfalls to be avoided which act as an impediment for the growth. The initial stages of the IT Services firm growth is fuelled by close involvement of the entrepreneur/founders/ senior management team who take charge from contract negotiation to day-to-day delivery. But once, the size of the enterprise starts to grow, its starts becoming bureaucratic and sluggish. Its overhead increases and also its responsiveness decreases. However, as the company grows its operations become more stable and quality of work more dependable. Mid-size companies do not grow easily as they are not able to differentiate themselves. They do not possess business domain skills, and find it difficult to develop any unique value proposition. Large IT Services company hit the *growth block*[10]. Since they have grown to a significant size (10000 + team) they start encountering increased attrition in their staff and end up being less responsive to their customers. All these must be controlled and avoided. Even Forrester, a leading research firm, has opined that as the major Indian providers grew and matured, they lost the flexibility and client responsiveness[11].

Factory led approach prevents flexibility

An interesting report by Avinash[12] presents that factory style adopted by large IT Services company leads to loss of flexibility. The reasons sighted are:

(i) Standardization leads to demand of a certain revenue and growth commitment every year;

(ii) Restrict commitments that a project manager can make on a project (in order to reduce value leakage, or value given away without charge)

(iii) Imposing a quota of fresher for each project, irrespective of complexity, to hold down costs in fixed price projects

---

10. In line with writer's block which every writer encounters when he./she is not able to write anything new for weeks or months together.

11. Forrester report ("Right and Wrong Reasons to Work with Tier Two Offshore Providers", Forrester Research Inc., Aug 17, 2010)

12. Factory as idiom for growth: Re-thinking the predominant Indian IT Services Supply Chain model Avinash Rao Principal Consultant, Enterprise Solutions Consulting Group, MindTree Ltd.

(iv) Need to replace experienced resources to seed other engagements after 18 months, where they can be paired with freshers.

Avinash suggest that mid-size companies can follow the niche/specialization model in IT Services sector as German Mittlesand[13] do for manufacturing and physical services area.

Charting out unrelated growth

IT Services company every has a certain ingrained capability or style of working, which is also called its DNA. Expanding in unrelated area may lead to facing resistances, road block and at times loss of business and reputation. For example many companies who are not well-versed in managing large government contracts face this difficulties when they want to grow in this market.

Not able to invest in team building and creating a climate of excellence

Companies that fail to develop team and their skills and not able to retain their talents face this problem which impacts their growth.

13.8 Summary

Most ITSE firms growth in not an option, but a necessary imperative for the survival. This chapter discusses the concepts, processes and practices of managing growth of ITSE firms. IT Services company would not be able satisfy their employee needs as well as the needs of the stakeholders like investors, founders, suppliers and partners.

The chapter underlines three factors that propel growth which are demand, quality of the business environment and supply response of an enterprise. While the first two are the influencing factors needed to be taken into account, the last factor is one that the enterprise has to focus.

We discussed the stages of growth for IT Services firm and noted that it follows an evolutionary cycle, traversing through

(i) inception

(ii) start up

(iii) development

(iv) maturity and growth

(v) acquisition or merger

(vi) hiving off, selling or split up

The chapter then discussed the process of managing growth and its stages such as

(i) strategize

(ii) devise

(iii) operationalize

(iv) appraise

(v) keep innovating

---

13. http://www.businessweek.com/globalbiz/content/sep2010/gb20100929_905740.htm accessed 05092011

The chapter also discussed various growth alternatives for IT Services firm using organic as well as inorganic growth models.

In the end, it discussed the best practices and pitfalls for growth to be avoided during the growth stages.

Review Questions

13.1 Why ITSE must grow to remain viable?

13.2 What are the factors that propel growth?

13.3 What are the stages of growth for IT Services firm? Do you think it is an evolutionary cycle?

13.4 What is the process of managing growth? Describe its various stages.

13.5 We are the various growth alternatives for IT Services firm?

13.6 Describe some of the best practices to be adopted or pitfalls to be avoided during the growth stages of ITSE firms.

Suggested Further Reading

Christensen, Clayton M., "The Innovator's Dilemma: The Revolutionary National Bestseller that Changed the Way We Do Business", *Harper Business Review*, 2000.

Shane, Scott, A., *Finding Fertile Ground: Identifying Extraordinary Opportunities for New Ventures*, Wharton School Publishing, 2005.

Staples: A year in the life of a start-up, Boston, Harvard Business School, 2000.

Moore, Geoffrey, *Crossing the Chasm: Marketing and Selling High-Tech Products to Mainstream Customers*, Harper Business Review, August 2002.

Adams, Rob, "A Good Hard Kick in the Ass: Basic Training for Entrepreneurs", *Crown Business Review*, 2002.

Collins, James C., "Good to Great: Why Some Companies Make the Leap ... and Others Don't", *Harper Business Review*, 2001.

Moore, Geoffrey A., "Inside the Tornado: Marketing Strategies from Silicon Valley's Cutting Edge", *Harper Perennial*, 1999.

Chapter 14

Future Trends in IT Services Business

The future is already here, it's just not evenly distributed
—William Gibson

14.1 Introduction

Predicting the future that too for IT Services Business is interesting yet a daunting task. While there is no doubt that IT Services will only grow in form and volume, but it is also certain that it will change its form in future. We will capture some of the likely trends that are showing the writing in the wall as shape of things to come in the future in the IT Services arena. It may be noted that these are just likely trend that may happen not that these predictions will necessarily take place. In fact, no one can make any prediction in IT area as most will happen sooner than expected.

14.2 Understanding the Trends

All this trends will have an impact on the way ITSE will have to transform themselves. IT Services trends have been grouped into the following categories:

(i) **Business environment trends:** IT Services are oriented towards other industries and their anticipated changes due to economic environmental changes, will have a direct impact.

(ii) **Information and Communication Technology (ICT) trends:** IT Services are also woven around ICT technology, and therefore, new development will impact the way these services are being packaged and delivered including exploring new markets and new services.

(iii) **IT Services business model trends:** The next impacting trend is that of evolving business model in IT Services sector.

(iv) **IT governance trends:** Finally, the way IT governance decisions will be taken in future within corporate and government will shape the way IT Services will be sought and delivered.

IT Services future will depend on the combination of all these four trends.

By deeper study ITSE firm can visualize the direction and take necessary preparation to meet the emerging scenario. IT professional too can prepare themselves by acquiring skills that will become more relevant in the times to come.

These are also shown in Figure 14.1 to depict in a pictorial form.

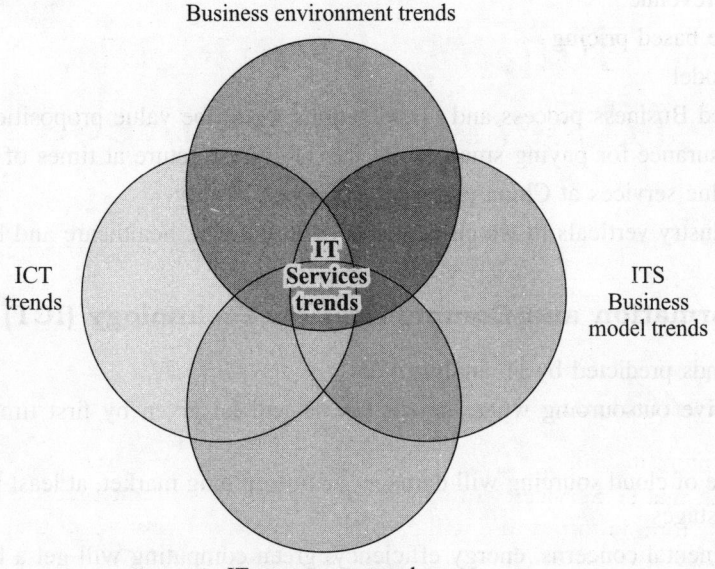

Figure 14.1 Four impacting trends for IT Services.

14.2.1 Business Trends

Let us examine some of the business trends across industries which have direct bearing in the way IT Services would be demanded.

(i) **Business uncertainties will force short term decisions:** The continued economic uncertainties which have become a norm that visits at regular and shorter intervals will prompt short-term IT decision of services outsourcing.

(ii) **Less spending from government, protectionism will increase:** Government of developed economies which spend sizable amount in IT Services, will cut spending and will not be off-shoring work to lower cost destination. This will lead to reduced market opportunities for IT Services company. It will also give rise to protectionism to some extent.

(iii) **Domestic IT Services market will increase:** Both government as well as private sector, especially SMEs will increase their IT Services spend.

(iv) **Robust economies of developing countries:** Economies of BRIC nations are growing fast. They will demand localized contents and local languages in IT applications and services.

14.2.2   Business Model Trends for IT Services

The existing model of seeking and offerings services will change. Some of the emerging trends are:

   (i) Pay as you use services

  (ii) Sharing revenue

 (iii) Outcome based pricing

 (iv) Opex model

  (v) Integrated Business process and IT operations would be value proposition

 (vi) IT as insurance for paying small fee to use IT infrastructure at times of failure

 (vii) High value services at China price will soon be a reality

(viii) New industry verticals to watch would be environment, healthcare and life sciences

14.2.3   Information and Communication Technology (ICT) Trends

Some of the trends predicted by IT analysts[1] are

   (i) Progressive outsourcing where smaller deals will be given by first time buyers of IT Services

  (ii) The hype of cloud sourcing will damage the outsourcing market, at least in the decision-making stages

 (iii) Environmental concerns, energy efficiency, green computing will get a boost.

 (iv) Customization will give way to standard offerings. Deloitt calls them "Almost-enterprise" solutions which may not have all the security of a robust corporate application, but quick deployment and availability on cloud will make them attractive.

  (v) Application will be smarter in days to come. Location, pattern and historical relevance have to be embedded in the applications

 (vi) Innovation will drive the growth and growth will accelerate the innovation.

 (vii) Mobile based applications for masses would spur a growth for application sachets that micro and small businesses and home users would like to use.

(viii) Data security, privacy, fraud, and ethical issues will become prominent. Data loss, Intellectual property pilferage will increase and necessary safeguards have to be built.

 (ix) Business analytics will become real time analytics that will converge voice, data image and pattern into one.

  (x) Increased investment on business continuity and resilience of IT systems and infrastructure.

---

1. http://www.globalservicesmedia.com/BPO/Market-Dynamics/11-Outsourcing-Trends-to-Watch-in-2011/23/28/0/GS101221259068

   http://www.deloitte.com/view/en_US/us/Services/consulting/all-offerings/hot-topics/technology-2011/e3c74a2a6179f210VgnVCM2000001b56f00aRCRD.htm

(xi) According to Gartner[2] report the following technology are likely to be a firm reality in next five years.

- Cloud computing
- Social software/Social networking in business
- Next generation analytics
- Mobile and real world web
- Context aware computing
- Augmented reality
- Future user interfaces
- 3D printing
- Mobile robots
- Fabric computing

14.2.3 IT Governance Trends

(i) **Increasing cost and dwindling profits:** IT Services will continue to face cost pressures. Wages in low cost countries and its management will be important.

(ii) **IT Services for the masses:** Consumer-based application on demand will be a new services to emerge.

(iii) **Apprehensions will increase:** The openness of IT, deployment across border, mobile work force, handheld computing away from corporate premises will lead to Customer apprehension while parting data. More and more safeguard, Audit and mistake proofing will be sought.

(iv) **Increased decision by business units:** Rather than IT decision of outsourcing by business units will lead to loss of disciplined outsourcing.

(v) **Mergers of some of Indian IT Services major with Global MNC:** Such merger will create new business entity and will increase competitiveness in IT Services Business.

(vi) **Future will witness more and more standardisation:** Is it possible to force services to a similar standardization process as products have been standardised? According to a study[3], standardization of services will play a principal role in the further development of a service economy. It was no wonder this study was sponsored by the government of a European nation[4] which is known for its engineering standards in automobile and product area for the last century or so.

Standardization process ensures commonality of terms used, people capability, technology, and organizational processes. For example, a Welder grade 'a' who is called to weld boiler

---

2. David Cearley VP & Gartner Fellow during his address in http://www.youtube.com/watch?v=_c2MTBYHBgk

3. Service Standardization by Ralf Reichwald, Kathrin M. Möslein, Anne Sigismund Huff, Marcus Kölling and Anne-Katrin Neyer The Center for Leading Innovation & Cooperation (CLIC), Federal Ministry of Education and Research Germany, CLIC Executive Briefing No. 012 ISSN 1866-4148

4. Germany

leakage is expected to have certain capability, expertise and will follow a process to ensure that high pressure boiler does not leak (or bursts) after the said services are performed. In the same manner, a business analyst should be expected to perform analytical task for business requirement using the standard process making sure that these requirements are comprehensive and complete. This is the demand customer organization would make and ITSEs have to ensure it in the future. This earlier study also gives three benefits of establishing standards for the business as:

   (i) Standards strengthen the innovative and competitive ability of individual service companies.

  (ii) Standards not only encourage economic growth and competition, but they protect the consumer and create conditions for fair and free trade.

 (iii) Service companies that implement both company-specific and sector-specific standards possess competitive advantages. They decrease their transaction costs and are perceived as businesses that actively promote the security of their customers.

Though this study was done on broad scale to transform Germany from being services desert to Services Made in Germany, the idea is very profound for ITSE firms to take note of. We have frequently seen services disruption in IT area just because a person leaves or a contract of one company is terminated. Even making multiple services provider to coexist in ecosystem that serves the entire services delivery chain to meet customers need in a seamless fashion seems next to impossible, just because the ITSEs have not embraced standards comprehensively and effectively.

One of the initiatives towards IT Services standards is being done by PAS[5] (Publicly Available Specification) which is a consultative document occupying its place between in-house and national standards written on the British Standard model which can be used to standardised best practices on a specific subject with BSI acceptance. Some notable standards and PAS[6] in IT Services areas are

   (i) PAS 77: IT Services continuity Management—Code of Practice

  (ii) PAS 700 Provision of ICT facilities and services in workplaces—Specification

 (iii) BS ISO/IEC 38500:2008 : Corporate governance of information technology

 (iv) BS ISO/IEC 27005:2008: Information technology—Security techniques—Information security risk management

  (v) BS ISO/IEC 27031:2011: Information technology—Security techniques.

 (vi) BS ISO/IEC 20000-1:2005 Information technology—Service management—Specification

 (vii) Information Technology Infrastructure Library (ITIL), contains best practices for IT service management (ITSM) Its current version is ITILv3 and ITIL 2011 edition—Its five core publications covers ITSM lifecycle stage—ITILv3 supports ISO/IEC 20000 (former BS15000)

---

5. http://en.wikipedia.org/wiki/Publicly_Available_Specification
6. http://shop.bsigroup.com/en/Browse-by-Subject/ICT/?t=r

14.3 Summary

This chapter outlined that the future of IT Services is tough as well as interesting. It is because the changes are taking place too fast and at unpredictable speed. In fact no one can make any prediction in IT area as most will happen sooner than expected.

In order to understand these trends trends they were grouped under four distinct themes such as:

(i) Business environment

(ii) Information and Communication Technology (ICT) trends

(iii) IT Services business model trends

(iv) IT governance trends

IT Services future will depend on the combination of all these four trends. Each of these themes were further discussed.

The important aspect of these trends is not to state that they will definitely happen, but they are likely as per the recent indications. It is for ITSE to visualize them, put their informed judgement and prepare for being successful by transformation. Similarly, IT professional should also embrace new skills that will make them more relevant and valuable for the future, if they keep a close watch on these trends.

Review Questions

14.1 Why it is difficult to predict future of IT Services?

14.2 What are the four distinct themes to categorize and understand the IT Services trends?

14.3 Write short notes on the major trends related to the following themes:

(i) Business environment trends

(ii) Information and Communication Technology (ICT) trends

(iii) IT Services business model trends

(iv) IT governance trends

14.4 What are the advantages and disadvantages for keeping a watch of the future trends for ITSE and IT professional?

Suggested Further Reading

The IT Management System of Tomorrow: Integrating IT Governance, Management Standards and ITIL best practice for business benefit Alan Calder, www.bsigroup.com/ictstandards

Making Metrics Work, 2nd ed., www.bsigroup.com/bip0032

BS ISO/IEC 26514:2008 Software and systems engineering. Requirements for designers and developers of user documentation. www.bsigroup.com/bsisoiec26514

Gartner, Meta group, Deloitte www.deloitte.com/in , PWC, Accenture websites.

Chapter 15

Summing It All

Tell them what you want to tell them, Then tell them,
Finally tell them what you have told them

Anonymous[1]

At the end of this book we will now summarise what we have learnt in all the fourteen chapters. The purpose is to briefly review the key concepts and draw its relevance to your learning objectives.

This is book is about IT Services Business Management. It is intended for a large cross section of IT services professionals. It is meant for all those who are about to take their first few baby steps in this exciting industry. I must admit that while writing all its fourteen chapters images of these young readers were floating in my vision. I am always enamoured by their starry eyes and inquisitive mind which is rearing to make the difference. This book is my humble contribution to their success. All these chapters have given the readers an insight of the management aspect of IT Services Business they are about to face. Let us take a quick recap of what these concepts were.

Chapter 1 gives a glimpse of the global and Indian IT Services industry by drawing the IT Services industry landscape. The chapter covers the industry size, its projected growth and major players. The chapter discussed why and how ITS is different than any other services and why it is necessary for us to understand its concepts process and practices. The absence of this knowledge will surely be felt in our professional value and ultimately impact our growth. The chapter also explain readers some of the challenges faced by IT Services Enterprises (especially Indian ones) and necessary actions required to maintain their growth. Our job as student of ITSBM is to build necessary skills, capabilities and best practices to contribute in ITSE success. For example the coveted Indian Civil Services exams which selects future civil servants has a well crafted syllabus of General Studies covering history/geography of the country, current affairs, Indian polity, structure of the government etc. This subject is a way to speed up the learning of civil service aspirants who have to prepare to pass the exams. This book is a similar effort to prepare aspiring ITS professionals for ITSE.

After building foundation knowledge about the ITS industry in Chapter 1, the Chapter 2 is devoted to dive deeper to understand the ITS industry value delivery chain. This discussion is aimed to provide structure to understand various IT Services by defining ITS Portfolio. The

---

1. A well-known advice for making good presentation

chapter categorise various ITS and then detailed their activities in this chapter. The various ITS heads are as follows:

(i) Advisory services

(ii) Build services

(iii) Perform services

(iv) IT Governance services

(v) Management of Quality

(vi) Software as service

Understanding the nature of these services is essential to choose and excel in our career in ITS industry. While you may start in any function or role in an ITSE, the ultimate goal for each one of you would be to find a specialization appropriate to your liking and capability. By learning about what entails in each of these ITS services category you can make much informed decision, preparation and navigation to the right slot.

Chapter 3 is devoted to provide IT Services business processes, models and functions overview, which is the main theme of this book. ITS is not just about software development that many may believe. Like any other business ITS business has to be understood by getting a comprehensive view of its processes and functions. The chapter describes several charts and tables each of these processes in detail by drawing inputs, activities and outputs from them. It covers IT Services business processes under the following theme:

(i) Strategy, Planning and Business Model design

(ii) Managing Finances, Support Infrastructure, Administration, HR

(iii) Business Development which includes

(a) Marketing

(b) Sales

(c) Opportunity Management and Customer Engagement

(iv) Delivery Management

(v) Managing Services Business Operations

In order to understand the business of IT Services, its cost elements and their relationship with revenue and profit, was presented in tabular form. This would help our readers to get appreciation of financial terminologies used in a typical ITSE. This chapter also discussed functional organization structure in IT Services firms which are typically adopted by major ITSE.

Chapter 4 covered Services business strategies. ITSE adopt various strategies for their growth and continuously fight competitive challenge. The chapter recalls the generic strategy theory and discusses its relevance with ITS. These are further divided into three main sub strategies:

(i) Organic Strategy covering expansion of the existing capabilities

(ii) Inorganic strategy covering mergers and acquisition, creating joint ventures, etc.

(iii) Hybrid strategies, a mix of the above two.

Several approaches adopted by leading ITSE firms under each one of these categories were discussed in detail giving examples of some of the most well-known names of the ITS industry. In addition this chapter presented evaluative framework titled ITSE "Strategic analysis Diamond" to evaluate practiced strategies by leading ITSEs.

Chapters 5, 6, 7, 8 and 9 are devoted to discuss the major processes and functions of IT Services business, in detail.

Chapter 5 discusses IT Services marketing to explain how it is different than any other services marketing. Giving deep theoretical background and practical insight this chapter would be most enjoying for those of you who want to build career in IT Services Marketing which is most rewarding and sought after role. ITS marketing is the most important function in any ITSE and has produced several ITSE organization leaders.

We laid the foundation of this topic through a well researched concept in the form 6 Ps of IT Services marketing as follows:

    (i) Promise

    (ii) Process

    (iii) People

    (iv) Performance measure

    (v) Past experience

    (vi) Price

This chapter then covers the sub processes of ITS marketing and developed the theme of how to successfully conduct each one of them by sharing best practises tips, stories and learning task (SALT), including how to measure marketing effectiveness and make continuous improvement.

Chapter 6 is covers an extension of chapter 5, focusing on business acquisition aspect of ITSE. This chapter discusses business development of ITS, i.e. soliciting new untapped business potential by reaching out to new customers, new opportunities and even launching new product or services. The chapter discusses what BD function is all about, why it is needed and what are the tasks performed. The chapter defines the role and business development process, its various steps through suitable diagrams and easy to remember approach titled 7 W and one H. The chapter described the necessary capabilities and skills required for doing Business Development. It also describes the career tracks for business development and tips, traps and pitfalls to be avoided for being a successful business development professional.

Chapter 7 is the last of the trilogy of ITS business acquisition functions which covered IT Services sales. The chapter covers various nuances which are typical of ITS sales. We started with identification of the likely buyers of the IT Services in any organization and preparations required to convince them. It also discusses the specific traits required in any sales person, and describes various steps of the sales process, giving useful tips, traps and best practices for successful sales. It includes process diagrams and tables to illustrate Sample sales funnel as well.

While sales process makes the customer agree to seek IT Services, it is the delivery function of the ITS firm which acts as the revenue realization engine. Customer pays only after getting the service, and therefore, having an efficient delivery process is important for the success of ITS business. Accordingly, as a natural next step of our ITSBM learning, delivery management is the theme of the Chapter 8. It opines that delivery management function in ITSE is what order fulfilment is to any manufacturing enterprise. We developed the delivery management topic by further categorising it into three major process groups Delivery Planning, Execution and Governance. Each of these process groups were further detailed out into sub processes for the better understanding of this most important process which employs the majority of ITS professionals. Understanding delivery management even if you are not a part of the function is necessary of success and survival in ITS industry. This chapter deals with various sub processes of delivery management to build the deep understanding for the readers.

Chapter 9 discusses concepts and processes to assure IT Services quality, which is important for the success of the ITSE and also to ensure uninterrupted operations of users of ITS. Without doubt IT Services quality is a competitive differentiator for an ITSE. The chapter defines Services quality by presenting views of several well-known researchers and explains why and how IT Services gap exists between customer expectation and service delivery reality. The chapter also underlines the role of a business consultant in minimizing these gaps, and examines Deming's philosophy to achieve IT Services quality. The chapter enunciates the concept of IT Services quality profit chain and advocates a right balance between customer delight.

Chapter 10 details on Measurement and Driving performance of ITSE. Managing IT Services Enterprise effectively and successfully cannot happen unless it adopts a rigorous process of measurement of performance and driving it towards perfection. However, measuring and driving performance is not an easy task, and we discussed the challenges involved. After defining the performance measure it was necessary to discuss the ways of aligning performance measurement in the organization so that the entire organization works towards the common goals. It discusses the tools that help capturing performance measures results and present them as suitable reports. The next important theme was to discuss about driving performance by identifying drivers and blockers of performance. The chapter presents performance measurement metrics template as an example and describes how individual performance can be improved. In addition, a simple mathematical model of target setting was also discussed. It also underlines the reasons of failure to drive performance within an ITSE.

Chapter 11 is devoted to the people aspect of ITSE by explaining concepts and processes for creating a winning ITS team. The chapter identifies various types of teams in an ITSE and defines their characteristics. It conceptualize a skill /capabilities cube and opined that developing skills continuously and undertaking certification programme can enhance the performance of the team. We also tabulated skills and expertise levels and certification required for various job roles in ITSE. Finally, it underlines the importance of creating right environment for people to give their best.

Given the widely accepted understanding that ITSE firm's growth and survival depends on continuous innovation and intellectual capital creation Chapter 12 is devoted on the concepts of managing knowledge, innovation and creating a learning organization. A successful ITSE is an adaptive organization which continuously goes up the path defined by lading researchers as learning spiral. The chapter explores the sources of new learnings for ITSE which is through customer, partners, independent researchers and competition, apart from their own employees. This chapter identifies enablers of knowledge creation and details on learning and knowledge management process through a suitable diagram. By identifying initiatives that ITSE can take for internalization of knowledge, further innovation can take place.

Chapter 13 deals with the topic of managing IT Services enterprise growth which is necessary for the ITSE viability and survival. It underlines the factors that propel growth and stages of growth for a typical ITSE. It lists various growth alternatives which can be adopted by ITSEs. It also describes some of the best practices for growth, and summarises best practices.

Chapter 14 deals with the future trends in IT Services to prepare ITSE and ITS professionals to build appropriate capabilities and skills. It outlines these future trends under following categories:

 (i) Business environment trends

 (ii) Information and Communication Technology (ICT) trends

 (iii) IT Services business model trends

 (iv) IT governance trends

It further examines each one of these trends into several themes being discussed in research reports and by several leading analysts. The purpose of this discussion is to encourage ITSE and IT professionals to prepare themselves for taking advantage and meeting upcoming challenges.

Future is all about preparation as it neither can be accurately predicted nor can be completely controlled, no matter whatever wishful thinking we may have. This is aptly true for ITS business as well as for all budding ITS professionals.

While the earlier fourteen chapters were a step towards this preparation for our readers the next recommended step for our readers would be to continue their learning with the help of references and website links provided in the chapters.

Index